Woman

vs

Womaniser

POWERFUL INSIGHTS TO HIS WORDS
ACTIONS, AND THEIR MEANINGS

J.C. Johnson

Insight Publication

This edition Published by Insight , 2015

ISBN: 978-0-9569083-9-1

Disclaimer: The following is a true story and events described
herein actually happened. For legal reasons and anonymity, certain
characters and other descriptive details have been changed.

Because of the dynamic nature of the Internet, any Web addresses or
links contained in this book may have changed since publication and
may no longer be valid.

To all the women I have hurt in my past, please forgive me. I was on a journey and genuinely didn't understand myself and the consequences of my actions.

To the one woman of my future, I have been through much in my life and it is through this that I am who I am today. It is because of this journey that I will cherish you so much more than I ever could have in my past.

J.C
JOHNSON

LONDON · NEW YORK · MONTE CARLO

WOMAN
VS
WOMANISER

POWERFUL INSIGHTS TO HIS WORDS
ACTIONS, AND THEIR MEANINGS

ACKNOWLEDGEMENTS

To everyone who took their time to share their thoughts... you all know who you are. As you know, my impatience sometimes gets the better of me, but you all helped me see it through to the end. For that I'm very grateful to you all: A Weir, R Dennis, V Grant, H Reid, S Alexis, N Cole, S Hewlit, L Foster, N Idelji, R De Silva, T Jordan, and D Luzi.

Wishing you all the very best.

To my three little angels, I love you more than the whole world.

To Mum, I will always love you, no matter what.

To P Paulusma, M Johnson and A Phillips for pulling more of the script out of me – I'm grateful.

Very special thanks to you, E Smith, for your support; you really are one in a million, of that I'm absolutely sure.

AUTHOR'S SPECIAL NOTE TO WOMEN

Over the years, as a womaniser I have learnt that love is the most powerful force on earth. My personal definition of being in love is this: the other person puts you before themselves. Don't forget this and you will never be tricked by a person like me.

However, love does not discriminate and will strike where it will. The only protection you can give yourself from falling in love with the wrong person is to control your emotions from the start. If you don't learn to control them, you will be riddled with 'blind spots'. What I mean by that is that our brains have two very real sides: the emotional and the rational. You have to use <u>**both**</u> sides of your brain if you are to see things accurately, as they really are, and if you are to make good decisions in life.

Whether it's a love situation or more general day-to-day stuff, your life will turn out so much better if you can manage not to get overcome by your emotional side and retain good judgement (no matter what you're feeling).

When you meet a new man, you must first and foremost make him do your brain (the rational side – not the emotional side) first! Always pay attention to behaviour patterns; they are the biggest clues you'll ever get to the person he really is. When you see patterns emerging that are not to your taste, cut your losses and move on. If you don't do that early and you get entangled in the love process, it will probably be too late and you'll be in for the worst rollercoaster ride of them all – the Misery Ride!

Here's my rule of thumb: you should never be in love with someone you don't know. Unfortunately, there is no shortcut for getting to know someone: it just takes time. Jumping in at the deep end is nothing more than letting your emotions run away with you.

Instinct: I cannot put enough emphasis on how important it is. We all have it; it's just a matter of learning to listen to it and developing it. My experiences have taught me that most, if not all, the women I went with as a womaniser had a bad gut feeling about me at some point. What is the point of God – or the universe, or whatever you choose to call it – giving you this amazing inner protection system if you don't use it?!

I've noticed that the more you follow your instinct, your gut reaction, the more accurate it becomes. Once you start using your instinct, you'll wonder how you ever lived without it. Here are a few examples of what your instinct will tell you about guys like me: this doesn't feel right; I really don't feel comfortable; he's a womaniser or player; he's using me; this is not what I really want; I don't like what I'm agreeing to or part of me doesn't; he has no respect for women; this feels the same as the last time; I'm making excuses for him; it just doesn't sound right; something's missing; my friends just don't understand; why am I always the one giving?

Ignore these instinctive responses to a man at your peril!

Contents

INTRODUCTION

My intention is to take you through the journey of my life and into the world and mind of a womaniser. I will reveal to you the abrasive manoeuvres and thoughts of a womaniser, giving a true account of his deceitfulness and the total pleasure he takes in using a woman to meet his own selfish needs.

It is almost impossible to cover every womanising experience, as each womaniser's encounters are legion, and each womaniser will have his own style. But it is possible for me to reveal the thought processes behind them, because they are broadly the same.

I'm sure that some women will be filled with disgust at the escapades I write about in this book; or they might find them hilarious! Or maybe both, even at the same time…? I'm also sure that the insights contained within these pages will make any woman who reads them impregnable to such characters. I hope that the benefits will by far outweigh the initial repulsion.

Some women make the same mistake over and over again: they fall for the same type of guy because they don't understand the psychology at play. Without knowing the mechanics, it leaves them with vulnerabilities, what I call 'blind spots'. It is by manipulating these blind spots to his advantage that the womaniser succeeds in turning so many women's worlds upside down!

The main aim of this book is to *show you these very same blind spots and in that same process reveal to you 101 manipulative ways of a womaniser,* to help you protect yourself and, at the same time, distinguish the womaniser from the genuine honest love partner who, at the end of the day, we all want to be with.

Enjoy the ride…

Part I
A WOMANISER IS BORN

CHAPTER 1
EARLY START

"I always knew you'd be a ladies' man!" I was only four years old when my true colours came to light. When my mother told me about it later, her smile exploded into uncontrolled laughter.

At the time we lived in a four-bedroom house in London with seven other family members – my grandparents and five aunties. I had no brothers or sisters at that time. I was the baby, the only one they could spoil. My memories of that particular period are hazy, but I do remember that I wanted to play with women, not toys.

According to Mum, on one occasion when I was four she returned home exhausted after a long day's work as a hospital nurse to find me asleep… or so she thought. She went straight to bed. Shortly after, she heard me creeping about and wondered where I was headed. Pretending to be asleep, she watched me tiptoe to my favourite auntie's bedroom across the hallway, open the door, and go in. She quietly followed and watched as I shook my auntie awake.

"Auntie, can I play with your titties?"

I still remember the beating.

Around my fifth birthday my mother and father decided they would take the big step and move in together. My father, who I hardly knew, bought us a three-bedroom house in North London and we took up residence. If it had been up to me, it never would have happened. I was happy living in my grandparents' house. Everyone adored me and spoiled me rotten. But what could I do? Nothing. I didn't take to my father – he was not like other members of my family, nor like my Godmother Aggie, who made me feel really special. I pleaded with my mother not to move us, but she reassured me things would turn out great.

How wrong could she be?

Not long after, my mum found a new nursing job at the local hospital. She worked tremendously long hours. My father had an easier time of it as a technician in a local university. I started school.

Everything seemed to be going fine until one day when I was waiting for my mum to collect me but she didn't show. Eventually, my father turned up, half an hour late. I knew something was wrong. Mum had never failed to pick me up, and my father was supposed to be at work. When I asked him where Mum was, he told me she wasn't feeling well. It wasn't until I got home that I found out why.

Liar! I knew he'd lied to me. I was intuitive even at that age, although I wasn't aware of what that meant. She wasn't feeling well, all right. *The bastard!* He had punched her in the eye! When I saw it, every colour of the rainbow, I cried and cried. I wanted him to disappear off the face of the earth. I wanted him to die. I never wanted to see his stupid, horrible face again. How could he do that to my mother, the person I loved so much? I guess my maternal grandfather felt the same way because that night he came over with my uncle, concealing a machete – he intended to take off the Monster's head. Unfortunately, my uncle intervened before he could slay him. *I cried again!*

From that day onwards, I always held a secret hatred for my father, and as the months and years went by, my hatred grew. The funny thing is, I believe he hated me too. When I was older, I asked my mother if she had cheated on him around the time I was born: maybe he thought I wasn't his son. It's not that I really thought my mother was that kind of a woman, but all the same I had to ask her because of his intense hostility towards me – I couldn't get my head around it. He was a naturally aggressive man, but over the years his aggression seemed to heighten when he was dealing with me. My mother told me later that she thought it started from the moment I saw her eye. She said that from that day onwards I couldn't stand the sight of him, and it showed big time.

But my mother forgave him soon enough. I never understood why, when he treated her the way he did: like a slave. He would do horrible things, like pulling the phone-wire out of the socket when she was talking to her friends and saying, "You chat too much rubbish, woman!" Or he would put the phone down when people phoned for her. Or he would turn off the heating and hot water just to spite her. Or he would lock her out of the bedroom… It took years for me to work out why she stayed. On many occasions I tried to tell her to leave his sorry arse and that she would be better off without him, but would she listen? *Of course not! She had blind spots!*

When I was seven years old, my mother gave birth to a little boy. We were all so happy – all except for the Monster, who showed no emotion. He was the typical cave-man type:

he always let tradition rule his life. I don't think he ever realised that the world keeps evolving, and that what may have seemed correct back in his day was not necessarily correct today. Over the years I have wanted to shout at him, "We don't ride horses anymore! They've bloody invented the automobile!" But he had been brought up with a rod of iron, and he expected everybody else to be brought up the same way. He ran the house like some kind of army camp:

"A woman's place is in the kitchen!"

"I'm the man of the house!"

"Everybody must obey my rules!"

"I don't speak to idiots!"

"Are you a donkey?"

You know the type: a Know-it-all-Charlie. He thought, because he was intellectually savvy, that he was above everyone else. And as a result he never reached his full potential, given his brains and talents. Why was he blind? Well, it's simple really: he only ever saw things from *his* point of view – no one else's. It didn't even appear on his radar that he could ever be wrong!

****

Here's an early tip: whatever happens to you in your life don't be a Know-it-all-Charlie; it will hinder you from reaching your full potential. It is a big character flaw, and will leave you with huge blind spots. Only through hindsight can I understand this now.

****

My mum named my little brother Paul. She was off work on maternity leave for a few months, which meant she was at home. I was glad she was there, because the Monster had picked up a bad habit of leaving me alone at home as soon as Mum left for the night shift. Not only God knew where he was going at such late hours of the night: it didn't take much brainpower for me, aged seven, to work it out. Even at that age, I seemed to have the ability to tap into anything that surrounded the opposite sex. I was a fast learner, as you picked up earlier! I decided to play it safe and not mention it to my mother. Why? Because I loved her, and I didn't want to cause her any unnecessary pain.

****

If I knew what I knew now I would have told her immediately. With hindsight, I'm sure my mother must have known something was up. Funnily enough, this a typical mistake that many women make: avoiding the situation and not realising that, in the long run, it delays an inevitable confrontation of the truth. The truth will come out.

****

He stopped slipping out when my mum was at home with Paul. *I didn't need it any clearer than that!*

Later that year, the Monster started to become stricter with me. *Imagine!* I was the only boy I knew who had his own maths book that hadn't been issued by the schoolteacher. My father bought me the book, and every day after school he would make me work from it until bedtime. If I got one answer wrong, his booming voice would holler "You fucking jackass" or "You're as thick as a two planks of wood" or any other insult he could think of. Then I would have to pick up a hundred stones in the back yard as a punishment. I remember I would be scared stiff whenever he yelled out for me, because I knew he was going to beat me down about something. When did I get time to play? Never; well, definitely not when he was around anyway. On a few occasions the local kids knocked on the door, wanting me to come out and play. But they soon got the message when Captain Cave-man answered the door, and they never came back.

I remember that the only happy moments I had around that period were when I got to see Simone, my babysitter, and when I got to play with my dog. Simone was my mum's best friend's daughter who looked after me occasionally. My dog Rasta was a black German Shepherd. Although Rasta wasn't allowed in the house, every chance I had, I would go out to the kennel and play with him. At night I would creep down into the kitchen and check he was okay. I could see his eyes shining through the glass door. I was unaware that the two things that brought me any peace in that house were about to be taken away from me at one fell swoop!

On my ninth birthday, I experienced both total ecstasy and extreme pain. The ecstasy far outweighed the pain: it was one of those things you never forget. *How could I? It was my starting point!*

I woke up early because I knew my mum would have a present for me. So I ran down to the kitchen where she was making breakfast.

"Happy birthday, son!" she said, handing me a birthday card. I wasn't interested in the card and she knew it. She said, "Your present is in the gar–"

Before she could finish her sentence, I was out the door and in there, admiring my new bike. It was a green striker with pedal back. Don't start thinking, *What the hell is* a strikerrrrrrrr!? That was the totally in bike to have back then.

You guessed it already: my father was a Monster, but my mother counteracted his abuse to me with gifts. I guess that was her conscience messing around with her because she knew the Monster was a git to me.

I ran back in. "Mum, can I take my bike and Rasta out into the alley?"

"Yes, after you've eaten your breakfast."

"Can Simone come around as well?"

"Well, I don't..."

"Go on, *please, please*... you know I don't have any life when he's around!"

****

Look at that - the first signs of me learning how to play on other people's emotions.

Here's the thing with my mother: she was beautiful, and not academically bright but full of wisdom in many ways that I wasn't able to appreciate at the time. She was also very soft-hearted and cared about people in general. But on the flip side, in my view she was weak-willed. Damn blind spots everywhere when it came to him!

Over the years she always claimed that she stayed with the Monster because of us kids - and, like a fool, I believed it. But I see it clearer now: she stayed with him out of fear - although she may not have admitted it to herself - fear of stepping out of her comfort zone into the unknown. She traded security for misery, not really understanding that she could have had security and happiness if she had not settled for less than what she wanted. Life only gives you what you are prepared to accept. The reason my mother settled for less than she deserved was because she convinced herself there was nothing she could do to change her situation. So many women who are being abused mentally or physically accept the apology, which usually ends with, "I love you." Blind spot! The rational side of the brain has left the crime scene, and all that's left is the emotional side, which justifies it all with something dumb like, but I know he loves me. Fantasy land!!! To be abused by someone and then be told "I love you" is an insult and nothing but nonsense - he is in love with himself. I'll repeat this again just in case you didn't grasp it the first time: if someone is in love with you, they will put you before themselves. Love is SELFLESS - I know!

Now here's another thing: I know when my mother met the Monster that he must have had the same characteristics that he always had, because that's just the way he was. I do not doubt that he had some charisma when he was younger. But the point is this: if my mother had looked at him rationally rather than emotionally from the very beginning, she might have seen the patterns of a monster and got the hell out. As it was, it was ten times more difficult for her to leave him later.

But I need to be careful - if she had been rational, I would never have been born!

****

Back to my ninth birthday.

"Oh, all right. I'll go and collect Simone later," my mother said.

Simone was three years older than me and, just like some of my aunties, she always made me feel special. She would always squeeze my cheek and give me love and affection and tell me how cute I was. Simone was the typical nine-year-old's imaginary girlfriend, although I must admit I hadn't built up enough courage to ask her if she would be my real-life one. I always got excited when she was coming over; I adored her. She was beautiful, with light brown eyes. Whenever the Monster did one of his turns on me I would retreat into my own little world where the only consistent beings were Simone and my dog Rasta. Thinking or being around them both made me happy.

I skipped with joy all the way to my bedroom, passing the Monster on the stairs. For a brief moment I wondered whether he might have got me a present. I decided against it, as he had never even bought me a bar of chocolate in the past.

I went down for breakfast, but when I sat down at the table I knew I wasn't hungry so I threw it all in the bin and covered it up with the newspaper. Just as I was taking the bike into the alley behind the house, the Monster sprang on me.

"Where are you going, boy?"

Boy! That used to really piss me off. He never called me Jay like everyone else. At times, I would swear under my breath, *Why don't you call me by my bloody name?* I never said it loud enough for him to hear though: I wasn't that brave. Not yet.

I said, "I'm going to ride my bike out in the alley."

"That's what you think! Have you finished those fucking sums I set you?"

"No, Dad."

"Then get your backside upstairs and finish them."

My mum appeared. "Let him go outside," she said. "It's his birthday, if you hadn't noticed?"

The Monster turned red with rage. "Shut your fucking mouth, woman! You can't see further than the end of your nose!"

I hated him!

I went to my room where I was out of earshot of the ensuing argument. As I sat there, deep in thought, wondering why my mum put up with all this, she came into my room.

"Don't worry, Jay. He's going to cricket soon. When he's gone, I'll go and get Simone and the both of you can go out and play."

I sighed with relief, knowing maybe my birthday was going to turn out all right after all. Getting stuck into my sums, my mind began drifting to Simone. Then the Monster interrupted my thoughts.

"I'm going to cricket now, boy. You make sure those sums are finished by the time I come back, you hear me?!"

"Yes, Dad."

Playtime! I waited restlessly for Mum to collect Simone, but I didn't have to wait too long. The first thing Simone said when she arrived was that she was staying over. I asked her nicely to do my sums because I didn't want to be picking up a hundred stones later on. When the sums were finished, we made our way out to the alley, with Rasta in tow.

We played most of the day, riding on bikes and talking about whatever came to mind. At the time I was intent on turning Simone from my imaginary girlfriend into my real girlfriend. All the same, we had a lot of fun, but it had to come to an end. *Or so I thought!*

Mum left for work shortly after the Monster got home. He was more concerned with checking my sums than anything else; with everything in order, he sent us to bed – Simone in the spare room. Some time afterwards, I heard the Monster sneak out of the house – off on one of his missions, I guessed.

I was about to go on one of my own!

I thought about Simone, all alone in the room across the hallway. I yearned to go and lie down beside her and... God knows why I was so horny at such a young age. It must have been in my genes! I made a split-second decision and committed myself. I made my way to the spare room; the door was ajar so I walked in.

"Simone, are you sleeping?" I whispered.

"No, I'm still awake. Where's your dad?"

"He left."

"Where's he gone?"

"I don't know. Can I get in the bed with you?"

"Of course you can," she replied innocently, oblivious of my intentions.

****

Now that I think about it, I'm not so sure she was so innocent after all; the older I get, the more I'm convinced women want it more than men do.

****

I slipped in beside her. And then it came out all wrong. I said, "Simone, can you play with my willy?"

"What?!" she replied.

"Nothing…"

"Did you say to play with your willy?"

"Yeah, but I didn't mean…"

"I'll do it, if you want me to."

Boing, boing, boinggggggg! It may have been small at the time, but it was still hard as a rock.

"All right then," I said, half-shocked. I couldn't believe my luck.

Without a word, Simone did her thing. It was the first time I was aware I had a beauty spot down there. When she was finished, she suggested we go all the way. Well, I wasn't about to object!

I remember that sweet fruity feeling I felt as the Monster burst through the door with diabolical timing! He took off his belt and beat me there and then, until Simone begged him to stop. But I remember thinking at the time, *The beating was totally worth the experience!*

When my mum got home the next morning, she didn't appear to be shocked in the slightest, although I know she must have been. She gave me a stiff talking to and that was that. As for the Monster, he made my life hell. He banned any kind of contact with Simone, and coincidently, that same week Rasta ran away! I was devastated.

With hindsight, it was clear I was getting these behaviour patterns from him. I'm pretty sure the Monster had come in from getting his own little groove on. My mum told me later that she had known he was a womaniser when she met him. What had he expected me to be doing in there with Simone? Playing footsie? If anyone should have understood, it was him.

Thinking back, I can recall times when he used to drag me along to watch him play cricket. Hundreds of times, en route to the game in his green Capri, I'd watch him wind down his window and deliver his favourite chat-up line to random women: "Hey, woman! Do you want to come stretch your legs?" Although it wasn't the most delicate of approaches, even with his cave-man technique he did surprisingly well! He would leave me outside for what seemed hours on end, just sitting in the car watching people walk by, while he did his business. I hated him for leaving me there so long.

But I must admit, there was a part of me that admired him, the way he eventually got them eating out of his hand. I could notice the subtle changes in their body language. Sometimes I would sit there and repeat his words: "Hey, woman! Do you want to come stretch your legs?" The funny thing is, looking back I wasn't mimicking him; *I was practising!* When he came back to the car, he would always have a grin on his face, as if he had just caught the biggest fish in the sea. I remember, I used to think, don't they have a daughter or something for me?! I often wanted to talk to him about girls and women, but he just wasn't that kind of person. All in all, as much as I hated him, that womanising side had me intrigued.

Around this time I was developing a reputation as a bully. Just as the Monster made it clear to me who ruled in his home, my school was my home and I ruled there. Everyone went out of their way to ensure that I was happy, not because they wanted to, but because they knew I would protect them if any problems came their way.

You would think with all the bullying I got from the Monster at home that a bully would be the last thing I would be. But I don't think it works that way. The abused always kick downwards; I had to vent my anger somewhere, and boy was I angry. Although I couldn't see it at the time, my hating my father was really an underlying wish for us to have a normal father and son relationship – not a son and Monster one. The only place I could vent was at school, so I took my feelings out on the other pupils.

How did I do it? After a few fights, amazingly I noticed I had a lot of friends and I got a reputation for being someone who was not to be messed with. From that point on it was easy: just keep the fear instilled. I guess I'd had a good teacher! A few times the school summoned my parents; I'd be wobbling at the knees thinking about what the Monster would do to me. It always ended the same way – ten lashes to each hand with the belt followed by serious book-work and no TV or play.

When I turned eleven, the Monster really turned up the torture and began doing crazy stuff. He would be sitting downstairs watching TV late at night, and I would be fast asleep in my bed so I would be fresh for school the next morning. He would start banging on the ceiling with a broomstick handle, shouting, "Hey, boy, come and get the remote!" When I came down, I'd find the remote right in front of him. Then he would say, "Now, go back to your bed, boy." Then, when he would leave for work at five-thirty a.m., he would make sure I was out of bed and say something dumb like, "Get up, boy! Do you plan on spending your whole life asleep?" And woe betide me if he caught me watching TV when he came home – he would even feel the back of the TV to see whether it was warm.

I hated him even more!

It was time for me to start secondary school. My mum wanted me to go where all the brainboxes went – Lehman Guild. I passed the entrance exam but they refused to accept me because of my bad reports that detailed my bullying. Although I was accepted by my second choice, St Raymond Mixed, I had no idea how short my school career would be.

Amazingly, I managed to maintain good grades in most subjects, even though my first year consisted of playing football, establishing a bad-boy reputation, and girls telling me that other girls fancied me. At the time I thought their attraction was because I had power and I was the top sports boy – and to be honest, I'm sure it did play some part. The thing is, when I looked in the mirror, I didn't see a good-looking boy: I just saw average. It wasn't until later that I became aware that I'd been fairly blessed in the looks department.

By the time I was halfway through the second year, I was hanging around with pupils a few years older than me. One in particular turned out to be a lifelong friend: his name was Wayne Whiter, nicknamed *Stretch* because of his incredible height.

It was around this period the Monster found another torture method. If I happened to come home late, the door would be locked from the inside. On countless occasions I would have to sleep in the porch, to be woken up by the sound of the milkman placing the milk bottles. The first few times it happened, my mother had tried to open the door, but the Monster had done his nut. Now my hate for him turned up even more. (I still did not realise that my anger was more to do with the fact that I wanted him to be my dad and guide me.) But for the first time my attention also turned to my mother, and I felt negative. Many of those nights when I was squeezed into this box and freezing cold, I would lie there thinking about the two of them hugged up in bed. I felt abandoned, and that she was putting the Monster before me.

During my third year I was picked to play for Tottenham Hotspur Juniors' team by my PE teacher, who happened to be a Tottenham scout. There was a lot of talk about how talented I was. Later on, I was also scouted by Arsenal, but I turned them down to stay with Tottenham. They would pick me up from my house every Thursday for the training sessions, and weekends for the matches. But soon I started refusing to go to the training sessions: I believed I didn't have to train as I could see I was a cut above the rest of the players, and I only wanted to play in the matches. And sometimes the Monster wouldn't let me go either, preferring to take me to cricket with him. After some time, they sacked me, and the reason they gave me was – my attitude. I cursed the manager to his face and the Monster under my breath.

It was later on that same year that I got expelled from school for beating up a pupil. For two weeks I pretended to go to school, until the last day of term when I returned home to see the Monster waiting for me, cricket bat in hand.

"Where you coming from, boy?"

Straight away, I knew he had found out, but I lied all the same: "I'm coming from school."

"So what's that letter I found under your bed?" He didn't wait for my answer. The cricket bat came swinging through the air and struck my shoulder over and over again. "Pack your things, and get the fuck out!" he blasted.

I wondered whether he knew what he was saying. *Didn't he realise I wanted out anyway? He was doing me a favour!* Him saying that to me was like a prison warden telling an inmate to go and pack his stuff and get out of jail! It was a no-brainer, as far as I was concerned.

When I was in my room packing my things, dreaming of the days of freedom ahead, my mum came in. "Where are you going? Have you got somewhere to go?"

"No, I…"

"Exactly! Your father's angry at the moment. He'll calm down by the morning. Just stay in your room until tomorrow."

The next morning, the Monster woke me up with a bucket of water. "If you want to carry on living under my roof, you had better find a job."

"Yes, Dad," I replied. *Are you sick? I thought. Find a job! I'm only fourteen, for fuck's sake.*

Two weeks later, I sneaked an older girl into my bedroom for the night. The Monster burst into my room at around four a.m., catching us stark naked and completely in full swing. I stopped immediately and turned around; our eyes met. There was a long pause. He was resting his hand on top of the door, looking at me and then at her and then back to me. The look in his eyes said, *You piece of shit.* Suddenly, he dropped his arm. I braced myself; I thought he was about to attack me. But he didn't. To my surprise, he turned around and walked out. I heard him go back into his own bedroom and heard muffled cursing. I was in total shock; I thought he would have done his nut.

He did – *the next morning*! The minute the girl was gone, he flipped and threw me and all my stuff out. He was shouting at the top of his voice, "You think this is a *bloodclart* hotel? You good-for-nothing piece of shit…"

Mum was begging me not to go, and I started begging her to come with me. Well, you can guess what decision she made! I was really hurt, but I made my decision and stuck to it. There was no way I was staying. I was outta there.

CHAPTER 2
FIRST NIGHT OUT WITH STRETCH AND THE CREW

The Monster had stomped his brutal foot on ten years of my young life, but now I was out, I planned to make up for it. I was nearly 15, but as everyone kept reminding me, I looked closer to 18. Perhaps it was the company I was keeping.

My mother made half-hearted attempts to get me to come home, but when she finally realised my mind was set, she said, "You don't even know what life is about. I feel sorry for you; you'll just have to learn the hard way."

Feel sorry, indeed! It was me who felt sorry for her! It wasn't me living with the Monster, and having to put up with his cave-man ways. Out of everyone, though, I felt most sorry for my younger brother Paul; I guess he was going to be next in line for the Monster's brutality.

What a day! I was excited and worried all at the same time. I picked my bags up off the driveway and made for the bus stop. I didn't even know where I was going. As I got to the bus stop, I threw down the two bin liners stuffed with my teenage belongings – some clothes, trainers, a cassette recorder and my music tapes. I decided I would go to my grandfather's, who had recently split from my grandmother and was living in South London in a two-bedroom flat. I knew he would be happy to have me stay. I had always been his favourite.

Then I checked my pocket and found I only had one measly fifty pence piece. *Shit, fifty p won't even get me halfway,* I thought. For a moment, I wondered whether I should go back home and apologise. *Yeah right!* I found a phone box, took out my phone book and dialled the number.

I said, "Hello, is Wayne there, please?"

"Yeah, it's me. Who's that?"

"Stretch, it's me, Jay…"

"What's happening?" he said.

"Guess what: my dad has just kicked me out, and I haven't got any money to get to my grandfather's."

"Listen, you can stay here if you want. I've got a spare room."

I weighed it up – Granddad's or Stretch's – and swiftly deciding I wanted fun! "What about your dad?"

"Ah, don't worry about him," he chuckled. "I run things in this house!"

"Well, if it's not too much bother…"

"Nah, it's cool! I'll get my dad to pick you up. Where are you?"

"The phone box on Pembury Road."

"All right, we'll be there soon." And he hung up.

That was it. As I waited, I wondered whether I was doing the right thing. I just wasn't sure.

Stretch turned up ten minutes later with his dad, Duncan. We did the introductions, and then Stretch helped me put my stuff in the boot of the car. When we set off, Duncan quizzed me on what had happened. I explained everything, only from my point of view, of course. While Stretch agreed with me, Duncan didn't. He said, "I think you're making a big mistake, leaving home…"

Stretch butted in. "Shut up! You don't know what you're talking about!" Stretch had no respect for his dad. I remember thinking, *You wouldn't get away with that with my dad – he'd take your damn head off!*

Duncan muttered weakly, "Well, just make sure you call your mother as soon as you get to the house, and let her know where you are."

"Yeah, I will," I murmured quietly.

When we arrived, I called home. The Monster answered, and hung up. I dialled back, and this time my mother answered.

"Where are you?"

"I'm all right, Mum. I'm at Stretch's house."

"Jay, come back home, please! Your father's sorry!"

She was lying – I could hear him in the background: "Sorry, my arse! He's going to be a thief and a robber… He's not living under my roof!"

"Mum, I can't stand him and you know that. I'm going to Granddad's tomorrow morning, okay?"

"Phone me when you get there… I love you."

"I love you too, Mum," I replied, and hung up, and thinking, *Love didn't make you stick by me, your son.*

I wasn't to know that by the next morning I would be fast asleep in some sprat's bed.

****

As much as I don't like to say this, my mother put the Monster before me, and it hurt like hell. I couldn't really understand why. I loved her to bits, and rather than leave him she preferred to let me, her fourteen-year-old son, go. It didn't make any sense at the time; it was very confusing, to say the least.

****

Back then, we called girls and women *sprats*. A sprat is a type of fish, and I guess we saw women as so many fishes – plenty of fish in the sea – ready for fishing!

Stretch showed me to the spare room and helped me to unpack a few things before taking me to his own room to catch up on some small talk. He told me that later on he and some of his crew were going to see some sprats, to have some fun and a laugh. *Sprats and a laugh!* That sounded great to me! Obviously, I talked him into taking me. I wasn't going to stay in and get lectured by his dad!

Stretch was older than me and in many ways I admired him: the way he controlled his father, the way he could go anywhere he wanted when he wanted, even the brands of clothes he wore.

****

It wasn't until years later that I worked out that it was the other way around – *he* admired *me*. I became aware he would always try to be like me. He had a blind spot. Trying to be like someone else never works! He never realised that my manner was a part of me, a part of my DNA, and no matter how much he tried to copy me it never rang true because he just wasn't me.

I was the type of person who could say something downright rude to a woman and get away with it. I said things in such an ambiguous, jokey way that women couldn't really tell whether I was serious or not. Whenever he tried, Stretch would end up in a full-blown argument. And he just wasn't as good-looking as me. We could say exactly the same thing to a woman, and she would see him as having an attitude problem and see me as just cute and cheeky: it really was that simple.

****

Later that night, Stretch introduced me to the Crew: Wesley, Sweeny, Karl, and David – all of them at least three years my senior. We all squeezed into Wesley's car and drove to an all-girls hostel in a part of town called Holloway. When we arrived I was led into a room packed with sprats smoking weed and drinking alcohol. This was all new to me, but it was a scene I knew I was very quickly going to grow to like.

As Stretch was introducing me to the sprats, I noticed a few of them were giving me that look... you know the one: that 'Damn, he's nice!' kind of look. I might have been young, but I was not stupid. In fact, I would even go as far as saying from a young age I had quite a high awareness. I spotted a lot of stuff that went over most people's heads. I had an ability to perceive and feel things a cut above the people around me. I became aware that I could pick up subtleties in women's body language, and detect patterns that enabled me to read them fairly well – no matter what they were communicating verbally. It was clear to me even then that bodies were a 24-hour broadcasting station. No matter what, I could 'hear' and 'see' what people were feeling. A body could be saying to me "You bore me" or "You intrigue me" or "You're not my type" or "I'm totally besotted by you!". Although both men and women were emitting these signals, I only cared about the women, so that was all I tuned in to. This receptiveness enabled me to tweak how I handled women to get the outcomes I required. Of course I could make mistakes, but I was aware of them to some degree and could steer myself out of bad situations.

Now here's the thing with the Crew: they didn't appear to have anything like this awareness or intuition, apart from Stretch, who had some awareness. Some of the stupid things they would say and do would make me think, *Wow! How could he not have seen that?!*

****

I don't know why I had this intuition so young – it just came naturally to me. However, through the years I have noticed it in many people, young and old. I found that they are usually kinesthetic people, and therefore hyper-aware of bodily motion. I do know this: awareness has a lot to do with paying attention! Do I believe it can be nurtured? Yes, I do. Do you have the discipline? Well, that's entirely up to you!

****

At the time, I had no idea what awareness was, but I had it.

As far as I was concerned, my only close competition in the Crew was David. He had that caramel-baby-face-dimples thing going on. He was what many people would call a 'sweet boy'. I thought he was weak, and he laughed (a laugh like a cartoon dog called Muttley, a strange wheeze of a laugh) too often – it used to annoy the hell out of me. I had the baby face and the dimples too, but I had a rough edge to me. Sprats would feel protected if any sticky situations arose. They knew I could hold my own. David was the wimpy type. So I guess I had the edge on him.

Back to the hostel. The Crew wasted no time pouring the drinks and wrapping some spliffs. One of the girls, Karen, offered me a strong drink and a spliff. I accepted the drink and rejected the spliff politely. As she poured me the drink, she asked, "Jay, how old are you?"

I didn't want them to know my real age. "How old do you think I am?" I responded.

"Seventeen, eighteen?"

"Bang on – I'm eighteen," I lied.

"Arrr... I think you're so cute."

I heard a few agree with her, particularly Louise, who said, "I think he's more than cute!"

As time passed, the more the drink was blowing my head, the more I wanted action. I did my best to hold it together. If this was what Stretch called fun, just sitting around smoking and chatting rubbish, he must have come from a different planet to mine. As young as I was, even I could tell the sprats wanted a little more than conversation. I found it incredible that the Crew had known these girls for some time and couldn't see that they wanted more than talk. The drink was starting to take over, so I weighed up which sprat would be the easiest target for me. I decided it was Louise: I guessed the comment she had made earlier was an invitation for me to chat her up.

"Louise, where's your room?" I said, slurring my words a little.

They all laughed.

"Why's that, cutie?" she replied.

"I want to talk to you in private."

"What about?"

"About the weather, what else?" I said with a grin on my face. Now she probably took that as a joke, but I was really being sarcastic and thinking, *Sh*t! Why do sprats always play dumb?*

"Okay, big boy. I just hope your sun shines where it counts," she joked. This time, it was the girls who laughed.

"It definitely does…" I answered cockily.

****

My ego was getting ahead of itself already here. Later I was to learn that too much vanity and an unhealthily large ego are both major character flaws. They are traits that womanisers often show. Take heed, ladies - they should be a red light to warn you to keep away!

****

"Damn, he's in the fast lane!" I heard Sweeny mutter as Louise and I left the drug den.

I remember thinking, *It's you who's in the slow lane!* I was much younger than the other guys, but even I could see these sprats were hot and horny, and the type that always will!

Sweeny was one of those characters who complain about everything. The world was always against him, and he was constantly fighting thin air. He had a frame that looked as if it were chiselled out. I suspected that women just used him for sex, hoping he'd give it to them without talking. He only went for black girls; he believed that people should stay with their own kind. So I'm not sure what his exact purpose for being there that night was: all the sprats in the room were white. *More fool him!* I never really could get my head around why people have that racist thing going on. As far as I was concerned, I was colour-blind. *And I had no intention of reducing my market share!*

****

The way I looked at it even back then, anybody on earth who is racist is nothing short of ignorant. Why? I'll tell you why: it's obvious that as time goes by everybody is going to be mixed race eventually. It's a losing battle, whether the racists like it or not. They have lost even before they start. Why can't they see that?

I now draw the conclusion that many people don't question stuff. They follow the crowd like sheep rather than allowing themselves to be who <u>they really are</u>. I don't see anything wrong if someone's sexual preference is a certain colour or race, but to be racist is just plain old stupid.

And personally... anything goes!

****

Back to Louise. She led me to her room at the top of the building, a bottle of brandy in her hand. It was me who started the conversation, using formulas to make her think she knew me better than she really did. During the conversation, I started a play fight – just a little one. *Deliberately, of course!* Sometimes it worked, sometimes it didn't. This time it did.

I threw the pillow at her. Louise threw it back. I threw it back again. She threw it back at me again. I rushed her. She rushed me. I deliberately fell on top of her and put the pillow in her face. I let her spin me over and put the pillow in my face. I removed the pillow and kissed her. She kissed me back. Then POW! Before she realised what was going on, it was in there and I was giving it to the sprat.

Quite simple, really. Play-fighting with a sprat usually breaks the ice and gets things rolling, especially if you've both been drinking. That's not to say that she wasn't going to give it to me anyway – I just made it a lot easier for her to justify to herself why she was giving in so easily!

As soon as I had finished, my mind drifted back to my current situation. I thought about my parents and for a moment I felt all alone. I shook it off. *I'll fucking survive,* I concluded. Next I began to worry about how I was actually going to survive, it was niggling away at the back of mind and it really troubled me. I was fourteen years old, I couldn't work and even if I was old enough to I had no inkling about what I wanted to do. My thoughts jumped back and forth from thinking about work to the Monster's words ringing in my ears telling me how stupid I was; that I was a donkey; that I had two peanuts for brains; that I was good for nothing and I would be a robber and a thief. Every time I thought about something positive, his words always seem to overpower it and haunt me. Finally, there was the deep pain I felt at my mother not fighting or standing in my corner like I had done so many times for her.

I fell asleep begging for a solution. I was unaware that my solution to survival was around the corner, but not exactly how I would have necessarily planned it!

CHAPTER 3
A WOMANISER IS BORN

Things were looking up. It gave me a great feeling to be able to do whatever I wanted whenever I wanted to do it.

But this new-found freedom didn't come without a fight. Fourteen-year-old boys don't usually drop out of school and disappear. Oh no. The authorities tracked me down and sent me to a unit where all the bad boys who have been kicked out of mainstream school go. I lasted two weeks before I got into a fight and was expelled. Then they tried to put me into a children's home, but I wasn't having any of it. And in those days I don't think laws existed that got parents of delinquent children into hot water for their kids not attending school, because I don't recall hearing about my parents ever being held to account. So the episodes of my life involving school and the Monster came to a premature close, and I stood on the brink of a sparkling new beginning.

And life just kept rolling out one excitement after another. First Stretch got me in with the Crew, then I got my own flat. Can you believe it? Fourteen years old and I had my own place. It came about like this: when my mother told my uncle the whole sorry tale, he offered me his empty flat, since he had moved in with his girlfriend. My mother initially thought the idea was ridiculous, but what could she do? Let me live on the streets? So arrangements were finalised and I moved in.

A few times my mum talked about me going back to school; when she did, I ignored her. The truth was, no other school was going to accept me. Even if they did, I had no intention of going back anyway – I mean, why on earth would I want to go back to school when I had just been freed from hell and everything was going so great?

I was raving every night with the Crew, and sleeping with more girls than I could possibly imagine. I boned three more of Louise's friends back at that hostel in Holloway. I had been right that night – they were the kind of sprats that always will! Now here's a prime example of what I mean with the Crew. They were still pondering whether or not to make their advances known or not. Now, looking through my eyes, I found that absurd!

I also met a sprat who was so besotted with me that she gave me anything I wanted. I remember the first time she gave me three gold bracelets and a chain. Although I cheekily orchestrated it, I knew it was above her awareness to see how I was taking advantage of her. I was still blown away by how easy it was. I could see the excitement on her face: she was as ecstatic about giving as I was receiving. It made sense for me to get as much from her as possible – if it made her happy too, I was doing her a favour, right?! When it happened, my worries for survival evaporated there and then.

It wasn't long after I got in with the Crew that I started to get this insane urge: I felt that I had to bone as many sprats as I possibly could. I know this doesn't sound cool, but it did at the time: I started writing down the sprats' names in a little black book, numbering them in order. I boned a few sprats so quick I didn't even catch their names. When I was referring to them in my book I wrote *Slapper from -, Number -!*

The more sprats I boned, the more their friends wanted to sleep with me: it was unbelievable. First of all, I started with the ones I was attracted to, but soon I was doing every sprat I met. Somehow I couldn't find it in myself to refuse them. The range was diverse: black, white, blonde, brunette, skinny, meaty, beautiful, big tits, fried eggs, long legs, short legs. I didn't see a reason why I should refuse any of them. At the time I would justify to myself, what idiot said faithfulness was good anyway? Maybe God was sitting up there on his throne thinking, *I never told anyone to be faithful... Why the hell do you think I made women so sexy in the first place?!* Regardless of right or wrong, I really did love pu*sy, and I loved new pu*sy even more. *Nothing like new P-U-*-S-Yyyy!* I was like a vacuum cleaner, picking up anything I could find, even the trash. I noticed that most sprats picked one man in the club and marked him: *'If I don't get him tonight, I don't want anyone'.* Unfortunately for those sprats, they kept choosing me!

And now I had this sprat giving me anything I wanted. How could a fourteen-year-old boy like me turn womaniser overnight and manage to find this magic sprat? I'll tell you.

It all began one wonderful night at a club in Essex we used to call the Pum-pum Market. It wasn't until the Crew took me there that my womanising really began in earnest. You can guess how the place got its nickname? If you don't know, pum-pum is a slang word for pu*sy. The club was like a dream come true for someone like me. The very first time I went there I could feel the excitement flooding through my body as I walked in past the bouncers, who all looked like carbon copies of each other – Robocop! As I walked up the stairs, I instantly sensed that this place was going to bring me some good times. I could feel the sprats' eyes all over me as they passed me on the steps – I was new fish and I was good fish! When I walked through the double doors at the top, I paused briefly, taking in as much as I could. The atmosphere was buzzing. My attention was drawn towards the stage. It was packed with sprats dancing to Whitney Houston.

As I followed the Crew, I noticed there were sprats everywhere, at the bar, in corners, on the dance floor. The further I walked, the more I realised how big the club was, with big sweeping staircases that took you upstairs to the lounge and another bar. The dance floor was huge and heaving; it felt as if this were the only club in town. We went to the bar, ordered drinks and settled in a corner where I began to focus on a few females. I caught a whiff of cologne followed by a strong scent of weed, but lingering beneath these aromas, I could smell the real good stuff – Pu*sy!

Within the first fifteen minutes there were two pretty sprats hovering around, and every two minutes they would pass our corner, smiling. Amongst the Crew a disagreement arose as to who it was they were actually smiling at, and who should approach them. Not surprisingly, everyone suspected that the smiles were directed at him, apart from Wesley who, I must be honest, looked like the back end of a bus (his nickname was Wugly, although no one had the balls to say it to his face).

Wugly was the oldest member of the Crew. He was dark-skinned and had a big head with a receding hairline, and his stomach was distended like an alcoholic's. I sussed him out early on; he was the type of guy who knew he wasn't that good looking so he always attempted the 'back-door route' to get women. He would play the cry-on-my-shoulder card.

You know the type: when women are feeling low, he says, "Come on, cry on Uncle Wesley's shoulder!" He waits until they are at their weakest point, and then he strikes. The next morning, the woman wakes up and has a heart attack when she sees him with a big fat grin on his face! He was definitely not a threat to me. I was a super-confident person who never ever saw anyone as a threat. I guess my confidence stemmed from my belief – which was rapidly building momentum – that I was untouchable, and as far as sprats were concerned, I was realising I was more fortunate than many. The more time passed and the more attention I received, the more my confidence was rising.

Eventually, Stretch and David swaggered over to the two pretty girls; their swift return made everyone laugh. I knew who they were really smiling at.

"Jay, they both said that you're *criss* [which means you're really good–looking] and that they were smiling with you," Stretch said when the laughter had died down. They couldn't believe they had chosen a young boy like me over themselves.

"He's a little face, man," said David, as if knowing what the others were thinking.

That's pretty much how it went all night… the sprats were all over me. I was almost as shocked as they were, although I never let it show.

Eventually, the club wound down. Back in the car, I emptied out all the phone numbers I had collected. I felt good! *Wouldn't you? Be honest?* It was dawning on me how many sprats thought I was handsome. Even the Crew started calling me *galist*, which means womaniser.

Pum-pum Market had become my second home – it felt so comfortable... so right!

The Crew talked about me all the way home. "Shiiiiiiiiit, you weren't playing with those sprats tonight, *gal-ist!*" Stretch said, and everyone agreed with him. By the time I got home, I felt like some kind of idol.

That night, just before I closed my eyes, I thought back to Pum-pum Market and all those sprats who were all over me. It wasn't as if I had sweet-talked them into going for me; they had gone for me strictly because of my looks, which I hadn't even known were so striking until then. *I'm going to bone all of them*, I thought as I drifted off to sleep.

I woke up early the next morning. The sun was bright. I decided I would give my flat a thorough clean before I planned what I would do for the day. I hated untidiness. So, picking up a rag, I started to dust the place down. *Shit, I thought, there's nothing here to dust!* My uncle had decorated the flat well, but there was no furniture. I had one armchair, a couple of stools and a cheap table. The bedroom had only a double bed, with no cupboards or wardrobes. All my clothes were piled neatly in the corner of the bedroom. The kitchen was great – it had everything I needed: neatly arranged cupboards all around, a washing machine and a dishwasher, all colour-coordinated in a creamy white. But the rest of the flat definitely needed some additions. The only question was – where would I get furniture? I didn't work, so I had no money.

It wasn't until later that evening that the solution hit me straight in the face. After a long lie in the bath, I decided to go and check Stretch and Wugly, and suggest we invite some sprats down from the club. As I was leaving my flat I bumped into the old lady next door, Ms Carlton. She was a really nice lady but she always stopped me and kept me chatting for longer than I really wanted. She would tell me about her son over and over again. He used to do everything for her but he had committed suicide. I always waited until she ran out of breath, as the old lady was sweet in a funny sort of way. When she had finished I said my goodbyes and headed to Wugly's.

When I arrived, they were talking about going to the local park to play football. *Football indeed!* In my mind I just wanted to be with the sprats, and they were talking about playing football. I mean, I was an ace footballer, but when it came to sprats, football didn't stand a chance.

In the end, I convinced the boys that sprats were the best thing on the day's menu. Using Wugly's mobile, I phoned one of the club sprats.

"Hello, is Jennifer there, please?"

"Yes, it's Jennifer speaking. Who is this?"

"It's Jay."

"Hiya! I didn't think you'd call."

"Why's that?" I asked.

"I don't know; just didn't think you would."

****

Interpret this – what she really meant was, "I think you're out of my league so I didn't think you'd call me." I made a mental note that she had already put me on some kind of pedestal. I was learning my value, and fast. I was also learning to tap into sprats' vulnerabilities.

Ladies, here is the number one mistake many women make: putting the person on a pedestal as if the person has more value in life than themselves. Here is a tip: when you meet someone new and you really like them, act in the same way as you would if the person was someone you're not very fond of. Here's why: women and men _value_ what they have to work for!

The reason most people never seem to be able to hold on to the one they really want and the one they don't want is always hanging on is simple. It has very little to do with the other person, but has everything to do with your behaviour towards that person! The first thing to do is stop putting him on a pedestal and chasing him around, dropping everything for him, and always making yourself available. Do it back to front, ladies!

When you instantly show you like a womaniser, you have given him an early Christmas present: a good angle to manipulate your arse! (Sorry to be so blunt, but it's deliberate as my main focus is to make my words sink in.) But the minute you pull back (this is only for the early stages of dating), you make the womaniser less sure of himself and your feelings for him. And womanisers hate uncertainty.

What's funny, though, is that this can also bring womanisers to their knees if they are not aware of this human behaviour pattern. He may find himself falling in love and not know why. The reason is that every woman has always been predictable to him, but now she isn't (he has to work for it!!!). He's intrigued and eventually falls for her but doesn't know why!

Here is the golden rule: resist telling him he is your world and giving the impression it would be difficult to be without him. Men are great, but not the be all and end all. The key is to leave an element of doubt!

****

Back to the phone call.

"So what are you doing today?"

"I'm not doing anything today: it's my day off."

"How about coming down to see me?"

"I don't mind, okay then!" She jumped at the invitation.

"My friends are asking, have you got any friends you can bring down with you?"

"I don't know. I don't know what they're doing. I tell you what – I'll call you back in ten minutes. Is this your number?"

I gave her the number and hung up.

She phoned back quickly, confirming she would be down with five of her friends. Well, of course that was fine with us! I phoned the rest of the Crew and told them to be at Wugly's for six. With everything for the evening settled, they persuaded me into a game of football.

Wugly, Stretch, David, Sweeny, and I were ready and waiting at six. I told them Jennifer was mine: the rest they could sort out between them. I wasn't to know there would be a stunner amongst Jennifer's friends.

Eventually, they arrived, an hour late. I answered the door and ushered them into Wugly's cramped front room. Jennifer introduced her friends: Tiffany, Lisa, Doreen, and Tasha. Once everyone was introduced, Wugly offered them a drink and a smoke, and they all accepted, except for the stunner, Tiffany, who declined the smoke. *We have something in common*, I thought. Secretly, I hadn't been able to take my eyes off her since she arrived.

Soon the sprats were all settled and normal conversations started to flow until I started turning it into slack talk. I wasn't really one for beating around the bush; my confidence was growing by the day, by the hour.

I watched Tiffany intently. There was something different about her, the way she lifted her glass, the way she tilted her head at just the right angle, something sexier. She was just stunning: short brown hair and perfect features and striking eyes. She almost looked better than money. *I said almost!* Damn, why did I have to chat up Jennifer? Tiffany and I suited each other; somehow I knew I had to have her.

Stretch started firing questions at them, such as how many men they'd slept with. I listened intently to their answers, trying to detect who were the ones that always will. Tiffany was the only one who refused to answer. I tried to work out why she wouldn't answer. *Maybe she's slept with too many men and she's ashamed of it*, I thought. No, that couldn't be it, I decided. She looked too sweet and innocent.

****

I later learnt never to take someone on face value, whether they are pretty, or sweet, or innocent-looking: it's a character flaw to do that. It is quite difficult not to, as apparently we perceive people fifty-five per cent visually, but judging someone from the outside can be very deceiving.

I have also judged people negatively by their appearance and later found out they were absolute angels. It works both ways to trip you up.

The best thing to do is look for behaviour patterns before you make your call - they will eventually reveal to you who that person really is.

****

My attention was on Tiffany, but when I heard Jennifer say that she worked in a jewellery shop and that all the gold she was wearing she had stolen, my subconscious zoomed in and connected: gold + stolen + jewellery = furniture! But what about Tiffany? *I can't have them both*, I told myself. *Or can I?* Jennifer and all her gold would have to wait – Tiffany was the one I wanted now!

As the years passed I learnt (incorrectly of course) that the one with the loot always gets first priority!

By ten o'clock everyone was smashed either from the drink or the weed (or both) that Wugly was ensuring was circulating – another part of his back-door technique! I felt horny as hell. I was starting to notice that drink always made me feel that way. I wanted to get the ball rolling. By the looks of things, the Crew would have been happy to play tiddly-winks all night. So I suggested we play a game of truths. They were all up for a laugh. I only wanted the answer to the one question on my mind. I waited for my turn to come around, listening patiently to all the sprats' answers. It was Tiffany's answer to David's question that nearly made me fall off my chair.

"Tiffany, how many men have you slept with?"

For the second time she refused to answer, but the Crew put pressure on her.

"I haven't," she said quietly, as if she were ashamed of it. At first I didn't believe it, but the rest of the sprats swore that she was telling the truth. *Jesus!* This just made me want her ten times more.

Eventually, it was my turn. I stalled and thought about the question I would ask. I was going to ask them who they fancied in the room. I decided they might lie and say they didn't fancy anyone in the room. So I reworded the question. I said, "If you had to go out with someone in this room, who would you choose?" I popped it to Tiffany first.

All the crew leaned forward: they were on full alert awaiting her response.

"None of you," she replied.

"You have to say one!" we all cried in unison.

Looking around, she locked eyes with me for a hundredth of a second too long. "If I had to, I suppose it would be Jay."

I smiled. From that moment, I knew I would have to have her.

I guessed that she had made her confession reluctantly, because everyone knew I was meant to be hooking up with Jennifer. Jennifer was next. She also picked me. But I was really surprised when all the other sprats picked me too. I was happy about it – don't get me wrong – but it also made me feel uncomfortable: I didn't want the Crew getting jealous. I had already picked up some jealousy vibes. Sweeny had made a comment to me once: "Mr Galist, the man who can do no wrong," followed by an insincere smile. Now, I can't speak for anybody else, but what I *heard* him really say was, "You think you're God's bloody gift to women!" I had to be careful.

****

Personally, I have never been jealous of anyone or anything (hard to believe, I know, but true nonetheless), but over the years I have had many people jealous of me. I have observed that the jealousy was always because I outshined them. But in a more detailed observation, I realised that people's jealousy stemmed from their lack of belief in themselves. The number one reason I have noticed that men fail to get their fair amount of chicks (which can also apply to women getting their fair amount of men) is first and foremost their inner dialogue with themselves, which leads secondly to their expectations.

Let me explain... All my life when I have approached or chatted up women my inner dialogue has been "I have her"; in other words, I don't doubt it. I really believe that I'm already spreading the bed sheets on the bed, so to speak!! So when I approach a woman, it's already a done deal. That kind of belief radiates out in my body language and the way I say and do things. So just because a man can't consciously see his doubt, he may be radiating it outwards and the subconscious mind of the other person may be picking it up. I talk as if I expect it. Even if I get rejected, my inner dialogue says, "You can't get every woman you meet. It's her loss. Silly woman." It's not a problem with me; it's a problem with them.

Everything you do and believe comes across: people pick it up subconsciously.

****

The girls fired the same question back at us, and all the Crew picked Tiffany except Stretch and me. He picked Tasha, and I remember thinking, smart move! I didn't pick anybody: I wasn't going to shoot myself in the foot. The sprats made a big fuss about me not answering but I held out, so that was the end of that. Now that I knew the script, it was time to read it out. "Listen everyone." All eyes turned to me. "Let's stop playing footsies. There's five men and five women, and I know we all want things to happen."

Stretch jumped up and, rubbing his hands together, announced, "For real, enough of this. Tasha, come out onto the balcony. I want to talk to you."

Now personally, Tasha wasn't to my taste – empty-headed, big-breasted, and easy. Stretch had a weakness for big breasts. Sometimes I thought he was slow, but he definitely wasn't stupid: if I had wanted a guaranteed bone, I would have gone for her because she was plastered and looked like she was up for anything.

At that point Lisa, Tiffany, Jennifer, and Doreen decided they wanted to go. I could see Tiffany's mind was made up but Jennifer was easier prey so I persuaded her to stay. When the three girls were leaving, I pulled Tiffany into the toilet.

"Tiffany, I really like you…"

"What are you talking about? I thought you liked Jennifer."

"I did, until I saw you. Can't you see? I haven't been able to take my eyes off you all night. Can I have your number?"

"I can't because… Jennifer."

"Listen, I want you, not Jennifer. Trust me…"

She gave me her number, and I tried to kiss her full on the lips but she didn't respond. She simply walked out.

Now, there was no point in the rest of the Crew sticking around, so Stretch and I hinted that they were getting in the way. They all left except for Wugly, who retired to his room, maybe to have a five-finger shuffle.

Stretch and Tasha took the sofa while Jennifer and I took the floor. I almost burst out laughing when I touched her breasts. *What the hell am I supposed to do with these?* I thought. They were like two fried eggs! But it wasn't until later that we got it on. In the middle of the night, when I guessed everybody else was sleeping, I woke her up. We crept into the kitchen and closed the door quietly. Stripping her naked, I laid her down on the floor, undid my zip and sprung on her. If I'm honest, I was no expert at this stage of my life, but she was like a corpse; it was ridiculous – no movement. As soon as I let my load out, I got up and went to the bathroom. I turned on the light, and as I was just about to wash my baton... *Blood!* I flipped and marched back to the kitchen. I saw Stretch wake up but I didn't stop.

"You was on your fucking period, wasn't you?" I shouted, turning on the light.

"I'm not on my period," she whispered.

I paced the kitchen. As I did so, I noticed blood on the floor. "What the fuck is that then?" I said, pointing to it and thinking, *You lying little piece...*

****

Yes, I know what you're thinking – here's the pot calling the kettle black! Another common trait I've observed in womanisers is double standards, so it's fine for me to lie, but the woman mustn't ever! *And some men are just like that because of tradition.*

How do you distinguish between the two? Look for other womanising patterns that help build the true personality picture.

****

"It's not my blood, Jay. It must be yours."

Stretch opened the door. "What's up, mate?"

I didn't answer; I was too vexed. I marched back to the bathroom.

After a closer examination I realised she was right; it was my blood. She had messed up my foreskin. Well, if she thought I was going to apologise, she had another thing coming. As far as I was concerned, it was her barbed-wire! If she had put some bloody movement into it, it would never have happened.

The next morning, before the sprats caught a cab home, Jennifer asked me to come to her house later. I wasn't thinking about the blood by now, I was thinking about the gold, so of course I said yes. I told her I would come, but I really planned to get back to her later than that. I had other plans for the little stunner Tiffany.

When they left, Stretch confessed to me that he had heard everything. He also told me he had boned Tasha and that he had got a bloody good polish in return. *Lucky him!*

From that day onwards I realised that the Pum-pum Market was the place to be, so I made it my duty to go there every day it opened, come rain or shine.

Jennifer fell for me so hard that I could get anything I wanted from her. She started stealing around five hundred pounds' worth of gold for me every week – sometimes it would be substantially more – and because I knew it made her happy, I continued taking it. At first she was giving me stuff to make me happy, and then it turned into her giving me stuff to hang on to me!

I comforted myself with the fact that she hadn't started to steal because of me: she had been stealing before she knew me; I had just upped the frequency. I have no idea why she had started stealing in the first place, and it was frankly of no concern to me at the time. How, why, or where from made no difference to me – I was only interested in the cash. *I couldn't see what a bad thing this was at the time, because I never questioned it!! With hindsight, the reality was that I was just after the cash.* If I was to guess why she had begun, I reckoned it had just been an easy opportunity for her that she grabbed, and that's probably how she always looked at it.

****

Now here's the thing with Jennifer. She was naïve – I'd classify her as a type of sprat I called Naïve Nadine, and there are a lot of them about. I would describe Naïve Nadines as inexperienced and lacking good judgement. (They are taken in by the loveable side that every womaniser has; it's a huge part of what blinds them!) They generally take everything you say as the gospel truth: "Mummy never lies, and Daddy never lies, so nobody lies."

Naïve Nadines come in all shapes and sizes, but they have one thing in common: when they have had enough experiences with womanisers, more often than not they metamorphose overnight into Cynical Sues, who hardly believe anything a man says. But even as Cynical Sues, there are still abrasive manoeuvres that get past their fortress!!! So keep reading.

****

As it happens, Jennifer wasn't bad looking; she just didn't do it for me personally. She had long blonde hair, and she was very slim – which for me means no arse and two fried eggs. Don't get me wrong, many men love women that way. One thing I did like about her was her stunning green eyes. (And with hindsight, she was actually a beautiful person.)

By now I was sleeping with her friend Tiffany, and many people she knew. Tiffany, to her credit, had been the hardest nut to crack. But it still wasn't a tremendous effort. It had been clear that she liked me physically from the first time I met her, so I knew it was just about winning her over.

How did I do that? I deployed what I call the 'Me Too' technique. Whatever she liked, I made out I absolutely loved it too. Tiffany loved her dog, so guess what I did? "Me too." She loved her music. "Me too!" Then I tapped into aspects of her personality, things that she really liked about herself, and I used the Me Too in reverse. So I would say, "Do you know what I love about you the most, Tiffany?" and then I would tell her. I knew this would leave her with a (Me Too effect) proud feeling. In her case, she generally cared about people: people she knew and people she barely knew. She just cared about people's feelings, full stop. For me it was all about making her feel that I thought she was special and more comfortable with me and closer to me than she actually was. Slowly, I broke her down, and once I had her virginity it was all over.

Now, that wasn't what I did with every sprat; most of them didn't need that kind of effort. But eventually, my technique paid off and she was hooked. But unlike the rest of them, she had me coming back for more, over and over again. Don't ask me why – I couldn't quite work it out myself – (*maybe because I had to work for it?!*) I was just aware she had something special.

****

Even though Tiffany had something special that kept me coming back, she had some major blind spots. If she had used the rational side of her brain it would have said, "This guy can't be any good if he's trying it on with me as well as Jennifer!" Still, she went with me even though she knew I'd boned Jennifer the same night I'd asked for her number. The fact that Jennifer had stayed that night should have sent alarm bells ringing.

****

Everything was going so well. I had sprats chasing me around and I loved it. But then something happened with one of the Crew and I was out in the cold. As a result, they all stopped talking to me, apart from Stretch. My days with the Crew were over.

Suddenly, I was on the move again.

CHAPTER 4
FALLING INTO HELL

I guess my plummet towards hell began when the Crew abandoned me. My fall was a steep one.

To replace the Crew, I became best friends with Rocky (real name Justin, but no one called him that) who, by the time he was nineteen, had already done a stretch at Her Majesty's pleasure, for burglary. The name stuck to him because whenever he got in a fight, he always knocked out his opponent. His short, stocky build could have been that of a boxer; he was also what some women would refer to as a pretty boy. He was hyperactive, delusional, and in some of his saner periods he was very amusing, and very generous, I must say.

But there was one thing about Rocky that annoyed the hell out of me: he always wanted to get with the women that I'd been with. He was jealous of me, always in competition with me, and I believe it left him confused why I wasn't in competition with him as well. He was playing a game with himself; I simply didn't think he was in my league.

The day I first met Rocky I was standing outside the shopping centre waiting for a bus when I saw two guys I knew from the area, Kurt and Kenneth. I high-fived them and nodded my head towards the guy they were with. As I waited for my bus, they started telling me the latest crap going on in the area. I wasn't really that interested; I didn't get involved in 'mixup.com'.

We'd been talking for about five minutes when three white youths came over and started talking to Kurt. Kurt was a big drug dealer in the neighbourhood, so I assumed he was dealing. I heard the small one ask Kurt whether he had a cigarette. Kurt didn't have any, so he asked me whether I had a spare one.

Checking my pocket, I realised I only had two left. I looked at the kid and guessed he was about sixteen and a crack-head (incidentally, I guessed wrong: he was 25 and definitely not a freak). "I haven't got any for him," I said, looking him up and down. He looked back at me as if I were the freak. "Who the fuck you looking at?" I asked, ready to knock his lights out.

"Come around the corner, ya cunt. I'm gonna teach you a lesson," he said in a full Cockney accent.

Teach me a lesson! "Come on, then," I said, putting my hand in my back pocket and gripping my 007 knife. I never left home without it now, as it could come in handy when pricks like this one got above their station.

****

Back then, carrying a knife was standard procedure for me. Just as most people perform that check as they leave the house - "Got my keys - my money - my phone" - I had one last one: "Got my knife". Circumstances made me believe I had to carry one at the time.

****

So the little prick and I were making for a space behind the public toilets when Kurt got between us. He said, "Sly, forget this. It's not worth it."

Sly! The name sounded familiar; I tried to remember where I had heard that name before, but I couldn't. Right then, I didn't really care who he was anyway. I was confident I could deal with him swiftly. A couple of stabs and it'd be over.

Now Kenneth and one of the other guys were starting to plead with this Sly guy. "It's not worth it," they kept saying to him.

It didn't make sense. I thought to myself, *Why the fuck are they pleading with him? They should be pleading with me to cool it! They know I'm going to stab him!* Something wasn't right. Surely they knew I was going to beat him, but they were acting as if I were the underdog.

I'm not having none of it. I'll show them, I thought. I took out my 007 and in a split second I lunged at him. I missed.

Sly backed off and pulled out a long Rambo knife. "I'm going to teach you a lesson, you mug." He was laughing now, as if it were some kind of sick joke.

For a moment I lost my confidence. My mind was ticking fast now: *Shall I make a run for it? No! No way! I'll screw up my reputation!* That reputation that suddenly didn't seem to carry any weight.

From my school days up until this moment my reputation had been a straightforward, no-nonsense one: everybody who was somebody knew me, or knew of me, and knew that

I was not to be messed with. I was undefeated. Some time ago I had had a fight with a well-known local youth and, to be honest, nobody had won. But in my head, my rep had been damaged, and my rep was a key part of my pulling power. So what had I done to fix it? That same evening, I had paid him a visit at his house. I had rung the doorbell and when he answered I had battered him with a piece of wood right there on his doorstep. Then the next time I saw him I had stuck my knife in his back and taken everything he had on him.

I was fearless, I didn't care who the person was; they could be anybody. Well, nearly anybody – there was one character who I would never want to get into any problems with, and neither would anyone I knew: his name was Kain, and he was notorious. I avoided Kain at all costs.

That day facing Sly, it seemed as if they had all lost their minds.

One of Sly's friends said, "Don't kill him!" *Don't kill him!* Smiling, Sly advanced towards me. I was thinking, *He must be a lunatic.*

"Put down the knife," someone shouted.

Sly took a wild stab at me. I jumped back; he missed. I returned a wild effort, but it didn't connect. The next thing I knew, Sly was lying on the floor. It happened so fast I almost missed it. The person who'd called out, a stranger, had sprung from nowhere and connected a right hook to Sly's jawbone.

Taking the knife out of his hand, he said, "I told you to put down the knife. He's my cousin." Sly looked at him and never said a word.

This stranger had saved me a life sentence or perhaps even my life, who knows? One thing I was sure of – I was glad he intervened when he did.

My bus came just at the right moment. The stranger jumped onboard too; it turned out he was going to his dad's, who lived in the same block of flats as me.

We settled down together on the back seat. I took out my cigarettes, gave one to him and introduced myself. He told me his name was Justin, but that everyone called him Rocky. I told him I could see why. He told me about Sly, that he was sick and that he wouldn't leave it there. He told me how Sly had stabbed loads of people and actually murdered one, but he had got off with five years for manslaughter. He also told me that Sly wasn't sixteen but twenty-five.

We talked all the way to the bus stop; he seemed like a cool guy. I gave him the rundown on Pum-pum Market. He asked if he could come the next time I was going. As I had fallen out with the Crew, I was only too pleased he asked. We exchanged numbers and went our different ways.

Thirty seconds later my phone rang. It was Jennifer. She said, "Are you coming down?"

"Are you paying my cab?"

"You know I am."

"Then I'll leave in a little bit," I said, and hung up.

She had good timing. I felt in the mood for some sex. I was also broke and I knew she would line my pocket with some pounds.

The phone rang constantly, one after the other, my sprats calling in. They all wanted to see me. I was in demand and

I felt happy, so I arranged dates with all of them. They say too much of one thing isn't good, but I guessed whoever made that up was drunk!

Why is it the more sprats I had, the better I felt? At that point I was proud I was good at this womanising stuff; it gave me a sense of power. With every woman I hurdled, I felt as if I had won a hundred-metre sprint. The more I hurdled, the more I wanted to win!

I got to Jennifer's at half ten. Frantic to sock it to her, I wasted no time stripping her off and jumping inside her. She had definitely improved since the dead body days. *I guess I was a good teacher!* Contented, I turned over onto my back. My performance wasn't up to scratch and I knew it. I didn't really care; the only one who got top performance was Tiffany. Shiiiiiiiiiit! She had learnt a lot but not to the extent I would go all out to compete.

Now that the sex was over, I started to think of how to get some loot. I needed a car. The buses and cabs were starting to piss me off.

"Jay, why do you always have to wear a condom?" she asked.

"Are you stupid?" I shouted. She had hit a nerve. This question was starting to crop up too frequently. "Why the hell would you want me to take off my boots?"

I decided it could only be one of four things:

1. She wanted a baby.

2. She wanted to feel closer to me – skin to skin.

3. She needed reassurance that I really cared for her.

4.   She wanted to infect me!

Okay, so the last one was unlikely. But whichever other one it was, I wasn't about to do it – I didn't want her in my life forever.

But I remembered myself quickly – I knew I had to be nice to her so that I could get what I wanted. So I said, "Listen, Jennifer, sorry for jumping down your throat like that, but you know how it is. With AIDS going around, I might even have it. It's better to be safe than sorry."

"You most probably have, after sleeping with all them slags."

I ignored her, just as much as she was ignoring her own instincts! I knew that answering her would lead to an argument, and that was the last thing I needed. Many times she had accused me of sleeping with her friends or girls she knew. Whenever she did, it was as if she expected me to confess everything. *I was no fool!* I had no intention of cutting off the hand that fed me. In any case a womaniser has three rules when dealing with sprats: *Deny, Deny, and Deny!* I got my scam together in my head and waited.

She said, "Are you going to the club tomorrow?"

"Leave me alone, will you." I waited for several minutes. Then, "Jennifer, I'm sorry, I'm sorry I'm so jumpy tonight, it's just that... It's nothing." *I knew damned well she would push to find out what was wrong!*

"Tell me what's wrong, Jay?"

I paused, "Well, my parents have gone on holiday. I found my dad's car keys and took it for spin and I ended up in an accident. I wasn't hurt or anything, but the car is a wreck and he's going to murder me when he gets back." I poured it on.

"How much is the repair?" she asked.

"A grand eight."

"I've only got five hundred on me. It's in that drawer. Take it. It'll help," she said, feeling sorry for me.

Five hundred my foot! "I wish it could help, but where am I going to get the rest from?"

There was a long pause. Then she said, "I suppose I could get it. There's a diamond ring in the shop…"

"Do you think you can get it?" I asked a little too eagerly.

"Yeah. But you'll have to wait until Tuesday, until I'm in there on my own."

Gullible, I thought. "Thanks, Jennifer," I said. "You're always there for me. I'll pay you back as soon as I can." *Like hell I would!*

****

Ladies, beware of men who are always coming up with sudden scenarios that end with money!! They are playing on your emotions. Later on I will reveal all of the different kinds of emotions men use to manipulate women.

Now here's the thing with Jennifer. Her intuition, instinct, gut feeling – whatever you want to call it – told her I was a cheating money-grabber. I could tell even then. The problem for her was that, like so many women, she didn't want to listen. Even a couple of her close friends had said it to her. She didn't want it to be true, so she allowed her emotional side to come up with all the reasons why they were all lying. "My friends don't understand", or "They're just jealous because they're not with him", that sort of thing. Or perhaps she got caught up in the Time Investment Principle. You think you have put so much time and effort into a man that one day he's going to change and everything will turn out perfect.

Jennifer was ignoring the signs, and was well and truly on the Misery Ride! If before she met me one of her friends had told her they wanted to introduce her to a good-looking guy who was a cheating money-grabber, her rational side would have clearly rejected the offer. However, here she was, letting her emotional side override her instincts.

There is an old saying: if one person tells you you're a horse, they are crazy; if three people tell you you're a horse, they are conspiring; if five people tell you you're a horse, go get a saddle! She obviously had never heard the saying before.

Ladies, here's another tip, which goes over the heads of most people. (Don't take this to mean I think I'm better than anyone else, because I don't: it's just that I can see it so clearly after all these years of misbehaviour.) Most human beings don't – can't – see themselves accurately! The only way you can get a good view of yourself is from people who have a good overall view of you and who won't hold back the last ten per cent. These are the people that are brave enough to tell the truth to your face. More often than not, they are your real friends! Constructive criticism can hurt, but it usually reveals something to you that you were unaware of – it is always given with your best interests at heart.

Try to put the unhealthy egos and prides to one side - they are weaknesses, not strengths.

****

Knowing that the money was in the bag, I laid back and thought about what had happened earlier. Rocky seemed to be a cool guy. I had an idea that I would set him up with Lisa, one of Jennifer's friends. "Make sure Lisa is at the club tomorrow. I've got a friend who wants to meet her."

"What about David?" she asked.

David was Lisa's current boyfriend, and one of the Crew who'd abandoned me. I remember thinking, *That will teach him a lesson.* "Forget about him – he's a punk," I replied.

Rolling over, I gave Jennifer her money's worth: a grand-eight's worth of sex!

The next morning when I got home I jumped straight into the bath and had a good scrub. Then I got dressed and ready to go shopping with the five hundred pounds in cash I'd got from her. Just before I left, I phoned Tiffany. Her mother answered.

"Hi. Is Tiffany there, please?" I asked.

"Is that my little prince? When are you coming round to see your mother-in-law then?" she joked. *Or so I thought!*

"Maybe tomorrow, Sally," I replied.

"Okay, hold on. I'll just get her."

I could hear Sally shouting to her daughter and telling her I was on the phone. Tiffany picked up the other line and called to her mother to put down the other end.

"Hiya, handsome! Am I going to see you tonight?"

"Yeah, I'm going to stay over after the club. Is that all right?"

"That's fine with me."

"Listen, baby, I'll call you later. I'm in a rush."

"All right, see you later, handsome. I can't wait!"

The phone clicked as she put down the receiver. But then – yes definitely! There was a second click! Her mother had been listening in on the other line! But why? There was something about her mother I couldn't quite put my finger on. It wasn't until some time later that everything in that department really started making sense…

So I called Rocky next, and told him I had set him up with a sprat and that I would meet him later. Just as I got downstairs I saw Ms Carlton struggling with her shopping, so I gave her a hand taking it upstairs. As we were going up she kept going on about what a nice good-looking boy I was and that I must have all the ladies running after me. I denied this, of course. "I can see you must have had all the men running after you, and you probably still have," I said, stroking her ego and attempting to make her feel good about herself. She did; I saw the grin on her face as she reminisced. From then on I always made a point of complimenting her because I knew it brightened up her day. The truth was, you could tell she had been a looker in her day.

Just as I said my goodbyes and turned to leave, Ms Carlton said, "Jay, where are you going? Sit down for a minute. You're always in a rush." As I sat down I noticed how dilapidated the sofa was; in fact, the flat needed refurbishment. When I was settled she asked me to tell her about my childhood.

She caught me off guard and put me on the spot; I was not expecting that. I was reluctant to go into my past but she prised it out of me. What began as a brief outline turned into deep detail about the Monster and my school days.

When I had finished she asked me about my mother. I began to tell her that my mother wasn't strong enough to stand up to him, but then Ms Carlton abruptly changed the subject and said, "I'm sure you have things to do. We can continue this another time." As I went through the door and said bye, it appeared to me that she was tearful but I wasn't exactly sure. It wasn't until some time later that I realised that she had been actually crying and the reason why!

At the shopping centre it was rush-hour busy. I must have looked in five different sports shops before returning to the first one. I bought a crisp pair of Nike trainers to put that extra bounce in my step. En route to the clothes store I chatted up numerous sprats – nothing special, but it was good to keep in practice. It so happened that the next girl I bedded would make sixty. How did I know? Because I wrote them all in my black book, of course! I badly wanted to make my first century. *Yes, many men do make it!*

One shop had the latest fashion. I saw it instantly – it had my name on it, 'Womaniser'! – a C17 pair of jeans with matching shirt, the *in* style of the time. A womaniser is usually very particular about his appearance; he'll do everything he can to enhance himself and stand out from the crowd. Slapping the money in the assistant's hands, I walked out and made tracks to Rocky's. There was no doubt in my mind I would be the one tonight.

When I got to Rocky's place, he was entertaining some of his friends and they were all smoking cocaine. He offered me some and I accepted. I had never been anywhere near that devil-stuff before, but I thought, *It's time to celebrate! My first car is on its way, my new trainers are 'live and kicking, and just this once won't hurt.* I took a puff. The stuff was wicked. I wasn't to know at that moment how it would play a massive role in my downfall.

After what seemed to be a hard session, I filled Rocky in on Lisa. It turned out he knew David and also thought he was a punk. When I told him she was stealing money from the safe at her job in Covent Garden, his eyes lit up.

The Pum-pum Market was banging, as usual. Rocky took to the club instantly, just as I knew he would. Pointing over to the far corner, I said, "You see that crew over there? That's who I used to hang around with."

He said, "How comes you don't hang with them any more?"

"Well, you see David..."

"Yeah...."

"He found out I slept with the mother of his son. Because of that, he lied to the whole Crew and told them I stole some money from his house. He told them before I could tell them what *really* happened. So I thought, fuck 'em, they can believe what they want..."

****

As woman hungry as I was back then, the whole affair with Jackie, David's kid's mother, did play on my conscience. It wasn't something I had planned; it just happened. But Jackie got two for the price of one: not only had she fancied me for some time, but she also knew David was cheating on her and she wanted revenge.

Most women in her situation would have done anything to hide such an indiscretion, but not her. David was the wimpy type, and after we had been together she decided she wanted me to be her boyfriend. So she made sure he found out about us.

****

At that point in my story to Rocky, Jennifer arrived with Lisa. I introduced him to the ladies, pulled Jennifer to one side, and left him and Lisa to it.

"Jay, you look really nice today!" she said, admiring my new clothes, not realising it was her money that had bought them.

I didn't want her staying close to me, as I knew this would have a detrimental effect on my game plan, so I said, "I'll catch you up in a minute, babe, okay? I got to deal with something."

I went upstairs and did my rounds, touching and feeling all the sprats I'd been with, and chatting up new sprats and taking down their numbers – discreetly, of course!

Tiffany was by the bar with her friend. I approached her and politely asked her friend to disappear. Once we were alone I pulled her into a corner and slipped my hand slightly in between her thighs, my manhood standing to attention. There was something about Tiffany that made me like her more than any of the rest of them. She was just sweet and innocent. If I had to sum her up, I would say cool, calm, collected, and just downright sexy.

"Stop! People can see us!"

"I don't care," I said, pushing my hand further up her skirt. If she would have allowed it, I swear I would have boned her there and then.

"Come on, handsome, can't you wait until later?" she said, blushing.

I eased off, and just in the nick of time because Jennifer was now coming up the stairs and heading in my direction. She would have flipped if she saw me talking to the Enemy. She gave Tiffany a dirty look and walked passed. *PHEW!* I was glad she didn't stop. I would have been in a sticky situation, because Jennifer and Tiffany were no longer friends. Their friendship had broken down shortly after they met me. Although they both denied that fact, I knew better. Jennifer suspected I was boning Tiffany, and Tiffany knew I had boned Jennifer but didn't think I was still going there. I wasn't about to tip my hand about that.

I didn't want Jennifer to get vexed, so I told Tiffany I would catch her later. Really I wanted to stay put, but now was not the time to be playing with Jennifer's head. My car depended on her.

I started circulating the club. I noticed Rocky was still chatting to Lisa. I couldn't help thinking that he should have had her wrapped up by now. I mean, if he couldn't get her then he just didn't have what it takes. I had heard all the pillow talk about Lisa from Jennifer, and she wasn't exactly a nun. As I passed David, I gave him a dirty look. *What a punk*, I thought. He couldn't even see his girl was getting chatted up right under his nose. Then again, maybe he could!

The bright lights came on, signalling it was time to leave. I headed straight for the exit because I wanted to make sure I didn't miss out on any sprats. There was nothing that pissed me off more when coming out of a club than a friend telling me about some fit, sexy sprat inside who was nowhere to be found. I hated missing out.

Jennifer came out, looking pissed off.

"What's up, babe?"

"I want you to come and stay at mine tonight!"

No way! It's Tiffany's turn tonight! "I wish I could, but I can't – my friend is staying at mine tonight. I'll come tomorrow night, I promise."

"Okay," she said, flagging down a cab.

Rocky came out from behind the crowd. "Wicked…" he said.

Wicked! I couldn't see what the hell he found wicked about chatting up one sprat. "You wasted your night! Look how many sprats were in there!" I said. I was disappointed in him.

"Not really. I like her. She needed a lot of speeching."

I nearly laughed! Shiiiiiiiit! It had taken David approximately forty-five minutes to get a polish out of her, and here Rocky was telling me that she needed a lot of speeching.

"I'm staying at Tiffany's house tonight," I told him. "Here's some cab fare. I'll catch you tomorrow."

"All right, nice one. Tomorrow it is."

As I waited for Tiffany to come out, a sprat approached me and said, "Jay, Yasmin said to give you a message. She wants you to stay at her place tonight."

"Who's Yasmin?" I answered, totally dumbfounded.

"Don't you know who she is?" she asked, looking shocked.

"No."

"Well, she's around the corner."

I followed the girl hesitantly. I wondered whether Jennifer was setting me up. It wasn't until I got around the corner that I remembered who this Yasmin was. I had chatted her up a couple weeks back and promised to phone her, but I'd never got round to it.

"Oh, I never realised it was you. You want me to stay at yours?" I asked.

"If you want," she replied.

Well, it was obvious what she was after. The only problem was Tiffany. I weighed up the situation. I liked sleeping with Tiffany – in fact, I liked just being in her company. But to be frank, the way I was then there was nothing like fresh pu*sy. I badly wanted to make a hundred on my list and the only way to do this was to sex everything.

"Come on then," I said, hurrying her so that I wouldn't be seen.

We caught a cab from the back of the club. It was a short journey. I thought I'd had all the slappers from that club. *I was wrong!* She was the best even to this day, as you will find out later!

As soon as I got in her flat she took me into the bedroom. Closing the curtains, she wasted no time taking off my jeans. *I thought I was fast!* Flipping it out of my boxers, she caressed it slowly, licking and teasing me. She said, "I wanted to sleep with you the first time I saw you." I didn't answer; what could I say to that? I couldn't believe this sprat I'd known for little more than twenty minutes was actually going down on me. "I love sex. I can't help it," she said, licking my baton from base to tip and all around my balls, and just underneath. *Wow, the bit underneath the balls!*

By this time I was on fire and ready to release my load in her mouth. As if reading my mind, she said, "Don't come yet." I thought it was too late. "I'm coming," I said, losing control. Yasmin squeezed the base of my baton firmly. It stopped me dead in my tracks. *Damn, that was a new one to me!* She carried on sucking and French-kissing me down below. It wasn't long before I felt the tidal wave build up once again. This time she let it all out, swallowing every last drop. She said, "That was nice," as if she had just had a refreshing glass of water after spending a day in the desert.

Slowly, she took off the rest of my clothes and licked me from head to toe. Once again I was hard and stiff. Quickly ripping off her clothes, I laid her on the bed. Climbing on top, I started with deep steady strokes, then increased my pace, making her feel every last inch as I pounded her. "Faster, harder!" she shouted out as her orgasm rocketed through her; a moment later, I came again.

To my surprise, I still had a lot of energy left, and boy did I need it as that night she taught me all she knew, which was far more than I had experienced.

I left Yasmin's at midday the next day. Totally exhausted, I made tracks home. I knew I would be back for some of her crazy sex. But it wasn't to be until a year or so later.

When I got home, the first thing I did was call Tiffany to apologise for disappearing after the club. I told her Rocky had lost his door key and had had to stay at my place. Not a good lie, but she bought it all the same. When I hung up I called Jennifer: I had to keep her sweet because Tuesday (when she would be on her own in the shop and able to swipe the ring) was round the corner.

After a long bath I went to check up on Ms Carlton to see how she was doing. I was also curious as to why she had seemed so upset the day before. After Ms Carlton made me a cup of tea, I quizzed her. That's when she said, "Jay, you remind me so much of my son." She paused for a long while holding her hand on her forehead. Then she continued: "My son was just like you, a play boy. My Jamie was such a nice boy inside."

At this point she became tearful. I got Ms Carlton some tissue and patiently waited for her to continue. I wasn't sure where she was going with this.

"His father abused him mentally... He didn't have one positive thing to say about my son, even when Jamie continually went out of his way to please his father. His father always focused on the negative, making Jamie feel worthless. Jamie couldn't do anything right. I thought it was helping to toughen him up at the time. Unlike you, Jamie didn't vent his frustrations outwards; he didn't bully other people like you. He internalised everything, and I didn't realise how much it was eating away at him. I did nothing; I stood back and let it happen... He eventually committed suicide. If I'd only been strong enough, my son would still be here."

"But it wasn't your fault..." I interrupted her, trying to take away her pain somehow.

"Jay, you don't understand. You're too young to understand the effects. My Jamie wasn't as strong as you are."

I consoled Ms Carlton as best as I could before I made a swift exit. When I was outside I remember I felt a bit confused as to how she could compare me to someone who had committed suicide. I mean how could she look at me and think I would commit suicide? I had too much going on, sprats everywhere! *What I didn't realise at the time was that the suicide was not actually the point Ms Carlton was making!!*

I headed to Rocky's to indulge in some of that sweet cocaine I had had the day before. When we had smoked all of it, he said, "Do you want to come on a robbery with me?"

For a moment I felt tempted. The devil-stuff was making me feel up for it. But I said, "You know what? I don't need to rob. If I need money I just get it from Jennifer."

"You're lucky."

"Lisa's got money, my friend. Don't let her fool you."

"I know, I know, I'm working on it. But in the meantime I want something to smoke," he replied, deadly serious.

Seeing he wasn't getting through to me, he phoned one of his friends, who said he would go with him. I was tired so I called a cab and went home. It was seven-twenty when I got in. I went straight to bed. I had promised Jennifer I would stay at hers but I wasn't up to it. I knew she would call, so I took the phone off the hook.

I woke up the next morning not knowing that this was the day I was in for a surprise I would never forget. Even a fortune-teller wouldn't have seen this one coming...

I got dressed and decided I would surprise Tiffany with an early visit. I caught a cab to her house, and when I arrived her mother, Sally, answered the door in her dressing gown.

"Arrrgh! My little baby, you've just missed her! She's gone shopping with her grandmother. She shouldn't be too long. Come in and wait."

I wasn't exactly going to turn back now, was I? The cab had cost fifteen pounds! So I went into the living room, turned on the TV, and relaxed back on the sofa.

"Do you want a cup of tea," Sally asked from the kitchen.

"I wouldn't mind one – two sugars, please!"

She returned with two cups of tea, placing mine on the sofa arm as she sat down beside me. I could see her knickers in between the gap in her dressing gown. I tried not to think about it, and kept my eyes on the TV. How could I do anything else? She was a married woman, and she was old enough to be my mother.

"How old are you now, Jay?" she asked, as if she had known me for years.

"You know I'm eighteen," I lied.

"You're very handsome; you must have all the girls chasing you."

"Only Tiffany," I said, lying again.

"Have you ever been with an older woman?" she said, as calmly as when she had offered me a cup of tea.

Boing, boing, boingggg! I have found that a man's penis appears to detect stuff even before the brain registers what's going on. Don't ask me how – ask a bloody doctor.

"What do you mean…?"

"I mean…" She put her hand on mine.

Could she be suggesting – no, she couldn't be. She was!

"Don't be shy," she said, at the same time getting up and pulling me up straight.

Shy!

She kissed me. It took a moment for reality to sink in. Then I responded, tracing her every lip movement. Pulling her closer, we dropped back onto the sofa with her on top of me. Trying to adjust myself, I knocked over the cup of tea. I made a move to clean it up. She tugged me back. Slipping out of her dressing gown and knickers, she said, "Have you ever gone down on a woman?"

Have you ever had a brick smashed in your face! That was against the rules. You're probably thinking, some kind of bloody womaniser you are. That was then! I later mastered that too!

Eating under the table was one thing I hadn't done and had no intention of doing. Had it been Tiffany who asked, I would have probably given her one of Rocky's specials.

I said, "I'm not into that."

"You're young. You don't know what you're missing."

Accepting I was going to do no such thing, Sally took charge. Sitting upright on me, she inserted my baton. She boned me like a depraved woman, like an animal, scratching and biting me. It's crazy but I loved it. Maybe a little too much!

But I was feeling ashamed of my performance, so I decided I wanted out before Tiffany came back and caught us out.

"We'd better get dressed before your daughter gets back." I emphasised the word 'daughter', thinking it might prick her conscience.

"Relax! She's in London; she won't be back for a while yet."

Sally was a smart – she'd had it all planned. She had made out to me that Tiffany was shopping locally. She knew full well that I wouldn't have stayed if I'd known she was in town.

"Are you trying to get away from me?"

"No."

"Then just relax…"

Sally was sexy for a forty-year-old woman. She was what I like to call 'tick', which means she was voluptuous with those amazing gravity-defying breasts. She had long curly blonde hair and curves in all the right places. I wasn't ready for round two just yet, but she was the type that was very forceful. Soon, changing positions, we were at it again.

I left Tiffany's before she came back. I wasn't up for seeing her after boning her mum all day. I caught the train back to London. I wanted time to think. I knew I hadn't performed as well as I could have with Sally. But I tapped that pu*sy all the same. I felt good: sixty sprats and a woman – hey! I wasn't doing badly! I decided I would give her a better one next time round. I didn't know that the next time I was to see her, she would act as if nothing of the sort had happened. *Fine by me!* Perhaps my performance had been that lousy.

When I told Rocky, he kept saying, "You're lying!" *Lie my arse!* Okay, so I lied about a few things when it came to sprats – who doesn't? – but to say I'd slept with one when I hadn't was a definite no-no. I had come across a few of those kinds of people, and I usually didn't take to them. Maybe that's why I didn't take to David: he was definitely one of those kinds of guy, always saying he slept with sprats when he hadn't. After a while, I guessed he was just saying things to impress me. It had the reverse effect.

Jennifer came through as she promised she would – and some! She gave me two grand, cash. I guess the bonus was for good behaviour!

Three days later I gave the money to Rocky, who bought me a red Peugeot 205 GTI. It cost a thousand six; the change went on cocaine. Slowly but surely, the coke was getting a grip on me.

That night, I drove to Jennifer's and dropped Rocky off at Lisa's. Finally, he had got through to her. I parked the car at the bottom of Jennifer's road and pretended I hadn't bought it yet. *Just so I could collect the cab fare!* I boned Jennifer good and proper that night. How do I know? She told me so. If only she knew why!

When I woke up, Jennifer was shaking me vigorously. "The police are at the door!"

My first thought was, *Shit, it's something to do with my car!* The next thing Jennifer said made me think otherwise.

"They must have found out about the gold."

Phew... not my car! "Don't worry," I said, trying to reassure her. "There's no proof it's you who's been stealing."

The police took her bedroom apart, and they found a bag of gold and correspondence neatly concealed under the bottom draw of her dressing table. One of the officers read Jennifer her rights and arrested her for theft.

Did I go to the police station? *You can't be serious - of course I didn't!* I jumped into my car and paid a visit to Tiffany, who happened to live five minutes away.

Later that evening, when I saw Jennifer, I asked, "What happened?" a little too casually.

"I've lost my job – that's what happened! And they've charged me with thirty thousand pounds' worth of theft!"

Thirty thousand! I thought. I don't remember getting that much money... Maybe I'm the one getting robbed!

I consoled her for a few hours before leaving to pick up Rocky from Lisa's. It wasn't until I hit the motorway that it sunk in. Sh*t! *No more loot!*

When I talked it all through with Rocky, the outcome wasn't good. It was a Friday, payday for most people, including us. I was on the London underground, and my hands were shaking with the nerves already.

"You ready?" he asked.

"Yep," I replied, taking out my 007.

Rocky approached a man with his knife. "Take off your gold and give me your fucking money, and hurry up before I…" he demanded.

The man was rightly scared for his life, and did exactly as he was told, handing over his possessions. Moving on to the next victim, it was my turn. I repeated the process. It all seemed too easy. We attacked the whole carriage and fled to safety. It was a good haul: seven hundred cash, nine gold rings, and two watches. We smoked the money out in two days. The devil-stuff was starting to take over me.

Eventually, the robberies turned into a weekly occurrence, until one night I was on the train on my way home and I saw Yasmin. I hadn't seen her for almost a year, so you can imagine how all the memories came flooding back.

I wasted no time, and sat down beside her. "Where you been, stranger? I haven't seen you for ages!" I said.

For a split second there was no recognition; then she said, "Oh, it's you, Jay…!" She began telling me that she had moved in with a friend in London now.

"So where are you going?"

"I'm going home."

"Forget that! Come back to my place. Look how long it is since I've seen you." I pointed downwards.

"Okay then," she said without hesitation.

Once a slapper, always a slapper, I thought.

****

I would find out later that this is not always the case - people do change but it usually takes outside circumstances to shake you out of your comfort zone first!!

****

That night we fucked, fucked, and fuckd again. The next morning Yasmin poured out her heart to me. She told me her friend was kicking her out because she suspected her of sleeping with her boyfriend. To be honest, I bet she had done it. I told her she could stay at my place – unknown to her, I had plans for her.

She asked what had happened to Jennifer. Jennifer? *Wasn't that the sprat with no further use?* I told her Jennifer was in the past. That was part truth; the whole truth was that after Jennifer received community service, I couldn't find any other use for her – after all, she was jobless. So that episode had come to a sharp end.

Just as I was about to tell her about my eureka moment! Yasmin confessed that she had done prostitution before. Well, well, well, talk about beat me too it – I was just about to suggest it to her. After all, she had said she loved sex! I convinced her that we could make some serious money and then get out of there.

****

Yasmin was the kind of girl I suspect had been abused at some point. I got the feeling her parents hated her; perhaps she had been an accidental pregnancy.

These types of girls have no self-belief; their confidence is ruined at some time during their childhood. I've noticed they usually try their best to please everyone – everyone, that is, except themselves.

****

On her opening night, she brought back three hundred and fifty. I wasn't pleased; *I was ecstatic!* I was back in business! Didn't some wise-arse once say, "As one door closes, so another one opens," or something like that? Well, whoever he was, he was right! Jennifer came to an end, and in walked slack-bag Yasmin. Well, that's what I thought at the time anyway.

It only lasted for a month before it came to a very sharp end. But it was a happy time for me – not least because during that month I made it: I reached my goal and I was over the moon. *One hundred!* It felt a phenomenal achievement for me at the time. I was back out there again before too long, but from that day onwards I stopped counting.

But everything was about to change. One night, after returning from a nightclub, I jumped straight into bed – to sleep. I couldn't have been asleep for more than ten minutes when I heard someone frantically banging on the door. I assumed it was Yasmin returning from the graveyard shift. I knew she had a key but I was half asleep. When I opened the door, to my amazement there stood two policemen.

"Is your name Jay Jayson?" one of the men said.

"Yeah, why?" I asked with attitude.

"You're under arrest for suspicion of robbery."

Robbery! Bullsh*t! I hadn't done a robbery in a month! They searched my flat and found a bundle of credit cards under the carpet. All of them belonged to victims.

It was my first time in a police cell. I remember thinking, *I'm only fifteen - I'm still a juvenile. They can't touch me.* I couldn't have been more wrong.

I was approaching hell, fast.

CHAPTER 5
REMANDED IN HELL

The entry to hell consisted of a big electronic gate: the court had remanded me to Feltham Young Offenders' Prison. The gate closed slowly as the sweat-box rolled into the prison grounds. A moment later, it ground to a halt at a smaller iron gate, which had the word RECEPTION written above it in bold. With the sweat-box unloaded, the screw told me and the five other convicts to enter the reception area. Terrified of what was to come, I trailed behind the rest.

In the reception area, we were strip-searched and told to take a shower. Just as I finished, one of the screws shouted out, "Johnson, your number is NX0123. You're going to Meddler wing. Collect your bedding and follow me." I followed the screw for what felt like a ten-minute walk down long homogeneous corridors, all secured with either bricks or iron bars. Finally, we arrived; I was shoved into cell twenty-one, and the door was slammed behind me.

The tiny cell was bare except for a metal table, a chair, a bed, and a messy formation of cigarette butts stubbed into the floor. I started to make the bed, but I was interrupted by a bang on the wall, followed by, "What you in here for, mate?"

"Robberies," I replied.

"What's your name?"

"Jay," I answered.

"Jay, my name's Otis... I'll chat to you later."

"All right then."

I didn't bother to question him about my new surroundings. I didn't want to talk to anyone. Relieved that he'd gone quiet, I jumped into bed, only to discover that the bed had no spring to it. I could just as well have been lying on the floor.

I tried to calm my mind and to think of all the possible ways I could get myself out of the situation I was in. A number of unresolved thoughts tumbled around my mind, and then suddenly, like a flash of light, I recalled something my solicitor had said to me after the judge sent me away: "Don't worry, Jay. I'll get you bail on your next appearance in a week's time." I let the words ring in my head, and they made me feel more comfortable that night as I fell asleep.

The week that followed felt like a month. For twenty-three hours a day, I was locked in my cell. The only time I got out was to collect my food, for visits, and for one hour's daily 'association'.

I spent most of the time talking to Otis. I thought he was bona fide until I found out he was in for rape. Obviously, he said he had been stitched up. I never did understand why men raped women – as far as I could tell, there was no need!

On my next appearance at court I was refused bail. All my solicitor could say was, "Don't worry; you'll have a different judge next week and he'll give you bail." If I didn't get bail the next time, I knew one thing: I was going to punch my solicitor straight on the chin and then fire him – what I would call 'sending him for a kip'.

The next day I found out Rocky was also in Feltham, but located in a different wing because he was two years older than me. I jumped for joy when I heard it – at least I wasn't in there on my own!

The next week went even slower than the first. And at the end of it, my solicitor's prediction was wrong again. This time he said, "Maybe next week." So I asked him loads of questions, memorising every answer as best I could, and then, deciding he was of no further use to me, I sent him for a kip!

When I got back to Feltham after the hearing, I phoned my mother and asked her to sort out a solicitor for me. Two weeks later, I was lying in my cell when a screw opened the door and told me to pack my kit – I had got bail. I thought he was pulling my leg, but it turned out I really had been released. It's amazing how one's situation can flip in the blink of an eye.

"Otis, I just got bail!" I shouted excitedly. "I'll leave you my cigarettes and toiletries."

When I got to reception, I was given my bail sheet with my conditions of release. Glancing at them, my eyes clocked two conditions in particular. The first one read: 'To reside in the SE15 area, not to travel north of the river Thames.' SE15 was my grandfather's address. The second condition read: 'To abide by a curfew of four p.m. and to sign on at the police station at twelve p.m.' I read the conditions in disbelief as I made my way to the iron exit.

This was going to be tricky.

CHAPTER **6**
ONE WEEK'S BAIL

The first thing I did on my release was pay a visit to my cousin 'T' in his flat in South London. As I was restricted to the South London area, I had very few places to go.

When I arrived, he greeted me with that sweet aroma of weed. After answering a thousand and one questions about Feltham, he handed me a Super Tennent's. I wrapped a spliff and gulped the Tennent's, thinking about which sprat I would bone first. It was going to be a bit tricky as most of the sprats I knew lived north of the river.

T was the quiet type; you know, kept himself to himself. He was working for the post office and I guess he just accepted that this was going to be his life forever and ever. Well, that was about to change — at least for that day anyway!

When I finished my beer, I realised I was feeling tipsy and horny as hell. Enough was enough. "Let's go up the high street and look for some sprats..."

As if reading my mind, T interrupted me: "There's this all-right-looking chick. She lives downstairs."

I wasn't a shy guy, so I slipped out and knocked on her door. I guess that was really the brew taking over, and the fact I had just been released. A little scruffy boy answered, looking like he hadn't seen a bath in months.

"Can you get...?" I paused. I hadn't even bothered to ask T what her name was. Putting it down to the drink, I continued, "Can you get your sister, please?"

Wiping his runny nose, he shouted, "Patricia, there's someone here to see you!" and he ran off.

As I stood there waiting I noticed there was no wallpaper or carpet in the hallway. For a split second I wondered if they were squatting. The next thing I spotted were a pair of huge breasts standing proud in a bra top that was blatantly too small. Smiling at the girl, I said, "I'm T's cousin upstairs. I want to talk to you."

"Okay, I'll be up in a minute," she said. "I'm just going to get my shoes."

BIONG, BOING, BOINGGGGGG! At first glance I knew I had met her type before. She was weak in character and easily convinced of anything. How was I sure? My instinct told me: she reminded me of Yasmin. It's difficult for me to put my finger on exactly what it was that reminded me of Yasmin. Sometimes when I listen to my intuition I don't exactly know the details, I just get the answer – which in her case was ABUSED, which made me think of Yasmin. However, maybe it was just that here I was, a complete stranger, and she had just agreed to come upstairs with me without any hesitation whatsoever – maybe that was the trigger. Either way, boy was I right!

Patricia wasn't as pretty as I'd hoped. She had long, scruffy dark hair and very light dirty-coloured skin. Her eyes were light brown and hollow, as if she had been through too much for her age. But the bust more than made up for the lack of looks.

Smiling to myself, I went back upstairs, and drank the rest of T's brew. Very nearly drunk, I asked T if he had any rubbers. Shaking his head, he replied, "No, why? Is she coming up?"

"Of course she is."

"Damn, do you know how long I have wanted to put one on her...?"

There was a knock at the door.

Sitting on the bed beside Patricia, I asked her if she drank or smoked weed. I wanted to get her plastered. She declined both. Looking at me, she said to T, "How comes you've never told me about your cousin? What's your name?"

Looking at her chest, rather than her face, I told her my name. Just then, I realised I was starting to slur my words. I decided I wasn't in the mood for talking; it wasn't as if she would take any hard work. So I got straight down to the nuts and bolts.

"Have you ever slept with two men before?"

T flashed me a look as if to say, "That's a bit forward."

The problem with T was this: he was the perfect gentleman type, but he was not able to distinguish between sprats who appreciated the overly nice gentleman stuff and those who did not.

"No, I haven't. Not yet anyway," she replied, expressionless.

The answer she gave and the way she said it was just what I was looking for – I knew she was up for it. And I guess T came to the same assumption, because he came and sat on the other side of her.

"So are you up for some fun then?" I asked.

After what seemed to be a moment of deep thought, she replied, "I'm not sure my boyfriend would like me to do that."

Boyfriend! Who was asking him anything?

I was in no mood for games, so I put my hand on her breast as a tester, motioning for T to do the same. She never said a word. I took her silence as a cue to go further. Taking her webbers out of the bra, I started to kiss the right one. T followed my every move on the left breast.

Gradually, we stripped her naked and laid her down on the bed. She kept completely silent. She started polishing off T as I attempted to bone her at the same time. It wasn't working – I couldn't get in – so I told T to have a try. We swapped places: he tried to insert himself and Patricia gave me a good old polish. After a few attempts T said, 'I can't get it in either." Changing positions for the second time, I gave it one more go. It was no use – something was wrong. But somehow, some way, I knew I was getting in there.

"T, you got any Vaseline?" I asked him.

"I haven't got any."

Racking my brain for a solution, my eyes caught sight of a broomstick on the floor. Sober, I probably wouldn't have dreamt of it! But without a word I picked it up and nudged it inside Patricia. She tensed up a bit, but never said anything. Five minutes of broomstick and I thought she would be as wet as ever. I tried again, but still no entry. By now I was really frustrated and totally at a loss for what to do next. Then, like a whirlwind, it came to me. Cooking oil!

"T, you got any cooking oil?"

"Cooking oil?" I could hear the shock in his voice.

"Yes, bloody cooking oil."

"Yeah, hold on, I'll just get it."

I could not believe my eyes; T came back shrugging his shoulders with a frying pan in his hand! *Unbelievable!*

Cooking oil worked like a dream.

T stood on the bed and held her legs back so I could pound her properly. The drink enhancing my performance, finally she was enjoying the threesome: I could hear little moans of pleasure. After ten minutes, T started begging me to hurry up and give him a go. The ten minutes turned into thirty minutes. Eventually, I gave into his whining and said, "Your turn." What happened next brought tears to my eyes.

"About fucking time!" In desperation, he slipped trying to position himself; when he did finally get on her, he gave three – and I mean three – flimsy pokes and then he screamed, "Ar... Arrrrrrrr... Arrrrrrrrrrrrrrrrr!" and collapsed on Patricia. If I hadn't let him on her when I did, I guess he would have come just watching me paste her. Dragging him off her, I went back into action, until I let my juice all come flooding out, leaving me drained and sober.

Just as I was getting up, there was a tap at the window.

"Patricia, what are you doing in there?"

It was her mother. Patricia sprang out of bed and got dressed in a flash, shooting out of the door without as much as a "Goodbye" or a "See you later" or even a "Thanks, guys, that was a great time!".

When she was outside, I heard her mother ask, "What the hell were you doing in there?"

Patricia said, "I was..." That was all I heard as the voices faded away.

Fully sober now, I started to get dressed. Now Mr Paranoia paid me a visit and took over my thoughts. "What if Patricia lies and says we raped her?" The thought had me trembling.

I didn't realise I was thinking aloud until T said, "You're just being paranoid."

Paranoid or not, I was taking no risks. Prison was too fresh in my mind. Quickly getting dressed I said to T, "I'll come and see you later."

I lied. I had no intention of seeing him any time soon. It turned out I wouldn't see T again for another four years, and it would be two years before I heard Patricia's name mentioned again.

When I left T's, I went straight to see my godmother, Aggie: I needed some money. Now my godmother was the type of godparent every parent dreams of having for their kids. There was not one bad bone in her body; she was a real Mother Theresa: a caring, loving, and trustworthy woman. Throughout the years, I always went to her when I needed her, and she was always there for me. Before I left, she gave me the usual talking to about staying away from trouble.

It only took me five days to break my bail conditions. Five days after sleeping with Patricia, I was caught north of the river. I had actually been minding my own business chatting to a girl I knew on the high street when the police pulled me over for a routine stop. After numerous lies, they eventually found out who I was and arrested me.

The next day when I went before the judge he took my bail away. I was gutted. I couldn't come to terms with how stupid I had been. My bail condition had been clear: don't go over the Thames. Now, for not abiding by this simple condition, I was on my way to hell once again.

Boy was I a fool!

CHAPTER 7
A LONG STRETCH IN HELL

At Feltham Young Offenders', one month before sentence, I left my cell for a legal visit. A tall, conservative-looking man sat at the table smiling at me. He opened his briefcase and took out a bundle of papers. He said, "Well, Mr Johnson, I have some good news and some bad news. I am Michael Plackard, a barrister selected to defend you by your solicitor, Mr Williams. How are you doing?"

My eyes sent a ferocious look across the table to that toffee-nosed bastard. I said, "Don't worry about how I'm doing. Just get me out of this fucking place."

Fidgeting nervously with the collar of his blazer, he said, "I'm afraid it may not be as simple as that. These are very serious charges that could well carry a lengthy custodial sentence."

Sh*t! Why was he talking about a lengthy sentence when I hadn't even been on trial yet? I was confused. This guy was meant to be on my side but it sounded as though he had already tried and convicted me.

Waving my hands like a crazy man I said, "What the fuck are you talking about, sentence? I haven't even been on trial…?"

"Calm down, Mr Johnson, that's what I wanted to talk to you about."

"Calm down?! You listen…"

"If you'll just let me finish," he interrupted. "As I was saying earlier, I have some good news and bad news. The good news is that I've just received a letter from the prosecution stating that they want to plea bargain with you."

"What's a plea bargain?" I asked. I was totally lost.

Pulling out a single sheet of paper from his case, he studied it briefly and then said, "Well, they've decided that if you plead guilty to nine counts of robbery, they're willing to drop the rest. As your barrister, I tell you that your chances of getting off on all fifteen counts are extremely slim. I'm sure you're aware that if you plead not guilty and are deemed guilty, the judge will deal with you much more severely."

The truth was, I hardly knew anything. Who was I to tell this barrister he was talking bullsh*t? It wasn't until the day of sentencing that I would realised that Mr Plackard had led me into the lion's den to be slaughtered.

Pulling out a second piece of paper, he said, "Now for the bad news: your case has been filed to be heard by the learned Judge Jones."

At hearing that name, suddenly I had a headache; my anger drained out of me and I was dazed, dumbstruck. I knew I was in trouble. I had heard from other convicts about this Judge Jones guy; he was notorious. He had passed a string of ridiculous sentences to anyone who dared to come before him.

He noticed the shock on my face. "I take it you have come across his name before?" I nodded my head. "Not to worry too much; he's not as bad as everyone claims him to be." This was cold comfort and I didn't believe it. "Now I need some details on your background."

I gave him the information he required, and in a trance I made my way back to my cell.

The next day, I saw Rocky at the gym. He told me that he too had agreed to a plea bargain. For the rest of that month, I was detained in the GOD block (Good Order and Discipline). I don't remember why I was sent there; I just remember I was there. I spent most of my time perfecting a letter to the notorious judge, pleading for leniency and community service. I wasn't to know Judge Jones was as heartless as they get!

On the day of sentencing in the Crown Court, Mr Barrister was so nervous before the bench when pleading for my lenience that his speech broke into a stammer, and he nearly forgot to give my letter to the judge. The old judge appeared to be a different judge to the one I had heard so much about. He was in his oversized throne and seemed to have a pleasant look about him; that is, until he pulled down his half-cut glasses to the very tip of his nose. Then, staring down at me, he sneered, "Well, Mr Johnson, I have read your letter and, to be perfectly honest, I'm not impressed."

My mouth turned dry. I turned and looked up to find my mother in the gallery. Her eyes were glued to the bench. Turning back to look into the eyes of the judge, now frosty and hard, I heard Rocky whisper, "Fucking idiot."

"You are a vicious young man. Your crimes against all these innocent people are inexcusable. The very nature of the crime excludes any possibility of community service. For your own good and that of society I sentence you to six years under section fifty-three on all indictments to run concurrent. Take him out of my court."

I could hear my mother sobbing in the background as the guards took me down to the court cells. A moment later, Rocky appeared, hissing through his teeth. Jones had also given him six years but not under section fifty-three. I would have to serve longer than him as section fifty-three meant I didn't have an early release date and more than likely would have to serve the entire sentence.

Well, that was how it was supposed to be, anyway. But I had no idea that a certain lady, a Ms James, would be thrown into my path! If there was a gender I got on with best… need I say more? We'll meet her later.

As we waited for the coach to take us to Pentonville Prison as a stopover, the screw came and gave me a note from my mother. It read: 'Son, I love you no matter what. Please be strong. All of us love you out here. Always love you, Mother x'.

It wasn't until a few weeks later, when I was transferred from Pentonville Prison back to Feltham, that the reality of what had happened sank in. Rocky and I were separated, and I was put back in my original wing. The only difference from last time was that the word REMAND on my cell card had been replaced with the number six and the letters Y-E-A-R-S, in bold. I must have been in my cell five minutes when a convict known as Superman knocked on my cell flap. He said, "Damn – you got six years. Don't worry, just ride it. You've only got five years, eleven months, and two weeks left!" It was at that very point the reality sunk in. SIX *Fucking YEARS!*

I tried to picture myself in six years' time – I couldn't. I could barely think about one year into the future, let alone six. I felt depressed. I wanted to close my eyes and wake up when it was all over – or better still, never wake up at all. At that moment it really felt as if my life was over and there was no way to fix it.

For some time, I stared into thin air, my mind completely numb, to the point that I was actually looking at nothing – neither was I thinking of anything. I entered that state for roughly forty minutes before I snapped out of it. It was this place where nothing happens and I couldn't recall being in it. And when I did snap out of it, it wasn't long before I sank inside it again, a kind of waking trance. Why couldn't I just fall asleep and never wake up...?

In the first few months of my sentence letters flooded in every day, in fours and fives. Everyone had heard about my downfall, either through gossip or by reading the paper. When I did get a glimpse of the paper, out-of-date, there it was in black and white: GANG ROBBERS GET SIX YEARS.

The following months were very difficult for me. I was caught in a state of deep depression. The only things that kept me going were my fortnightly visits, and of course my affair with Lady Five-fingers! No convict misses his freedom more than a womaniser: he lives for his addiction to sprats, and my supply had been cruelly cut off. Could it get any worse? Oh, yes!

A week after Christmas, a screw opened my door and the look on his face told me I was in for a shocker – and I was right. My stomach churned. "Here's a late Christmas present for you," he said. "Pack your kit – you're going to Aylesbury."

My head pounded as I traced back through all the horror stories I had heard about Aylesbury. Aylesbury was well-known as the worst Young Offenders' Prison. It dealt only with long-termers, mainly lifers. Several convicts tried to console me while I waited for the coach to take me to the countryside. As the coach swooped through the stormy weather, I remember looking at the convict who was handcuffed to me and noticing he looked just as sad as I felt.

The prison looked ancient and filthy as we filed out of the sweat-box into the reception area. Checking through my personal stuff, the screw said, "You can't have these tapes."

"What do you mean, I can't have these tapes?" I asked, a little shocked.

"What do you mean, what do I mean?"

"I mean how comes…"

"Listen, you little piece of shit, and listen carefully. You're not in Feltham any more; this is Aylesbury. This is a totally different show, you understand?"

I didn't answer, but I understood all right. He was simply confirming everything I had heard already.

I arrived at the Induction Wing, where I was to stay for the next week. All the new cons were held here to receive a medical check and categorisation before being assigned to a wing in the main prison.

The single cell I was housed in could easily have been mistaken for a primitive cave. Unlike the cells at Feltham, there was no toilet or sink, just a little piss-pot and a bowl. The door was three times as thick, and a miniature glass panel at the rear end of the cell was a poor imitation of a window. I lay awake, wide-eyed, the whole night, wondering if I would be able to survive six years in a place like this.

After the medical checks and various visits from probation officers, we were taken out of induction on the seventh day and escorted to the main prison. As we headed to our new locations, I noticed some very big convicts were trying to intimidate us. I guess they were looking for potential victims to harass. The boy next to me's knees were having a boxing match as we shuffled past them into A Wing. I reckoned I would probably be the youngest convict in Aylesbury – and I was right.

It wasn't until later that evening on 'association' that I got a surprise. When my landing was unlocked I picked up my wash-kit and headed down the landing for a shower. The first person I saw was Horse Mouth, somebody I had known on the outside. No need to wonder why we called him Horse Mouth – it was simple – he had the mouth of a horse.

"Hey, Horse Mouth! What you doing in here?"

"I've been here six months now – robbery charge. There are loads of us here." He led me to a cell packed with cons. "Hey, everyone, look who's here!"

They all turned around at once and rushed to greet me. Rocky was leading. For the first time in months I didn't feel so alone. At some stage I had hung about or known all of them on the outside. And it was great to see Rocky again. He gave me the rundown on Aylesbury. He told me he had been shipped there two months before. His version didn't seem half as bad as everyone else's.

After association, I had a bowl wash and jumped into bed, getting stuck into a Harold Robbins novel. Just as I had got to a juicy part of the book, I heard banging on the ceiling above. I got out of bed and went to the window. "Yeah, yeah!" I shouted.

"What's your name, what you in for?" a voice bellowed from above.

I gave the stranger my name and a quick rundown on why I was there.

Switching to a Jamaican accent, he said, "Mi name is Chubby, and ah mi run this prison, ya hear mi?"

A few weeks later I found out he wasn't far off the truth.

Flipping again to his English accent he continued, "Anyway, I have some weed. Do you want a zoot?"

Prison is a funny place in many ways. I had never come across so many different characters and slang words.

"Yeah, yeah," I replied. Damn, that was exactly what I needed.

He ripped his bed sheet and attached it to a cup, put the weed in it, and stuffed tissue on top so it wouldn't fall out. He swung it down to me.

I slept like a baby.

That weekend Stretch, my mother, and Tiffany came to visit me. As I sat down at the table I noticed the stress on my mother's face. I said, "Don't worry, Mum. I'll get through." I didn't believe it myself, though.

After a little chat with Stretch and my mother, I asked them to leave so I could talk to Tiffany in private. Tiffany had a little present for me – some weed – hidden in her mouth. I got it just in time. Unfortunately, it was the only safe entrance into the prison!

Damn, I really missed Tiffany and she missed me. I found out years later that prison really does have that ability to heighten the sense of missing someone. You know the old saying 'Absence makes the heart grow fonder'? Well, it is true – at least until the circumstances change!

By the time I was fifteen months into my sentence, I had found out that Aylesbury wasn't that bad after all; it didn't live up to its notoriety. But I wasn't getting used to the piss-pot regime and I badly wanted to be transferred back to Feltham. I put in three applications: the SO (senior officer) laughed at the first one; the PO (principal officer) was in hysterics at the second; at the third, the governor had the cheek to ask me if I was feeling all right.

The next two months were sheer madness. They say things happen for a reason! I don't know why I did it, but I did. The victim had only been housed next door for two days, but I'd noticed it straight away: a Cartier watch. It wasn't a particularly good one, but it was a brand all the same. I could trade it for many other things.

"Take off the watch," I demanded on the second day.

"What do you mean, take off the watch?" he replied, trying to call my bluff. Pulling out a PP9 battery wrapped in a sock, he knew exactly what I meant now. "All right... all right... take it!"

So I did. Two hours later, I was being frog-marched to the block by eight screws. The governor put me in the block for fourteen days.

On the fifth day, a con was restrained and brought down for punishment. That night, when everything was quiet, we had a lengthy talk during which he gave me an idea. He said,

"If you want to go back to Feltham so badly, why don't you write to your MP?"

"What's he going to do?" I asked.

"Listen, all you have to do is tell your MP you want to do a brick-laying course or any course that they don't do here and the only place that does it is Feltham. Throw in a bit about getting bullied, and that should do it. Trust me!"

"So why haven't you done it?" I asked, a little bit sceptical.

"I don't want to go to Feltham. I'm from Aylesbury so it's much easier for me to get my visits here."

"Me personally, I'd prefer to have no visits than stay in this sh*t-hole..."

This MP business was all new to me, but I decided it was worth a try. The next morning I asked the screw for the address for Parliament.

The day before I was due to go back on the wing I got another visit from Tiffany. I told her I was down the block and she started to cry. I couldn't blame her: I felt like shedding a few tears myself. "Don't cry," I said, "I can handle it. Now listen, I want you to pass it to me as soon as the screws behind me aren't looking, okay?"

"All right, handsome."

Handsome, my foot. I knew I looked a mess. But I needed to hear that word. A womaniser is always conscious of his appearance.

"They're not looking," she said.

I leaned across the table and kissed her full on the mouth. I used my tongue to prise the weed out through her lips into the safety of my mouth. Everything seemed perfect and I assumed they had seen nothing so we settled down to some dry sex for the remaining minutes. When the visit came to a close, I waved goodbye to Tiffany. Boy did I miss her.

As I stepped into the search area, three screws jumped me. One of them had me by the throat. I tried to swallow it but I couldn't: his grip was too firm. I tried to bluff but they didn't fall for it. Fully equipped, one of them produced an oversized lolly stick; forcing it into my mouth, he dug out the drugs.

On adjudication, the governor sentenced me to a further seven days cell confinement (CC) and fourteen days' block with no privileges. CC is the worst; they even take out the bed during the day. I remember reading words etched on the floor: 'They think we're fucking animals.' Whoever wrote that must have felt exactly as I did. But amazingly, the seven days passed quickly. Finally, I was allowed a bed to finish off the remaining days in block.

Eventually, I was released from the block. When I returned to the wing, I was greeted with a round of applause from the cons. They were glad to see me: they had assumed I had been sent on the Ghost Train. The Ghost Train is a ride nobody wants to make. The inmate is shunted from one block of one prison to another block in another prison every month for twelve months. Nobody knows where you are – including your friends, your family, and anyone outside the prison system. And while you're riding the Ghost Train you're not entitled to anything – no letters, no phone calls, no contact. I had heard rumours that they drug you up along the way. It's really messed up. By the time the Ghost Train is over, you wouldn't know whether you were in heaven or hell. Everyone was glad I wasn't on that ride: especially me!

Two weeks later the screws gave me another surprise – but this time it blew up in their faces. Opening up my cell door, the screw said, "Who's a lucky boy then? Pack your kit – you're going to Feltham in the morning."

WOW! I was overjoyed! I punched the air with my fists. The letter had worked! "God bless that boy in the block who told me what to do!"

All the guys I had made friends with inside, and the ones I knew from the outside, were sad to see me go, especially Rocky. In a way I was a little sad to leave myself. Goodbye, Aylesbury; hello again, First Class Feltham!

Landing back on better ground, I decided it was time to further my education, so I took up a computer course. A year and a half later, I would realise the course was my early ticket back into society.

Around my eighteenth birthday, two things happened that I could only describe as a godsend. Firstly, the governor of my wing at Feltham was replaced with a tall red-head named Ms James. Now if there was one set of people I knew how to get around, it was females. Surely my track record proved that to some degree. Secondly, I passed my computer course with flying colours. The course was designed to last six months, but I finished it much earlier.

Fortunately for me, I got to meet the red-head soon, on my review board. The only people present were Ms James and my personal officer, Mr White.

"Hello, Jay, I'm Miss James, your new governor."

"Hello, Miss James. Is that Ms or Mrs?" I replied with a smile on my face.

Miss James refused to answer.

Mr White outlined my progress to the governor. Listening attentively, I could tell she was shocked but I wasn't sure why.

"I'm pleased to hear that you're trying to better yourself, Jay. What do you plan to do now that your course has finished?"

Jay! No screw or governor had ever called me by my first name. Was that a sign of an easygoing, laid-back person? Was it a sign of someone with good people skills? Or was she just attracted to me? I wasn't sure but I decided I would push my luck anyway.

I said, "I would really like to take a higher course in computer studies."

****

I knew where I was going with this. All womanisers seem to have the ability to know what they want but go indirectly to get it – I was no different. Although I must admit, some womanisers may not yet be aware or actually view it as manipulation.

****

"Well, it shouldn't be a problem. I'm sure Mr White can arrange something for you with the education department."

"Yeah, but they don't have any higher courses to offer me. It's a shame because I'm passionate about computers, and about furthering my education."

Passionate my arse... The only thing I was passionate about at that point was sticking her one!

"Oh, that's very unfortunate; something should be done about that..."

Exactly what I wanted her to say! "Maybe I could go to college on a temporary basis; that is, if it's possible, of course?"

Mr White shot me a look. I think he was trying to ask me if I was crazy or something.

"Is that possible, Mr White?"

"Er... Er... I've never heard of it being done before."

"How long have you served, Jay?"

"Two years convicted."

After a moment's silence she said, "I'll look into it, but I can't promise anything. I'll let you know as soon as possible." She gave me a warm smile as I left.

I liked her. She seemed to be a very nice lady. I wondered if this would be my break.

That night, for the first time in years, I thought about my future. What was I going to do when I got out? Crime was out of the question, but then again so was working for a living. The way I calculated at the time, nobody got rich from a job. I needed to find myself something else that wouldn't put me back in jail.

****

What I didn't know or understand at the time was simply this - nobody becomes successful without mastering their profession, field, or talent... The loot, recognition, and so on automatically follows behind. If you try to get there any other way, success will forever elude you. In other words, *there are no shortcuts apart from mastery. Take heed!!!*

****

I thought, *I'll find myself some rich sprats. Yeah, that's what I'll do.* I also decided to stop smoking drugs. I knew it was doing me no good. All of a sudden I was trying to eliminate anything that would possibly put me back in this sh*t-hole. That night I dreamt about the outside, and in my dream I found a million-pound sprat!

Two weeks later, I was summoned to see Ms James. I knew it had something to do with my college request. Hands sweating, I knocked on the door. I said, "You wanted to see me, Ms James?"

"Yes. Please sit down."

"Governor James, could you please contact admin on two-four-two?" a speaker announced.

"Could you give me a minute, Jay, while I check what they want? They don't give me a rest, you know..."

"Shall I wait outside?" I asked.

"No, you can wait right there. I won't be a sec."

Trying to relax, I noticed I had built up a sweat. The suspense was killing me, and Ms James wasn't giving anything away.

She closed her conversation.

"Yes, now where was I? Yes, about this college course. I've talked at length to various officers and Mr Carter, the head of education. I will tell you, most officers were totally against it, but Mr Carter spoke very highly of you. He convinced me that, given the chance, he believed you are capable of succeeding at any task given to you. I've also been informed you'll be the first to attend college from this institution. If you do well, you'll set a path for others to follow.

"Now, Mr Carter has already spoken to the college, and they say that they're willing to accept you. So it's just a matter of filling out the application form, which you should have by the end of the week. This particular course will not start until September, so in the meantime keep your nose clean. I've had to pull a lot of strings for you. I'm putting my neck on the line here; don't let me down, Jay."

"Yes, Ms James. I don't know how to thank you. I promise I won't let you down."

I phoned my mother straight away to tell her the news, and she was as ecstatic as me. She said, "Just make sure you don't slip up, okay, son?"

"Yes, I'll try my best. Mum, I suggest you give Ms James a call and thank her, and call every now and again so she knows I'm loved out there."

****

Again, my mind jumped forward. I reasoned that if my mother called Ms James often and I didn't mess up at college, when it came to my parole maybe she would put in an extra word. I knew that governors carried a lot of weight with the Home Office, which would ultimately decide if and when I was to be released early.

****

I struggled through the next few months with a cleaning job, scrubbing concrete floors on my hands and knees. It was degrading work, but I kept my head down and bided my time.

One day I was playing football on the prison field with another inmate when a man approached us; it turned out he was a Chelsea scout. He wanted to take us on and asked us how long we had left to serve on our sentences. When we told him, he said he would look into seeing if he could get us out early, but that we shouldn't get our hopes up as we both still had a long time left to serve. The next day, he gave me the bad news that he was unable to influence my current situation.

All the same, Ms James regularly checked up on me; on one occasion she confirmed that the acceptance letter for the City & Guilds Level 3 Information Technology course had been received.

On enrolment day for my course, a Wednesday in early September, I was awake at four a.m. I couldn't sleep a wink; I was too excited. In exactly three-and-a-half hours the screw would unlock my cell so that I could enrol at West London College. *Sweet, sweet Ms James!* I'd already got out of bed maybe five or six times to try on my new designer clothes that Tiffany had sent me. I admired myself in the mirror; the reflection I saw sparkled. It felt great to be in my own clothes. I don't want to sound conceited but ladies, imagine the man of your dreams!

I pictured the college, full of lovely long-legged sprats. As you can imagine, I was bursting at the seams. I craved a good old-fashioned shag more than anything. For years I had been entertaining myself with memories from the past, or the odd men's magazine. Now I was soon to be able to have it in the flesh. *The first person I catch is in trouble,* I thought to myself.

I imagine secretly boning all the girls at the college. I'd perform so well on the first sprat – maybe in the lift or somewhere exciting – that she would confide in her friend that I was the best lay she'd ever had; her friend would want to know what I'd got that was so great, and I wouldn't refuse to demonstrate it to her. Slowly, the word would spread, and the rest would be history. *Bang!*

The screw opened my door at exactly seven thirty. I must have showered and changed in five minutes flat, but due to a few administrative hold-ups I didn't get clear of the gates until nine thirty.

Stretch and Wugly were waiting outside for me in a convertible BMW. I was shocked to see Wugly; he hadn't spoken to me since the incident with David. It turned out he no longer spoke to David and had heard the real story. It looked like things were on the up for him! I jumped into the car. Stretch gave me a bottle of champagne and a bag of weed. I took the champagne and told him he could keep the weed – I no longer smoked.

I had roughly four hours to play with until I had to enrol; I decided to hang around the town centre, making sure I went very easy on the champs because I'd not drunk anything for over two years. The *last* thing I wanted was to get drunk and put my new-found freedom in jeopardy.

I arrived at the college half an hour early so as not to miss anything – or anyone. Gradually, the main hall started to fill with students. Standing fourth in the queue, I scanned the room slowly, taking in everything. As far as my eyes could see, there were beautiful-looking sprats flooding in by the second. Was I seeing things because I had been locked up for so long? I wasn't sure. They must have thought I was crazy by the way I was staring at them. I glimpsed two mixed-race girls joining the back of the queue. If my eyes weren't deceiving me, the lighter one of the two looked outstanding.

The process bell rang. I strolled forward behind the three students in front of me in the queue, and sat down at the only table available of the four situated in that section. I handed over my papers to the lady in front of me, and she ran her eyes over each sheet, stamping each at the bottom. The way she rushed through them, I found it almost impossible to believe that she had read anything, until she got to the very last page. Giving me a strange look, she glued her eyes to the paper. I was puzzled as to why she had looked at me in such a manner. I leaned forward and traced her eyes back to the paper.

She was reading the following entry on my form:

HOME ADDRESS: HMP FELTHAM,

                              BEDFONT ROAD,

                              MIDDLESEX TW13 4ND

That explained it.

Stamping the last sheet, she told me to move on to the next section. And so it went for the next two hours. When I had finally finished with all that bullsh*t, I went to the canteen where Stretch and Wugly were waiting for me. The canteen was only half full. Looking around, I spotted them sitting at the back of the hall. I sat down with them and asked Stretch to get me a steak and kidney pie; he kindly obliged. I was just about to start eating when in walked the two sprats I'd clocked earlier in the main hall.

Stretch noticed them too. "I'll take the lighter one," he said.

"No. I'll take the lighter one."

"You've been away too long, mate! You won't be able to handle her. I bet you've lost your touch, *gaɬ-ist!*"

He was challenging me! "Then I'll just have to show you," I replied.

We watched the girls glance around for somewhere to sit, eventually choosing a table directly in front of ours. *How convenient!*

"They look like sisters," observed Wugly.

"C'mon then, Jay, show us you haven't lost your touch then!"

I looked at the darker sister. She was fresher looking, but there was something more distinguished about the lighter one. I couldn't put my finger on the reason why, but given the choice I wanted the lighter one.

I stared at the lighter one, waiting for eye contact. There – I had it. I smiled, she smiled back, and we held each other's glance for that moment too long. In the space of that moment I knew I had to have her, and that I was going to have her.

"Did you see that, Stretch?"

"Did you see what?"

"Did you see the moment?"

"You're seeing things," he said.

Maybe it's my imagination, I thought, *but I'm not usually wrong about those things.* I knew it wouldn't be long before I found out. One week, to be precise.

I arrived back at the prison five minutes before my five p.m. deadline. Back in my cell, Ms James came by briefly to ask how my day had gone. I assured her everything had gone well.

Impatiently, I waited for the starting day of my course. The only thing on my mind was that sprat. I couldn't get her out my mind. To get her out of my system, I knew I had to bone her.

The big day came. From now on, I was out five days a week attending West London College, where there were sprats running wild all over the place – well, that was my view of it. It was just what I needed.

The first week for me was more about sussing things out. From the moment I walked onto the grounds, I tuned in. The college was divided into three sections, and in the middle was a mini-field. There were two main buildings, a large recreational hut with table-tennis, pool, and bar football, and the canteen, which I knew would end up being my favourite spot – everybody's got to eat, right?

The canteen was in need of an upgrade; it reminded me of a prison visit hall with all the chairs and tables formulated in straight lines. In the first week I sussed out who were the cool cats and who were the nobodies. The cool cats had the best seats right at the back, where they had an almost panoramic view of the grounds and the other buildings and all the exits. The nobodies were scattered everywhere else. I knew I had to find a way to get in with the cool guys and girls.

As usual, I didn't have to put much brain power into it. Cool cats have a habit of recognising other cool cats and are drawn to each other. Very quickly, I was in with the in-crowd and eventually everybody found out I was coming from the prison, which turned me into the coolest cat of them all. Most male students were in awe of me and the sprats – well, they all started competing for my attention. Within a few weeks, I was the King of West London College and all of a sudden I was the person to know.

And now I suppose you're wondering what happened to the light-skinned sprat. *Need you ask?* I had approached her on the first day. Her name was Jackie Noel, and the sprat she was with wasn't her sister after all. After she told me her name, I told her in my own charming way that I was really feeling her.

"I've been with my man Sam for two years now, so the answer to that is no."

No indeed!

****

Rejection? That word doesn't exist in my world. I don't believe in no at all. To me, 'no' is just a word on the way to 'yes'. It's a good philosophy to have in life. If you want something and get rejected, big deal! You haven't lost anything – you are still in the same position you were before.

I don't let my pride get in the way – neither should you!

****

Two weeks later, Jackie approached me in the corridor. She touched me on the shoulder and said, "Hi, Jay. How are you?" Then she let me know in the subtle way females do that she had finished with her boyfriend. *Was she bright or what?*

"That was quick," I said.

"No, you don't understand. It's…"

I understood all right! I knew all the sprats were talking about me, and she wanted in first.

"It's all right," I replied. "You don't have to explain."

A few weeks later, Ms James gave me a home leave for the weekend. On the first day, I brought Jackie to my godmother's house. As soon as we were in the living room I wasted no time in unfolding the sofa bed. It was a bad move: she had me speeching her until two a.m. just to get in between her legs. I was on home leave! Didn't she realise I didn't have time for all that crap? But I had no intention of leaving without some, either – damn it! I'd been waiting nearly three years for this!

It took me so long to talk her round that when she finally succumbed I gave up the chance to get a condom from my jeans pocket because it was on the other side of the room. I was scared she was going to change her mind by the time I got back.

I was a man possessed: I ripped off her knickers and attacked her passion button with my tongue – like a cat tucking into a fresh bowl of milk. I was hungry! And I wanted her to feel my hunger. In next to no time she began to squirm and ever so slightly edge her pelvis forward. I couldn't help but slip my palms under both butt cheeks and give her a helping hand forward. As I did so I could see her mouth open and shut; she was lost in ecstasy somewhere.

I wasted no time. I could feel I was getting over-excited, and I wanted in. I climbed on top of her and with her hand she put me inside. She was soaking wet as I pumped away at her vagina. When I came, it was as if every single bit of energy was zapped out of my body.

As soon as I recuperated, I wanted her out – the job was done! But I didn't want to be so blunt, so I started to fidget and fumble for my exit strategy. Eventually, I came up with an excuse – I had to go and see my mother.

****

Ladies, I have always wondered why, with certain women, I've felt the urge to always find the exit door as soon as I have reached climax. Here is your answer: she simply was not the one! It's a dead give-away that you're not the one when a man looks restless or fidgets about straight after sex, then soon after makes an excuse and a swift exit.

If someone is really into you, it is never just about sex – it has a lot to do with just being together in each other's company. Take note!

****

A week later, I dumped Jackie for another sprat. But it wasn't all over because a month later she told me she was pregnant. The news was good and bad for me. Deep down, I wanted a kid, but I didn't want it with her. Luckily, it didn't turn out that way, thank God.

It wasn't long before everyone found out I was actually coming from the prison. I was the talk of the college. If only you could have seen it! I had all the sprats, boning them and dumping them like nobody's business. Before long, the girls were calling me a womaniser.

As for Feltham, I was hardly there.

Then one day I returned after college to be summoned to Ms James's office. I knew something bad had happened; I could feel it.

She said, "I received a phone call from the college dean today. He claims that an anonymous caller phoned him and said, 'There is a young man at your college from Feltham prison who is selling drugs and has got one of your students pregnant. If something isn't done about it I'm going to the newspapers.' Then he hung up. What do you have to say to that, Jay?"

I was sh*t-scared, and it probably showed. In the blink of an eye I could see myself back in my cell and in prison clothes.

But I hadn't been stupid: I had already told Ms James about Jackie; I could talk to her like that. Over the months we had developed a kind of mother–son relationship. It was the drug-selling part of the story that had me baffled. Why would someone make something like that up? I thought to myself.

"I wasn't selling drugs. Please believe me, Ms James."

"I believe you, but who do you think would want to say something like that?"

"Maybe it was Jackie, because I dumped her?"

"It was a man's voice."

I racked my brain but I couldn't think of anyone who would do that. Little did I know the culprit was right under my nose!

"Then I haven't got a clue," I said.

"Jay, I'm sorry but I have to suspend you. I have to investigate this allegation further. In the meantime, it's very important that you don't say a word to anyone about this."

The screws were only too happy to see me back on the wing. Although they had no idea why I was really back, they found it hard to disguise their joy at my apparent downfall, and insisted on making malicious comments poorly disguised as jokes.

As for the inmates on my wing, well, they couldn't say anything to me – the way I ran the wing was no different to the way I ran things at school. But I'm sure they were laughing at me in their heads, and thinking, *Good, he got what he deserved.*

Two weeks went by and all I did was hang around on the wing, half-listening to all the bullsh*t prison talk and wondering all that time how I could get myself back to college. I was absolutely devastated at the fact I was suspended for something I had not and could not have done. For some time I didn't want to speak to anyone.

Then, when I least expected it, Miss James called me to her office and let me know that I was back at college, and reminded me to keep my head down and to steer clear of any trouble.

So, finally, I was back on home ground, doing what I do best, which wasn't computers. I hardly went to the lessons, even though the college was told to report me if I missed any classes. The only teachers who were supposed to know I was coming from Feltham were the college dean and the head of information technology. It was simple really – I would tell the students to sign in my name; when the register was checked weekly, it showed me to have a one hundred per cent attendance record. No one noticed when I wasn't there.

The day I filled out my parole papers, I found out who that anonymous caller had been. It was a screw, can you believe it? Mr Brown, an ex-soldier, had a bit of a reputation himself. All the other screws were sh*t-scared of him. He was a loose cannon, and everybody knew it. He and I had been quite close until one day, when an inmate had got on the wrong side of me, I had asked Mr Brown if he could open the boy's cell door so I could punch his head in – and he did it. The inmate had told the governor (not Ms James at the time), and from that day onwards Mr Brown had treated me differently.

He told one of the inmates that he had phoned the college, and the inmate then told me. I reckoned he'd wanted me to know it was him, and had told the inmate because he knew I'd find out. He was crazy like that. He wouldn't have given two sh*ts if everybody knew it was him or not. Was I pissed about it? Of course, I was furious! Did I say anything to him? I decided not to. There were two reasons why I didn't. Firstly, he really was a nut-case. Secondly, I didn't want to lose my place in college. I told Miss James immediately, to cover my back, and she told me she wouldn't put anything past him and that I should forget about it.

With all this going on, I had put Jackie to the back of my mind. But then I bumped into her at the bus stop late one afternoon as I was making tracks back to the prison. She was holding a baby to her chest. I approached her and had a look at the baby. I nearly fell over in shock; the little girl was very dark-skinned – nothing wrong with that, but with me being quite light-skinned and Jackie mixed-raced, it didn't seem right.

"Whose baby is that?" I asked.

"What do you mean, 'Whose baby is that?'"

Turning my head away and then back to her, I shot back, "Did I stammer?"

She paused. I could tell she was uncomfortable and nervous.

I cut in before she could say anything. "There is no way that baby is mine! I want a blood test!"

Instantly, she gave me an 'I hate you' look. "You bastard!" she muttered, and stormed off.

But she wasn't fooling me with that bullsh*t act. Or maybe she actually believed it, I thought. Whichever one it was, I was at the age where I was learning to trust my instincts more and more, and they were clearly saying to me, *Hell, no way is that baby a Johnson!*

On the Saturday morning I was sitting in my cell, thinking about some big-breasted sprat that was next on my list, when a screw threw two letters on my bed.

The first letter made me laugh. It was from my cousin Roy, T's brother. He told me that he had swapped flats with T because he needed a change, and now he had a new girlfriend who lived downstairs and that her name was Patricia. *P-A-T-R-I-C-I-A*! I hadn't heard that name for ages! I guessed T had never filled him in on the cooking oil incident, otherwise he wouldn't be calling her his girlfriend! Roy was with a slapper, and he didn't even know it!

I made a mental note to fill him in when I saw him...

****

The truth is, Patricia probably wasn't a slapper at all – maybe she just made one mistake. Some women might think that what Patricia did is her business and no one else's. To a point, I definitely agree. But the thing is, most men don't see it that way. Most men think, 'Yes! She's a slag so I'll give her one! But if you think I'm making her my girlfriend or my wife, you're off your head!'

Our egos, to our shame, make us more concerned with what other people think of us. And what I find even funnier is that I use to call women slappers when I was the biggest of them all! What a huge blind spot that was. Tradition has it more or less that only women can be called slappers, but this is my point when I say most people just follow the crowd and don't question stuff. A little more thought will reveal it makes no difference whether it's a man or a woman!

****

The second letter, however, wasn't funny in the slightest. It was from the Child Support Agency and it was demanding that I pay child maintenance for a Lakisha Noel. *Are they fucking crazy?* I thought. *I'm in fucking prison, for fuck's sake! Where am I supposed to get money from?*

I was outraged – I put pen to paper immediately. In reply, I wrote a clinical description about the night in question, adding one little lie – that I had used a condom! After all, it was only one night. I made Jackie out to be the slapper. I then told myself she was, and stuffed the letter in the post.

Three weeks later, I received a letter stating that I was being taken to court to be ordered to take a blood test. *The nerve of some women!* I knew exactly what was going on in her mind. The guy I took her from wasn't a lot to write home about; he just didn't have it. She wanted me in her life forever. I put it down to what I put a lot of things down to – just plain old immaturity, and an inability to see further ahead.

****

You're probably thinking – God, Jay! You've got a bloody cheek, calling anyone immature...! To be honest, you're right and you're wrong! At this point of my life you're absolutely right; however, later on, well... you'll see!

****

A few weeks later I received another letter from the CSA stating that the case regarding Lakisha Noel was being dropped, and that I would no longer have to take a blood test. *Damn bloody right*, I thought. I never heard from the Noel family again.

The following October I got my parole. It was due to Ms James putting in a special report to the Home Office. I remember how I found out: I had just come back from college; as soon as I got on the wing a few of the inmates ran up to me and told me. At first I thought it was all some kind of cruel joke, until my personal officer confirmed it. My mind leapt back in time to that day when I had wanted to close my eyes and never wake up. Today I was overwhelmed with joy – my time was finally up.

The next day, Ms James came to my cell to congratulate me personally. She began by thanking me for not letting her down, then she sat down on my bed. I could sense a lecture was coming, and I was right.

"Jay, when I first read your file, I admit I prejudged you. You swaggered in to my office that very first day, with that cheeky, confident grin on your face. But I sensed something about you that was genuine which made me put my neck on the line for you. Your case is typical of those who've had an abusive childhood. Over time I've got to know you better, which enabled me to see past all your bravado and your file.

"Jay, you're obviously an intelligent person, but you just need to apply yourself well and channel your energy in a positive way. You're also a lovely person. The problem I've found is that you don't actually believe it. You have to start believing in yourself and put your childhood behind you. Get out there and prove to the world that you are someone. I believe in you, Jay. And stop breaking all those girls' hearts... Find the right girl and settle down, because you only want to be loved, I can see that."

When she left I laid on my bed. I felt really good about myself: nobody had ever told me I was a lovely person. I laid there lapping it up until my mental recorder came back on and sent me back to reality! *You're good for nothing... You got two peanuts for brains... You're a donkey... You're going to be a robber and a thief...* and so it went on, my mind churning out the Monster's voice.

Finally, after the longest three years and eight months of my life, I was finished with that sh*t-hole for good. The feeling as I walked out of those big electric gates for the last time was truly exhilarating for me, even though I'd spent the last stint of my sentence on the outside at college and on home leave.

As I walked over to Stretch's waiting car, I was conscious not to look back at the prison. My first stop was the flower shop. I picked up a huge bunch of flowers for Ms James to show my appreciation. The next stop was going to be

Mum's. I remember on the way there how I kept smiling and repeating to Stretch, "I'm free... I'M F-U-C-K-I-N-G F-R-E-E!"

CHAPTER **8**
A BIG BANG TO RIGHTS

I was now nineteen years of age, and everyone kept telling me I was looking more handsome than ever and much more mature. All I wanted to do was put all that prison crap behind me. Dwelling on the past is a mug's game; I wanted to plan ahead for better days to come.

I passed my course at West London College. Don't know how I did it, myself. I hardly went to any of the classes – I was too busy chasing sprats. Funny thing was that now I was out I noticed nobody used the word sprats any more.

I was living back with my folks. When I told my mother that I'd passed, she started nagging me to go to university. Well, I wasn't having any of that: I wasn't cut out for uni and I told her so. As for the Monster, he looked like he'd aged ten years since I last saw him, but he hadn't changed his ways. I could tell he didn't want me around. I guess he reckoned I'd be a bad influence on my twelve-year-old brother Paul. I knew I would have to move out, and sharpish. I didn't want to give him the satisfaction of kicking me out again.

Nobody knows what the future holds – except perhaps a clairvoyant. I planned to be the exception: I was going to make sure I knew exactly what my future held: something worthwhile. I had plans – big plans – and I intended to see them through to the very end. I planned to live in luxury, drive Porsches, BMWs, and Mercedes, and, last but not least, bone any woman I pleased. That was the only future I was going to accept.

There was something exciting about being a womaniser. It was as if there were no woman on earth I couldn't have if I really wanted her. I really believed I could get paid from women around the world and make a living, and a good one! It *sounds ridiculous to me now*, but back then, well, it sounded fantastic; that's how those women were making me feel. I suppose I should have known from the age of nine, when I lost my virginity, that I was destined for this kind of life.

Check it out!

I had not long been released from prison, and *all* I could think about was women, women, and rich women. That's not to say that prison didn't do me any good because it did – I would be lying if I said it didn't. It made me realise how much I love the female of the species, and that if I wanted to stay with them I would have to keep well clear of any criminal activities. I intended to do exactly that.

But this was easier said than done. To be totally truthful with you, and I always am, I'd committed one crime already since my release. But it was only a small one and it had to be done, as you'll see – in my mind there was no alternative. Two weeks after my release, I bought a hand gun. I had heard so many stories about so-called 'friends' who were no longer fighting with fists or knives. I panicked, buying it for my own protection; you know, 'if the worst comes to the worst' sort of thing. It's not as if I had plans to rob a bank or anything. When I bought it, I had no idea my own gun would be turned around and used against me. A few months out of prison and finally I was starting to get somewhere. I couldn't yet see the end of the tunnel, but I could just make out a glimmer of light.

I moved out of the family home swiftly, and was now living with a new girl called Mandy. Somehow Tiffany and I had drifted apart; I guess I didn't miss her as much as I thought I did. That's the illusion prison can create. I had accumulated a number of new girls, and Mandy was my current favourite. She was a nice girl, really loving and great in bed – that's really hard to find – all the good qualities in one girl. Of course, she had trust issues, but they were actually very much justified. For me, it was a good thing Mandy wasn't in touch with her instincts – she was the one currently giving me the most st£rling!

****

What Mandy failed to realise is that if you're with a man and you feel like you can't trust him, you're probably right. I have learned that these feelings come from your subconscious, which is capable of picking up the signs more accurately than rational thinking. In other words, if you can't trust him, knock it on the head. You're just setting yourself up for misery!

Ever met a man and, in the beginning, something inside told you, "This guy is a player or a liar"? Then some months down the road something dramatic happens to prove it? Well, that was your instinct talking, your hunch. Listen to it. It deserves your attention. The more you follow it, the more accurate it becomes.

****

Mandy's reason to doubt was Kizzy Blake. We met in a West End nightclub. I wasn't in the club more than five minutes when I noticed her; immediately I knew she would be my main target for the night. Then, for a split second, I thought I'd seen her before, but I figured it was impossible: I would never have let such a fit girl slip away. I would surely have put it on her.

****

That's how womanisers operate; they never let a criss sprat pass them without turning on the charm. Any other action is going against the womanising rulebook. They can't help it; it's a habit!

****

Fortunately for me, I didn't even have to make a move. She took it upon herself to come over to me. She said, "Excuse me, but isn't your name Jay?"

"Yeah, who are you?" I replied.

"Don't you remember me? I'm Kizzy, Janice's friend."

"Kizzy… Kizzy… Who?" I asked.

"Kizzy Blake from school. You used to go out with my friend Janice," she insisted.

Kizzy Blake. The name didn't ring any bells.

"Oh yeah, I remember now. You look so different, so nice…" I said, lying through my teeth.

"So do you. That's why I came over. My friends were saying how nice you look."

This girl was blatant, but in a way I preferred them to be upfront. She leeched on me for the rest of night. Did I mind? *Of course I bloody did!*

****

Womanisers never like to be leeched on in a club.
Maybe at the end of the night, yeah that's fine,
but not in the club. There's still work to be done!

****

Eventually, we had a dance, and boy was it a dance! She was totally wow! She almost had me coming on the dance floor. All right... okay... I confess it all now: she made me come on the dance floor in my pants. Sh*t *happens sometimes!*

Just as we finished our wet sex dance, it all came back to me – Janice! She was the girl I had mucked about with at school and Kizzy was her little scruffy friend she used to hang around with. I thought to myself, *No, it can't be: it's impossible!* But it was her... not so little any more, and the total opposite of scruffy. Classy!

I told her I had just come out of jail and that I was staying at my cousin Mandy's house until I got some accommodation sorted out. I then invited her round for a drink. She accepted, maybe a little too hastily.

I was starting to get used to all the women throwing themselves at me. When I had been younger I had thought I had it going on, but it wasn't half as much as I did at this point.

****

I could see right through Kizzy. She was one of those girls at school who had no confidence. She was chubby back then and the boys would always pay attention to her friends rather than her. But as she matured she dug out some confidence, lost some weight, and had a make-over, and the end result was a smashing, sexy lady. And she had decided she was going to milk everything out of this new look.

Her approach to me was probably a 'look at me now' sort of thing. I wondered if she'd wanted me back then and knew she wasn't in my league. And perhaps now she was simply thinking, 'I can have you now and I will.' It was a straightforward game, and I was very happy to play it with her!

****

I set the date for a few days later, when I knew my girl Mandy would be at her mother's overnight. For the rest of the night I kept it moving from girl to girl.

Kissy turned up for our date ten minutes late and looking as sexy as hell in black knee-length boots and a short top that revealed the valley between her breasts. Jesus! My baton stood to up like a jack-in-the-box. I thought to myself, *There is no way you're leaving here without some bump and grind!*

I welcomed her in, gave her a drink, and put on a video. Settling down, we talked, joked, and laughed. There was something about her that bedazzled me. She looked so damn sexy I couldn't wait to get up inside her.

She said, "How long did you do in prison?"

"Well, I got six years but I done three years eight months altogether," I replied.

"So how old were you when you went away?"

I was glad she had asked that question because, very soon, I would be swearing to her that I was a virgin. With her knowing the age when I got sent down and that I just got released, she might think it was true.

****

I told so many girls the same thing: I learned it was a quick shortcut to get in their knickers. It was a psychological game I played. My own little survey had proved that most girls preferred it if their partner was a virgin. They liked to think they were the one to break them. People's egos!!! Personally, I no longer had time for virgins. I preferred them to know what the hell they were doing!

My survey also revealed that if I told a girl who fancied me that I was a virgin, their first reaction was disbelief. The second reaction was to interrogate, and as long as I didn't slip up, which I never did, they would believe it to some extent. Their instinct must have been saying, "Ridiculous! He's talking a load of rubbish!" and then they would let their emotions take over. They _wanted_ it to be true, so they started convincing themselves of all the ways I could be telling the truth. Incredible. But that's females for you!

****

"I was fifteen."

"Argh!... You were just a baby! I hope you're not planning on going back."

"Don't worry. I'm not." I thought to myself, *Just a baby! Perfect – I'm glad you're thinking like that.*

Now I was starting to get impatient, scanning her big chest and her long legs. Oh God! She's sexy! My mind was communicating with my baton; it twitched back its approval. I was just about to get down to the nitty-gritty concerning sex when she fired out yet another question.

"So, did your girlfriend wait for you?"

"What girlfriend? If I had a girlfriend, do you think I would be here with you now?"

She smiled. "Do you have any kids?"

Now was my chance. "Have any kids? Have I any kids?" I repeated seriously.

"You heard me…"

"No, I haven't. I shouldn't even tell you this, but I feel so comfortable with you… Oh, it's nothing."

"No, please go on…"

"Well, I've never had sex before."

I glanced at her to check her reaction. It was the expected disbelief. She said, "You? A virgin? Pull the other one. God's gift to women maybe, but a virgin? No way! Didn't you sleep with anyone before you went inside?"

The interrogation had begun, just as my survey told me it would.

"I didn't have time for girls before; I was too interested in football – that was all I ever did."

"You don't look like a virgin."

"What does a virgin look like?"

"I don't know… I just don't believe you."

I was ready for that one. I said, "I don't blame you. My own mother didn't believe me when I told her." I ran my eyes in her direction and she was smiling slightly.

"I've never been with a virgin before, funnily enough," she laughed.

See - it's their dream! I knew it! I guessed she believed me now.

"What time is your cousin coming back?" she asked.

"She's not. She's staying at my aunt's until tomorrow."

Why had she asked me when my cousin was coming back? Was she thinking on my wavelength now? The next thing she said confirmed to me that she was thinking about bed.

She said, "Are you really a virgin!!!?"

I was ready again, one step ahead of her. "Yeah, I am, but does it really matter whether I am or not? You're making me feel uncomfortable talking about this."

"No, no course not..."

She answered too quickly – I read in between the lines. I had her right where I wanted her. I grinned to myself. Females at times can be so irrational, and she was gullible, just like the rest of them. That was good, good for me. My quest was in the bag, I was sure of it.

It was time to work on the second item on my agenda – her income. She told me she worked in a jewellery shop. My mind raced back some years to Jennifer. *I could be sitting on a gold mine!* I thought. I would pay close attention to this one.

Time was pushing on and my baton was throbbing. I couldn't wait any longer. I would get back to the pounds another time.

****

Ladies, this is what you really need to be careful of: womanisers know timing plays such an important role in womanising. Now wasn't the right time. The art is to make women fall in love, and give you their hearts completely. When they have fallen, that's the cue to swoop in for the pounds. That's the time they are running on pure emotion and blind as bats! To make a move on their money before then is risky, because the rational part of their brain is still operating!!

****

I patted my lap, gesturing Kizzy to sit there. She didn't object. I started kissing her intimately.

She pulled away. "Where did you learn to kiss like that?"

I remember thinking, *From all the girls I've had, Dumbo!*

****

Womanisers know that another part to getting a woman emotionally is in the kiss! They know if they get it right they will have your emotions flowing! They know women like to be fucked like a man and kissed and touched like a woman. They know passion is the key. They will kiss every woman like they are in love.

****

She was trying to catch me off-guard, but it didn't work: this was all routine stuff to me.

"I don't know – I'm just responding to you," I replied quietly.

She was about to say something else, but I stopped her with another intimate kiss. The next time we parted, it was me who pulled away. My baton was twitching signals, and my brain was receiving them. My baton was saying, "Forget this bullsh*t! Just get her into the bedroom and let me give it to her!"

"Let's go in the bedroom," I said, obeying my other head's orders. I linked my arms with hers as she followed me into my room – Mandy's room. I quickly glanced around the bedroom, double-checking that I hadn't left anything out of place when I had cleared up earlier. I briefly thought about Mandy – what if she came back early and caught me and Kizzy in her bed? I dismissed the thought as ludicrous: she wouldn't be back until tomorrow evening.

Soon there I was, thrusting away, *wap, wap, wap*, increasing the strokes. Her walls! Had a firm grip on me she started to shriek in pleasure, scratching my back frantically. "I love your cock," she whispered. It really turns me on when women talk dirty during sex. "I'm coming, Jay."

"So am I, I'm coming," I replied, releasing her legs from behind her head and collapsing face first on the bed.

When it was done, I lay back contented. I thought, *Shit! And I thought I could fuck before! Some of those girls must've thought I was a joke! Oh well, I know the business now.* My mind turned to Mandy for the second time. I couldn't understand why I was getting these repetitive thoughts. You know those thoughts that just keep popping into your head over and over again, even when you're having a great time?

****

I later learnt to tap into the meaning of repetitive thoughts. They are a red light - they mean: 'Stop! Evaluate the situation more carefully!' It's the subconscious part of your brain and it knows something isn't right. But on this occasion I dismissed them.

*** *** ** **

Mandy had an uncontrollable temper at times. On a few occasions, in the heat of an argument, she had picked up a knife, leaving me no choice but to vacate for a few hours.

Kizzy suspended my thoughts. She said, "I thought you said you were a virgin?"

That one always came after the sex, unsurprisingly. "Not any more, baby!" I replied, not really caring whether she believed it any more – it was too late.

I decided we should do the side-mirror. I said, "Kizzy, put your boots back on."

"Are you getting kinky on me?" she replied sarcastically.

I bypassed the comment. I led her into the front room, and I put on a tape, an R Kelly special. *"There ain't nothin' wrong with a little bump and grind..."* I bent her over a footstool in front of the long panelled mirror. She looked nice in the knee-length boots. My baton was standing stiff as a rock. I thumped it deep inside her – *wap*. Getting my rhythm, I gave it to her hard and fast.

It seemed like I was fucking her for hours. It always works that way the second time around, lasting three times longer. I don't know how or why, but it just does. It was definitely a buzz for me to see my baton sliding in and out, and to see Kizzy's facial reaction after every penetration.

After the sex we went back into the bedroom and flopped into bed. I was shattered, and by the look of things so was Kizzy. There was some reminiscing about our shared school days before I started to feel sleepy. Just before I dozed off, my mind turned once more to Mandy, and I couldn't work out why. It wasn't as if I felt bad about sleeping with a girl in her bed. I felt great about it! I tried to throw these thoughts to the back of my mind, but I couldn't – they just kept recurring. *Why didn't I listen?*

The last words I remember Kizzy saying were, "I have got to leave at eight. I've got work in the morning." Then I fell asleep in her arms.

A loud bang startled me from my sleep. Mandy was standing at the bottom of the bed. She was crying and her whole body was shaking. She had a gun in her hand – and it was pointed at me.

I was confused. My mind was racing in eighteen different directions. *It's a nightmare; I'm still sleeping!* was my first thought. Then, *This can't be for real! Why the hell is she pointing a gun at me? Is she mad?* My thoughts came sharply into focus (amazing how a gun has that effect) in a tenth of a second. It dawned on me: last night – cheating – Kizzy – it's my gun! I glanced to my left and there was Kizzy, the sheet pulled to her neck, a terrified, bewildered look on her face.

I looked back into Mandy's eyes, wondering if she really had the balls to shoot me. I wasn't sure as at that point she looked demented and capable of anything. I made a move towards her; at the same time, I shouted, "What the fuck are you doi–?"

Those were my last words before – BANG!

CHAPTER 9
THE CRAZY WOMAN AND MUM'S FAVOURITE

My next move was a foolish one: I left Mandy's and moved back in with my parents.

As usual, the Monster didn't want me there, and he made that fact very clear. He didn't mince his words: he just told me straight. Without asking me why I was back, he said to me one morning, "Listen, I don't want you here. So just make sure you find somewhere else to live. Fast." He walked off mumbling to himself, "Fucking good-for-nothing... useless..." I heard it all. Whenever our paths crossed in the house, he would hiss through his teeth. I guess he really wanted to throw me out straight away just like the old days, but he probably knew that sh*t wouldn't sit so easy this time around.

Mum did ask me why I was back, and when I told her what had happened, she barely batted an eyelid. That doesn't mean she wasn't shocked – things rarely rattled her. That was just the way she was. When I finished telling her the story she gave me a ticking off and told me never to see Mandy again.

As for my brother Paul, he was getting abused by the Monster just as I had, although in my view he was getting away with some things that I wouldn't have, back in the day. I noticed that he and my mother were very close. I wasn't that close to him; I guess I just saw him as a little kid. He didn't fight the abuse, which was probably why he still had the privilege of living there.

So here I was, back to square one. The whole situation made me think about Ms Carlton. I hadn't seen her since I went to prison. All of a sudden I had an urge to go and check on the old lady. I knocked on the door and waited patiently. It took a few seconds for her to register it was me. Then a huge smile appeared on her face.

"How are you, Jay? Where have you been? I was so worried about you?"

"I'm sorry, I've been in prison and I had no way of contacting you."

Ms Carlton sighed with disappointment and ushered me into her living room. Then she asked me to explain everything that had led up to me going to prison and my experience inside. After I told her the story she said, "Jay, you have to let go of the anger you have for your father because it will only lead to your own destruction." I remember thinking at the time, *Why is she going on about the Monster when I was talking about prison?* As I stood up to say goodbye Ms Carlton offered me a room, but I nicely declined. She made me promise to stay in touch.

When I got back to the Monster's I knew I had to make a move and fast. It wasn't good for my health to be living in such a tense environment.

I was anxious to get back to Mandy. She was my backbone until I could find someone better. She was the one who put money in my pocket and pampered me. I just loved being pampered – who doesn't? Tradition has it that the man should pamper the woman. But at the time I thought,

What idiot started that crap! That was not the rule in my world! I missed her, but I wasn't going to let her know that. I was going to let her sweat for a while. If she thought that calling me every minute of the day and giving me all that sweet-talk bullsh*t would get me running back to her, she had another thing coming. Of course, I had every intention of going back, but I wasn't about to let that sick stunt she had pulled slide so easily. *As far as I was concerned she would have to pay, and out of her hard-earned cash!* There was no way I was going to let her get away with trying to shoot me with my own gun.

It's a damn good thing she had never handled a gun before: what would have happened if she'd been on target? I later found out that when she had found me asleep in her bed with another woman, she had wanted to die. In a moment of madness, she had gone straight for the gun and let off a warning shot that was meant to wake us up. That shot had actually gone through the polystyrene ceiling cove and right into the top part of the wall. Then her intention had been to shoot me you know where!

One thing that puzzled me at the time was how she had managed to actually find the gun. She knew it was in the house, but I had moved it from its original hiding place and I hadn't told her where (not because I thought she might one day use it against me; I just found what I thought was a better hiding place: I had cut a hole in the bottom of the sofa and hid the gun and a box of bullets safely inside). How the hell she had found it was beyond me. It turned out she had lost her keys one day and dug out the sofa looking for it – and the bloody old sofa went all the way down to the base. So she had known all along it was there.

My stomach turns every time I recall the event. Could you imagine me then, in my prime, with no manhood? Some womaniser I would have been. Luckily for me, Mandy had thought two bullets would be sufficient. When she pulled the trigger the second time I can only guess the kick-back threw her off (or she didn't really have the guts to do it) and she fired instead just above my head. I jumped off the bed to grab her. Just as I reached her, she was pulling the trigger frantically as if there were still more bullets in the chamber.

Kizzy watched the whole thing in shock. I suppose there wasn't much Kizzy could say. She was probably confused by the whole situation.

Mandy told me all this afterwards, but I'll never really know whether or not she was aiming to kill. The day after I left, she started calling me at my parents' house, and every time I would tell her to fuck off.

****

Ladies, stay alert to this one!! Men who somehow have a way of making you feel bad for something they have done wrong! Whenever someone has done you bad, under no circumstances should you be made to feel bad about it. That is another form of manipulation!

****

After a while I told my mother and Paul that if anyone called the house for me they should say that I no longer lived there. I didn't bother to tell the Monster because he told them all that anyway.

I still hated him! The Monster was unbelievable. I mean aren't people supposed to mellow in their old age, see their bad ways and try to rectify them? Doesn't a man at some point realise his unhealthy ego is all a waste of time and energy? Doesn't the penny drop at some point that love is the most important thing to give your kids, give your family? Yeah, well that's what I thought too. The Monster still hadn't got any of that. He was still the same old, same old.

After two weeks of boredom at my parents' house I got it. *Imagine!* I woke up to find my balls were on fire. Itching like crazy they were. Could I have crabs? It wouldn't have surprised me if I did, the amount of girls I'd slept with since being released from prison. I tried to ignore the irritation, but by noon the blaze had increased. I pictured the little bastards moving around, swinging from hair to hair.

I ran to the surgery, demanding that the pig-face receptionist let me see a doctor. She tried to explain to me that it was impossible to see the doctor unless it was an emergency. *Emergency indeed!* The stupid woman didn't realise what was going on inside my trousers, and I wasn't about to tell her. I made such a commotion I guess she decided I wasn't worth all the embarrassment.

The waiting room was packed; I was in for a long wait. But considering my predicament, I couldn't have cared less. After all, how could I have left knowing what was going on down there…? Just the thought of it made me feel sick.

After ten minutes I started to get really paranoid; everyone was staring at me; they must've known what I had, given my fast hand movements every five seconds. And it was getting worse. I remember thinking, *Maybe one of those little shits is a womaniser crab - and he's having babies every second! Ouch!*

As I waited, I tried to work out which slapper had let her little friends bunny-hop onto me. It was no good; there were far too many possible culprits. I was just about to go back to Pig Face at reception when I heard my name on the speaker system. At last! I headed into Doctor Dyer's room.

"Yes, and what can I do for you today, Mr Johnson?"

"I think I've got crabs," I replied, acting as if it were a very common thing to happen.

"Oh dear. Could you pull down your shorts and lie on that bed over there, please." Doctor Dyer examined me. "Well, young man, if you've got crabs they must be invisible ones," he said, laughing at his own joke.

"Are you sure?" I asked.

"I'm sure all right. Crab louse can be seen quite clearly if you look close enough, and I can't see anything."

"So why am I itching like this?"

Doctor Dyer then examined my balls through a magnifying glass. "Probably a skin irritation."

Probably! My instinct told me he was wrong. "Can I have the treatment for crabs anyway?"

"Sure you can, but it will be of no use to you. Well, not now anyway," he said, laughing again. He really thought he was the funniest man in town.

Grabbing the prescription sheet, I did my fastest athlete impersonation all the way to the chemist, and then all the way home.

By the time I got in, it felt like I had a whole nation of crabs down there. I splashed on the treatment, and it burnt like hell. I quickly read the bottle in case I had done something wrong. The bottle read 'Ingredients: Alcohol...'. That explained it.

I lay down for a couple of hours to let the treatment dry as recommended. The first hour was pure torment! *What's the alcohol doing down there? I wondered. Killing the crabs or just getting them drunk?*

Eventually, the ointment was dry and the time was up. Feeling better, I raked a comb through my pubic area. *Fucking bastards!* They had revealed themselves: dead little fuckers on the teeth of my comb. *No wonder they're called g-e-n-e-r-a-l practitioners, I thought. PHEW!*

Later that evening, I went and stayed with one of my young girls. Her name was Sandra Manning. Sandra, one of the many girls I had been with since Feltham, was only seventeen. I hadn't seen her for some time, but she always called every day, asking how I was doing and saying if I needed her she would always be there for me, no matter what. Her head was screwed on. She was studying fashion and worked part-time in a designer store. She was fairly good looking – she looked a bit like Naomi Campbell. She could be a little stuck-up at times; she didn't see herself hanging around with the riff-raff. So why did she hang with me? I could only assume I wasn't the riff-raff!

Sandra was shocked to see me; she demanded an explanation for why I hadn't seen her for so long. I told her a string of lies – I was broke, I lost my chain, I was depressed. Her head shook in sympathy when she heard it all. Hugging me tight, she said, "Don't worry. I'm here for you now. I've missed you so much."

We went straight to the bedroom – we had a lot of catching up to do. *This time I kept my boxers on!* After all, she could be one of the culprits, even though I hadn't seen her for some time. I didn't know how long an incubation period these little fuckers had. Does it start with the egg or the crab...? Whichever way, I didn't want the termites on me again.

She woke me up with breakfast in bed. Handing over the tray she said, "Guess what, JJ. Because I've missed you so much, I'm taking you shopping."

Shopping! "For what?" I asked, grinning.

"I'm going to get you another gold chain, and a few Moschinos. I know you love your Moschinos."

She wasn't wrong. "You don't have to do that, babe," I said, lying through my teeth again.

****

Be mindful of men who always play that 'you don't have to' game. They do it to throw you off the scent to make you feel that you don't have to.

Let's say she turned round and said, "Okay, Jay, then I won't get it," which is unlikely - but it happens sometimes, especially if I've asked for something first without it being offered. Well, in that scenario you just work it from behind - I would come up with something a bit later like, "I really feel naked without my chain...", "I just hate being broke...", stuff like that. I would play on her emotions - obviously she wants to make me happy so she'll change her mind again. But it still leaves the lasting impression that the womaniser is not after one thing - the loot!

****

On this occasion she said, "Don't be silly. I want to."

After breakfast we took a shower together, got dressed, and went shopping. She took me to a gold shop in Bethnal Green where I picked out a six-ounce chap's chain. It was the size of a dog chain. Then we stopped at several designer stores and I scoured them for something I wanted, but I couldn't find anything. I suggested we go to a store in Haringey called Kriscross which boasted brands like Moschino, Versace, Valentino, and Armani. I tried on two shirts and two pairs of jeans at her request. They fitted perfectly. She bought them at a discounted price of four hundred and fifty pounds. As we left, the Italian owner smiled and said, "Don't hesitate to come back – I'll do you some good deals." The owner wasn't to know that I would soon be visiting the shop every week without fail.

That afternoon, Sandra asked to meet my mother. How could I say no? After all, she'd just splashed out on me.

****

Back then it was against the rules for me – introduce a girl to my mother, come to my home? That was a no-no! It is very rare that a womaniser will take a woman to meet his mother, unless there are some strong feelings. However, in this case it was more a case of getting strong currency!

****

I did like Sandra, and I knew she loved me.

When I brought her home, the Monster wasn't there – just as well.

"Mother, this is my girlfriend, Sandra."

"Is it really? Hello, Sandra," she said, shooting me a look that asked me how many bloody girlfriends I'd got.

My younger brother Paul's eyes were glued to the TV screen. I said, "Paul, this is my girlfriend Sandra."

"Not another one?" he said, not moving his gaze.

I felt like punching his little head in.

I took Sandra up to my room and closed the door.

"Jay, have you got another girl?" she asked seriously.

"Don't be silly, of course I haven't…"

"Then why did your brother say that? And yes, I did see the look your mother gave you."

Damn! She's alert! "Paul was joking. He likes to play games, he…"

"Well, I'm going down to talk to your mother," she replied, and rushed out of the door so quickly that I couldn't stop her.

Roughly two hours later, she came back up with a stupid grin on her face. "It's like that, is it!"

"It's like what?" I was very curious to know what my mother had said.

"Don't worry about it. I know, and that's enough."

****

She wasn't using that one on me! I was the master of that sh*t! I used it on girls all the time! Pretend to know some sh*t, and then let them spill the beans'- I was having none of that!

****

Later that night, my mother grilled me about being a womaniser. "Listen to me, Jay. I'm a woman too. Would you like someone to use me the way you use all these girls? Sandra seems like a very nice girl. She's good-looking and ambitious, not like all the trash I see you sneak in here. Why don't you settle down and do something good with your life? Look at that crazy girl who keeps phoning here. I've told her a thousand times you don't live here. She doesn't have any sense."

Fine one to talk, I thought, thinking about her and the Monster.

"Jay, please just settle down and sort out your life. Please, for your mother."

"All right, Mum. I'll try."

Me settle down! What the hell was she talking about! I knew exactly what I wanted out of life: girls, more girls, and more st£rling.

The Monster came back at around ten o'clock. Sandra and I were downstairs watching TV. She said hello to him. He hissed through his teeth and didn't even glance in her direction. We went to bed shortly afterwards. I wanted to see what the Monster had to say about that. I was now a grown man as far as I was concerned. He didn't say a word.

Sandra left early the next morning in time to get home and leave for work. I asked her for a hundred before she left. She gave it to me without hesitation. *Exactly the way I loved it!* I lay in bed thinking about her. She had potential when it came to looking after a man. In fact, she had a lot of potential, period. My mother was right: she was a nice girl; in fact, she was a very, very nice girl! I drifted back to sleep.

When I woke up, I put on my new garments and went to check on Stretch. I hadn't seen him for some time. Stretch insisted I give him the rundown on the new clothes. When I told him, he laughed and said, "Boy, why can't I find a girl like that? You always seem to find them!"

Stretch had just beaten a robbery charge. The police had charged him with robbing a policeman's daughter; the girl in question had picked him out in an ID parade. He had beaten the case because he really hadn't done it: he had been in college and the tutor could vouch he had been in a lesson at the time of the robbery. It was the only time education had done him any good! He was laughing when he told me about it.

Most of the original Crew were now in jail for either robbery or burglary. Everyone had split up and gone his own way. Even Rocky was doing his own thing: he never even let me know when he came out. I just heard about it through Stretch.

As I left, Stretch warned me, "I wouldn't wear that chain over your jacket if I were you. There are loads of jealous people out there."

"And your point is?" I asked, already understanding what he meant.

"You know what I mean."

Those very same words rang in my ears months later.

When I got home I received a call on my mobile. I answered. It was the crazy bitch Mandy.

"Why the fuck are you calling me? Leave me alone!"

"Jay, listen, I'm sorry! Can't you…"

"Where did you get my number from?"

"I'll buy you anything you want, just come back!"

"I don't care... What did you say? Buy anything I want? Where are you?"

"I'm at home."

I cut off the phone.

I didn't want to go. But I had to know what she was offering. I caught a cab there. She looked rough, as if she was cracking up. I did actually feel sorry for her but I never let it show.

****

What a huge blind spot! You can't say to a man, "I'll buy you anything you want if you come back." You lose what little power you had! If a man doesn't come back of his own accord but comes back because of gifts, it is clear to see that he doesn't love you. He will exploit your weakness. You must understand that you are just buying his love; in fact, you're not even buying his love - you are only buying his time! As sure as the sun comes up every day, you can bet he will be gone as soon as the loot runs out!

****

CHAPTER **10**
MY WRONG MOVE

Five days later, Mandy bought a Rover Coupe 216 GTI in exchange for my return. I moved back in. It was a wrong move but I wasn't to know.

I did have my reservations about going back. I wondered whether she would try to pull a similar stunt again. I couldn't be sure, even though I wasn't stupid enough to leave my gun in her house.

But there were a few points that made me overlook what she was capable of. Firstly, I couldn't bear the sight of the Monster any more. Secondly, Mandy had loot, so I couldn't afford to let her go.

After discussing the gun incident, I warned her that she'd better not try any bullsh*t like that again. She explained that she had felt so hurt and she would never repeat something like that, and that she would make it up to me.

But she lied. The crazy bitch started getting possessive. She made it her duty to keep a close eye on my every move. She went back to work a week later, calling me every hour to see what I was doing. She deliberately came home at unexpected hours, trying to catch me off-guard. She left me no breathing space, and as the days went by it got worse and worse.

After two weeks I hadn't seen Sandra or any of the other girls that I'd been messing around with. Sandra was speaking to my mother regularly, and I guess I allowed it. She was now Number One. I decided to call her. My pocket was running on 'E': it felt like it had a hole in it. And to be honest, I genuinely missed her. I told her so.

She told me she was missing me too. "JJ, I need to see you. I want you."

"I'm pissed off living here with my cousin. I need out but I don't want to go back home," I whispered, thinking about the crazy bitch Mandy in the bedroom. I had recently almost given her a slap for answering my mobile; only the memories of my mother's eyes stopped me. She was going too far. I needed my own place, and fast.

"Come over now, and we'll discuss your problems, then we'll make love."

Make love indeed! I needed some hardcore sex. Mandy was starting to get boring; she used the same positions and moves, even the same fucking moans. It was getting so bad I knew her every jig before she did it. It had been great when we first met, but now it was predictable. I had always wondered how men can stay faithful to one girl. It just seemed like total madness to me.

"I'm coming over now," I said, and hung up.

At ten thirty p.m. I pulled my new car up to the curb outside Sandra's family home. Her bedroom light was on. I beeped the horn and looked up at her window. She moved the curtains to one side and signalled for me to come in. She greeted me at the door in her dressing gown. She flung her arms round me and we kissed hungrily. I closed the door and took her there and then in the hallway. She whispered, "I love you, JJ."

Back in the bedroom I ran down my current situation with her, obviously not telling her that the 'cousin' I was living with was really the crazy bitch Mandy. It took me half an hour, with me even describing in detail the problems with living at the Monster's.

She was a good listener. She put her arms round me and said, "You know I would let you stay here, but my mother wouldn't allow it. You should call your probation officer and tell her you have nowhere to live. Surely she'll sort out something out."

What a clever girl! She was right: that was what probation officers were there for. I made a mental note to see her in the morning.

Then my mobile rang. Something told me it was the bitch checking on me, but it wasn't, it was Stretch. He wanted to go out raving. I hadn't been to the club for quite some time so I told him I would go. I put my hand on Sandra's thigh and rubbed it all the way up to her crotch. I said, "Babes, I'm raving tonight and I'm broke. Give me a hundred pound until next week." *Next week my arse!*

"No JJ, you always say that. No, I'm not giving into you this time. Anyway, I want you to stay tonight."

"I guess you don't love me any more then. We might as well finish." I looked at her seriously. I knew she didn't want to lose me. I didn't really want to lose her either.

****

Take note, ladies – a womaniser always knows his women; he knows how far he can push them. It's all an essential part of getting what he wants, enabling him to come at them from the right angle to hit the emotions right where it hurts.

****

"JJ, you know I love you. I'll always love you. So don't give me that rubbish."

"So why are you treating me like this?"

She paused to think, and kissed me on the cheek. "I don't know why I always give into you. I do it all the time. Hold on, I'll just get changed."

I drove us to the cash point, and she drew out a hundred. She gave it to me. I drove back to her place and slapped her on the bottom.

"Thank you, baby. See you soon!"

"Just remember I love you," she replied, "so behave yourself. I'm going to your mother's tomorrow."

I put my foot down. I went back to Mandy's and got changed. Just as I was leaving, the crazy bitch sprang out of the bedroom. She said, "Where you going?"

I turned and looked at her disdainfully, thinking, *You think you're my fucking mother or something?!* I slammed the door and made my way to Stretch's.

Stretch insisted he drive us to the club in his new car, which his dad had just bought him. All our roads back then led to a club called Bel Air. It wasn't until we arrived that I got a sudden jolt.

"Shit! Where's my phone?"

I searched the car inside out but it wasn't there. Maybe I'd left it at Stretch's house? I just couldn't be sure. Now I was panicking. What if I'd left it at Mandy's? My phone rang as if I was a drug dealer, but the truth was, it was just different girls.

Stretch started laughing. He knew why I was fretting. "You better hope she doesn't answer your phone!"

I didn't find it funny at all.

If that phone rang, she would answer it. I knew that for sure. I was sweating. I used Stretch's phone to call it. No answer – what a relief! *I must have left it at his house,* I thought.

****

But I was still worried. There they were again - repetitive thoughts. Something was up.

****

I remembered my battery was very low and would last maybe twenty minutes. But if the phone was at Mandy's it didn't matter – the charger was there too. I tried to put it all to the back of my mind.

The club was jam-packed with lovely-looking girls. It reminded me of the Pum-pum Market, back in the day. Stretch bought me a Hennessey; it was my favourite drink, mixed with coke or with champagne, and the only alcohol I would drink. After some trial and error with alcohol I had found that Hennessey made me lyrically smooth compared with others that would put downers on me.

So there we were, holding our normal favourite spot outside the ladies' toilets. Girls always visited the loo – not to use it, mind you; just to check their make-up! I would be waiting there for them.

****

As womanisers step up their game, they become more selective in their choice of ladies. They will eventually go for quality more than quantity. Quality ladies are the ones with the real loot! You may think you have these characters pinned down to certain actions, but I can assure you they will up their game. They may start off hanging outside the toilets, but eventually they will work out that behaviour pattern will make them look like a womaniser before they even make their move.

****

I was standing there, weighing up whether Mandy could have answered my mobile within that twenty-or-so-minute period, when I felt a tap on my shoulder. A voice said, "Can I have a dance, womaniser?"

I turned round to see Naomi, one of my old girls. Naomi was one of those typical ghetto chicks: she wore trainers rather than shoes and would fight anyone – really pretty but didn't take any crap. Too quick to lose her temper, she had many flaws. But she was definitely one of the prettiest girls I had ever met: perfect features and a great body – you wouldn't really realise it unless you were lucky enough to get her clothes off. It took some years before I decided I wouldn't mess with those kinds of chicks regardless of how pretty they are. They aim too low, and are too much hassle. I didn't want anybody who aimed too low in my world – that just meant less loot for me. But at the time, I was glad to see her. So much time had passed since we had last got together that it was as good as meeting a new girl.

I said, "Of course you can, beautiful!"

I left Stretch standing there.

Naomi gave me a slow rub.

I grabbed her bum. "Haven't you missed me?"

Pulling me closer to her, she hugged me tight. "Of course I have, but because I can't have you to myself, I've tried to forget you. You're always going to be a womaniser."

I've tried to forget you! The word 'tried' gave it all away! It told me I could have her once again.

"How's about I stay at yours tonight? Just to talk, of course. I still check for you a lot."

Pushing me away slightly, she looked into my eyes. "Come on, Jay. You're talking to me now. Why don't you just be honest? You just want to get in my knickers."

She was nearly right: I wanted to get into her...! "All right. Can I get into your knickers?" I asked cheekily.

"I should say no. I just don't know why I'm so weak when I see you. You always make me feel horny. I don't know what the hell it is about you."

I knew - The invisible stuff!!! There was a pattern when it came to women: I attracted them like magnets and they were always falling under my spell!

****

Back then I couldn't put my finger on exactly what it was at the time, but I was still aware I had something special with the ladies, and because I couldn't nail down precisely what it was, I always guessed it was that I was fairly handsome and manipulative.

Later on, I came to realise that it was more than that – it was what I call 'the invisible stuff' (some people may see it as personal magnetism) – a radiant aura, confidence, and charisma that radiates out of me and people like me. When that force radiates out, you can feel it but you can't exactly see it – like electricity. However you describe it, the fact is I had it, and it was built into my DNA.

I have also come to the conclusion that it cannot be nurtured; you either have it or you don't. Of course you can work on confidence and improve it, but it's a matter of having all the elements which makes it a very powerful thing.

Looks have very little to do with it.

****

I had arranged to meet Naomi outside when the club had finished, so I made my way to the spot. Stretch was there, staring gooey-eyed at some big-breasted girl like a kid who had just seen a new toy. I had been busy that night and chatted up loads of girls. Eventually, when I had cleaned up house, Stretch dropped me and Naomi back at her place.

I was unsettled; not having my phone was disturbing my normal rhythm. That night she did her best to let me know what I was missing out on. If she'd had pounds, dressed like a lady, and wasn't so aggressive she'd have been one hell of a girl. But unfortunately, she was caught up in her surroundings and was blind to the fact she had serious potential.

I left bright and early the next morning, promising her I would see her next week. *I wish I hadn't!* I caught a cab to Stretch's and jumped into my car. I headed straight to my probation officer's office. When I arrived, I ran over the details with her. She took out a folder and made some phone calls.

"There's a hostel room vacant on Westfield road. Are you interested?"

Interested indeed! "Yeah, I'm interested."

"Okay, fill out these papers; it should take about a week."

Yes! I thought. *I've got my own place; now I can organise these girls properly.*

I raced back home to Mandy's, to get some sleep. I thought she'd be at work. I was wrong. The crazy bitch was in – she was in bed. I looked for my phone. Damn! There it was, on the ironing board. It was switched off. I felt relieved. I was thinking I'd got away with it. I slipped into bed without saying a word.

"Have you missed me, JJ?" she asked as soon as I got comfortable.

I thought, *She's never called me JJ before, and why the hell is she asking if I missed her?* Something was wrong. I said, "Yeah, I missed you."

She got on top of me. She said, "I want you to fuck me."

I knew something was definitely up. She didn't normally speak like that. I pushed her off. "Not now, Mandy. I'm tired."

"Why's that, JJ?"

There it was again, calling me JJ. She was saying it in a really patronising way. Then it hit me. It was only Sandra who called me that. Sh*t! Sandra must have called my phone.

"I just am. Now let me get some fucking sleep!" I raised my voice as I knew war was about to break out.

"JJ, I'll tell you why you're fucking tired: because you're too busy sticking your dirty prick in that bitch Sandra. Well, I'm going to teach you a lesson. You won't be sticking it anywhere ever again…"

I quickly turned around. She had a knife in her hand.

Crazy bitch, not again!

CHAPTER 11
A STREAK OF BAD LUCK

She tried to stab me you know where. I jerked away just in the nick of time and the knife went into my thigh. I grabbed the knife and started pushing it into her throat.

"Go on, then... go on, do it..." she said very softly.

I looked into her eyes and they looked distant, as if her soul wasn't even there. Right there and then I realised I was destroying her, and she couldn't care less whether she was alive or dead. I removed the knife from her neck.

"You're not worth a murder charge."

I started to stem the bleeding on the outside of my thigh. Mandy just sat there, spaced out. Once I had tended to my leg, I started packing. Only then did she snap out of the twilight zone. She started crying and begged me to stay – but I couldn't.

For the first time, my conscience hit me like a ton of bricks.

I left her – I was convinced one day she would do me some serious damage and I was no longer prepared to take the risk. It became clear to me when Mandy got into that insane rage that she was not in control. It was like she was possessed.

When I eventually saw Sandra, she was furious. She ranted about me having said that Mandy was my cousin, and asked me how I could sleep with anyone else. Then, when I least expected it, she slapped me in the face.

My first reaction was rage. The way I had grown up, it was against the rules to take any kind of disrespect without retaliation. I was about to punch her lights out when I saw the frightened look on her face. Just as quickly as I had become angry, I calmed down. Hitting wasn't my thing, so I let it go.

I couldn't really blame her. I explained to her that Mandy was a mad girl who I had never wanted to live with but, because of my circumstances, I hadn't had a choice. I spun out another lie, and told her there was no way I had been sleeping with her.

She didn't believe me. *Would you?*

So I asked my mother to back up my story. Now at first my mum was reluctant to lie for me, but she really liked Sandra so she went along with it – but not without giving me a stern warning first that this was the last time she would cover for me.

In the end, Sandra forgave me, after a persuasive promise from me that I wouldn't cheat again. *That was like an alcoholic saying, "I'll never have another drink."*

My hostel room came through, as my probation officer had told me it would. I moved in instantly. My room was in the attic. Stretch helped me to move in. Sandra brought me a three-seater leather sofa and a nice mahogany table. I bought two champagne buckets and ten bottles of champagne. I placed the ice buckets in the centre of the table, the champers encircling it. The result was a sparkling sex parlour.

It had been a week since I had promised Naomi I would come back and see her. I decided now was the time to give her a call. I needed to be inside her; she definitely knew her stuff.

One of her friends answered her phone. She told me Naomi had popped out and that she wouldn't be back for ten minutes. I told her to tell her I was on my way down. I asked Stretch if he wanted to come and hook up with Naomi's friend: he said he couldn't come as he had a date with some other girl. So I left my hostel and headed to Naomi's place.

I was driving through Stoke Newington when I saw David standing at a bus stop. I tried to drive past, but he flagged me down. I stopped. I wondered if he still held a grudge against me. I guessed not. Acting as if we had never been enemies, he got in the passenger seat.

He said, "What's happening? I haven't seen you about in ages."

"I've been around, doing this and that."

Looking around at the car, he smiled and said, "I can believe it – when did you get the ride?"

"I've had it some time now."

"So where you going now?"

"I'm going to check some girls."

"So am I going to get a bring in?"

I had a good mind to tell him to fuck off, but then something made me change my mind. "Come on then."

When we arrived at Naomi's there was a group of guys outside, just loafing around. Naomi wasn't back yet. Her friend Alfia told us to come in and wait. Alfia looked very pretty. She was what I'd call coolie-looking: black mixed with Asian. She had mid-length curly hair and her chest was perfect. Even though the script was already set – I was on Naomi and David was on Alfia – I had a good mind to flip it. I decided I would give her my number on the sly. I wanted her, and in the moment when our eyes locked for that split second too long, I knew she wanted me.

David suggested we go to the off licence and get some alcohol, and I agreed. I wasn't to know we wouldn't even get there.

As we got outside I noticed three youths, roughly eighty metres ahead, walking away from us. I opened the car door and jumped in the driver's seat with the door still open. I leant over and opened the passenger door for David. I put my mobile on the dashboard.

Then I noticed that the three youths had changed direction and were coming quickly towards the car. One of them had an iron bar in his hand. Straight away my heart skips a beat. I glance at David; he is looking shaky. Two of the youths are already at the passenger door. Before they say anything, David says, "I haven't got anything!" and empties out his pockets. I think, *you punk*.

Now the third youth was on my side of the car, holding the bar above me. "Take off the chain before I put this bar above your head."

My mind was racing at a hundred miles an hour. I remembered Stretch's words of warning about this chain, how it was going to make people jealous. Then I thought,

No way am I giving up this chain! But I was trapped. Then I saw five more of them jump off a small building roof and head towards us. The reinforcements had arrived.

I say, "You take it off." I planned to rush him as soon as he bent down.

"Don't play games with me. I'm not going to tell you again."

I knew he wasn't bluffing. But I had to do something, and fast. So I leapt out of my seat and tried to grab the bar – but he moved back and it came cracking down on my skull. I almost went down, then I ran. He gave chase with the rest of them. I ran and ran, wiping my eyes as the blood from my head blurred my vision. I ran about half a mile, through estates, down alleys, until they eventually gave up.

Finally, when I knew I'd lost them, I stopped on a back street and knocked at the nearest house. A middle-aged woman answered.

"Could I please use your phone? It's an emergency."

She looked at me; I saw the shock on her face. "I'm sorry, I can't help you," she said, closing the door in my face. *Nice one, bitch!*

I could see a pub at the end of the road, so I ran down to it. When I walked in, the whole pub stopped dead and stared at me as if I had just arrived from outer space. I asked the barmaid if I could use the phone. She told me to go into the toilet and get myself cleaned up first. I told her politely that I'd do it the other way around.

So I called Stretch and told him to come down with some people. He said he'd leave immediately. I hung up and went to the toilet, and took my first look in the mirror. *What the fuck!* There was blood everywhere. The blood on my face had dried, I guess from running in the cold air. I did look strange. The gash on my head was still bleeding.

The barmaid came in and helped me clean myself up. She told me I was going to need stitches. As I was waiting for Stretch to arrive, I started getting dizzy spells. I ignored them as all I could think about was those pricks who had tried to rob me. I wanted them at whatever the cost, especially the one who'd put the bar over my head.

Stretch and a few guys I knew turned up half an hour later. We went back to the scene; it was like a ghost town. My car was still there, but my mobile and David were missing. Stretch tapped in my mobile number and it was switched off.

I said, "Come on. Let's go look for them."

We drove around for a while, but there was no sign of them. They'd vanished.

"I'm driving you to the hospital," Stretch said.

"Fuck the hospital…"

"Look at your head! It's like a fucking fountain!" piped up Wugly.

Look at your own fucking head, I thought. "I don't give a shit about my head; that's the last thing on my mind. If you want to drive me somewhere, drive me to go and get my machine."

Stretch drove me to the hospital. I went straight into Casualty. I was told right away I would need stitches. The doctor kept asking me what had happened, but I knew he was just fishing so he could report it to the police. I told him I had had an accident and fallen over. By the way he reacted, I could tell he didn't believe me, but I didn't care. After he had given me twelve stitches and was done, guess who showed up? The police were asking me all these bullsh*t questions that I had no intention of answering. So eventually I was discharged and made my exit.

Afterwards, Stretch dropped me round at my mother's house and said he would collect my car for me. They all promised me that we would go back and look for them the next day.

Within half an hour, David called my mother's. "Jay, you all right?"

"Where did you get this number from?" I asked.

"Stretch..."

"Where's my phone?"

"I got into a fight with them. They got it."

He was lying. He was trying to big himself up.

"I want the money for it in the morning."

"But..."

"No fucking buts," I said and hung up.

I was angry with him for acting so weak, and one thing I knew for sure was that he was going to damn well pay for my phone. In fact, if I had lost my chain he would have been paying for that too. If I had been with someone else we would have given them a run for their money, but not with David! With hindsight I can see I was taking my frustration out on him.

It was two thirty a.m. and everyone was sleeping. I went to sleep with one thing on my mind: murder. I was going to kill the one who had put that bar over my head.

When I opened my eyes again my head was pounding. I looked at my watch; it was seven a.m. The house was quiet. I got dressed and went downstairs. My car keys were on the doormat. Stretch had popped them through the letterbox. I picked them up, got into my car, and drove back to the hostel.

I showered and changed my clothes. I took out my machine from the base of my bed. I slid out the box of bullets and removed ten. I shined them and loaded up at the table. I took aim at the door handle. The door handle was that prick's head. I pretended to shoot. I was furious. My pride was killing me. I was prepared to go to the extreme.

Later that morning, I drove to David's house, my machine stuck in my waistband in a plastic bag. I rang the doorbell; his mother answered. I asked her to call David and a moment later he came to the door.

He said, "What's happening, Jay? You all right? That was some kind of joke, wasn't it?"

I had no time for conversation with this little punk. I said, "Where's my money?"

"What are you talking about…?"

"Listen, don't let me have to…"

"Is that how you're treating me…?"

"Yes."

"How much is it?" he asked.

"Sixty," I replied.

"What?"

"You fucking heard me."

"I've only got forty; I'll give you the rest tomorrow."

I had a good mind to mess him up there and then on his own doorstep. It wasn't the money that bothered me; it was his cowardice.

I took the money and drove off. I stopped at the nearest phone box. I dialled Stretch's mobile.

"Where are you?"

"I'm at home, where are you?"

"I'm on the road – I'm going to plot for those punks."

"Listen, Jay, forget about the gun thing. I know what you're like when you lose your head."

"What the fuck are you talking about... forget?"

"Listen, we can deal with it differently..."

I hung up. I didn't want to hear his bullsh*t. *Deal with things differently my foot!* There was only one way to deal with it: put two in that punk's head.

That afternoon I drove back to the scene and parked up on a side street where I had a good view. It was about two o'clock. With none of them in sight, I lay back in my seat and waited.

About an hour later I thought I saw one of them walking in my direction. I quickly drew out the machine and wound down the window. As he got closer I realised it wasn't one after all. Because of the way I was feeling, I felt like shooting him anyway, just to send a message. *I now know I was allowing my emotional side to override the rational part of my brain!!!* I let him pass.

By four o'clock I still hadn't seen any of them. So I decided to go and buy a new mobile. I told the man in the shop I wanted the same number I'd had before. He sorted it out within the hour, and assured me the line would be on at some point that day.

Feeling a bit better, I drove back to the same spot. *Even if these punks don't come out until eight, I thought, I'm going to sit here and wait for as long as it takes.*

Sometime afterwards I must have nodded off. My ringing mobile woke me. I looked around; there was no one in sight. I checked my watch; it was six forty-five p.m. I answered the mobile. There was no reply.

"Who the fuck is it?" I said.

No answer.

"Who is it?" I said for the second time.

"Jay?"

"Yeah."

"What, have you got your phone back?" It was Stretch.

"No, I got the same number in a new phone."

"So where are you?" he asked.

"I'm outside Naomi's, plotting for those pricks."

"All right, I'm coming. Be there soon."

Stretch arrived at half seven. He got into the passenger seat. "I take it you haven't seen any of them yet?"

"Nope."

"Have you considered they might not even come from around here?"

"I saw them hanging around here before, as if it was their patch."

"So how long are you going to wait?"

"Until ten."

"Night Moves tonight?"

"Maybe." I didn't have any real intention of going out that night.

Ten o'clock came soon enough. They hadn't shown up. I was pissed off, but what I could do? Stretch suggested we go to the club. Reluctantly, I agreed.

I didn't enjoy the club at all. All night my face was screwed up. I was begging someone to as much as step on my foot. We left at two a.m.; I was tired. But there were these two girls hanging around outside, and I had a hunch they were slappers looking for a good night. I approached them and let them know what was on my mind.

"Where are you lot off to?" I asked with little enthusiasm.

"We're going home."

"So are you not going to invite me and my friend back for an after-party?"

She consulted her friend, and then said, "If you want."

I was right. I could see a slapper a mile off. I guess I was a slapper myself; it takes one to know one – isn't that the old saying?

So they jumped into the car with Stretch and me. I don't even remember the name of the girl I was talking to, so I'll just call her 'the slapper' for reference; the other one's name was Pam, I think – something like that. I took out my machine and told the slapper to hold it, in case we got pulled over. There was no point taking unnecessary risks. I drove back to their place in Hackney. It was obvious they were both looking for a good time. I was only looking for a quick bone so I told Stretch to make sure this was a fast thing.

When we arrived at their place, I went straight into the bedroom with the slapper, leaving Stretch in the living room with Pam. I wondered how he could think of sleeping with her – she looked like a female wrestler who needed a shave... Sorry, I forgot! She had big breasts!

So Slapper handed me my machine and started giving me the third degree about why I was carrying it. I wasn't about to tell her anything. I told her to come over to me. She came like an obedient little puppy. I started caressing her breasts, and quickly stripped her clothes off. She tried to kiss me on the lips, but I told her I didn't like kissing. I had a feeling she was a blow job specialist. Why? *Because she had stretch marks around her mouth!* God only knows how many dicks she had sucked that day.

Once I'd stripped her, I picked up the machine. I rubbed it over her breasts, through the middle, and then all over her body. It was driving her crazy, I could tell. I started kissing her breasts and at the same time I slid the machine slowly until it was in between her thighs. She whispered, "Put it in." I shoved the muzzle right up there. "Harder!" she wailed, holding my hand and helping me — as if I wasn't using enough force already. I was just about to see whether the whole gun would fit up there when she said, "Put the bullets in."

"What?"

"Put the bullets in."

"What are you talking about?"

"Put the bullets in, and put it back in me."

I thought, *What the fuck is wrong with this slapper?* I stared at her for a moment. Then, "Listen, are you fucking sick? I'm outta here." I pulled it out and wiped it on her sheets.

I went to the living room. Stretch was getting a blow job.

I said, "I'm going. That girl's a fucking freak."

"Wait twenty minutes," he pleaded.

"I'm going now." I went to the front door, but the freak was trying to pull me back in. I shrugged her off.

The truth was, deep down, I wasn't really mad at her. I was still mad at the prick who'd put the iron bar over my head. She was just getting the tail end.

As I was driving home, Stretch fell asleep. I noticed I was feeling sleepy myself. My eyelids were closing slowly. I got to Edmonton Green, I turned onto Church Street, and then that's all I remember... until I felt a tremendous jolt. I opened my eyes. I was on the other side of the road heading straight into a parked car. I tried to brake but it was too late.

The windscreen caved in. The bottom of the dashboard was pinned to my knees. Stretch started to curse. I told him to shut the fuck up. I braced the dashboard and got out of the car. The car was fucked. I threw my machine into the nearest bushes. I thought, *I've got to do a runner.* I was only insured third-party. I knew the only way to get a claim was to say it was stolen. I waved to Stretch to come out.

I said, "Come on! We gotta get out of here."

But before he could even answer, the police had pulled up from out of nowhere. I was breathalysed and passed. I couldn't believe it. The police took us to hospital and kept saying how lucky we were to survive because we hadn't been wearing seat-belts. Once we got the all clear from the hospital, the police dropped us at home. It wasn't until I got to Mum's house that I realised I still had some bullets in my pocket.

That was too close for comfort. It was six forty a.m. As soon as the police had gone I went straight back to the scene to get my gun. When I saw my car I felt really depressed. I knew it was a write-off.

As soon as I got home and into bed my thoughts were consumed with those pricks who had tried to rob me along with the reality that I no longer had a car. I really felt like this was a streak of bad luck.

I woke up at two p.m. Sandra was by my bedside. She hugged me and said, "I think it was for the best."

"What?" I replied.

"God must have been looking out for us. I mean, now we can spend more time together."

I nearly floored her for those dumb comments, but then she climbed into bed and I turned over into the missionary position.

What else could possibly go wrong?

CHAPTER 12
THE LADY WITH THE STERLING

I had one choice and one choice only. I had to find a woman. I needed a car fast.

For three months, I was borderline depressed. It was due to a combination of no-car-and-not-enough-money-to-get-one combined with the fact that those punks had got away with trying to rob my chain. Every five minutes, my mobile was going mad. I was in demand, but I was finding it very difficult to keep up with my girls without wheels.

I decided that as much as Sandra and a few other girls were splashing out on me, it wasn't enough.

One Saturday I hooked up with Stretch. When I jumped in his car I could see he was pissed off: unlike me, he was chickless. I ran down my current situation for him. "Life's a bitch sometimes," I told him. "One minute you're doing all right and then the next, you're on your face."

"I know, Jay, but I'm sure it won't be long before you're back on your feet. You always land on your feet."

I prayed that he was right. "You know what? I have this funny feeling I'm going to meet a rich woman soon. All I need is one. You know me – I'll find a way into that bank account."

At that very same moment, I saw a BMW convertible with private plates coming towards us. A woman was driving with another lady in the passenger seat.

"Stretch, pip the horn!"

She looked over. I raised my hands and shoulder in gesture. She smiled, and I signalled to her to pull over. *No!* I thought. *This can't be for real!*

The driver came over so I wound down the window. She looked in and said, "Oh! I'm sorry. I thought you were someone else."

Someone else my foot! I played along all the same. "Aren't you glad you made a mistake?" I asked.

She ignored me and smiled. "So are you not going to tell me your names? My name's Denise. Nice to meet you," she said, looking straight at Stretch.

I thought, *Shit, don't tell me she likes him?* So I tried to divert her attention. "My name's Jay, and now that I have a good view of you, I'm very pleased to meet you."

"What's your name?" she said to Stretch.

"Hi, my name's Mickey," he lied, shaking her hand.

"Well, it's nice to meet you both. But I'm late for an appointment."

As she made to leave, I said, "Now, Denise, that wouldn't be a very wise move, to leave without exchanging numbers. After all, you don't know who I am yet, and I'm sure you're aware first impressions can be very deceptive. You appear to be very wise to me."

****

I was playing on her emotions. On first impressions I quickly surmised that she was well brought up because she spoke very well, and she was dressed very elegantly, and I guessed she saw herself as very wise. The chances are she wouldn't now want to be seen as not wise.

****

She paused for a second, and then took out a business card. "I don't usually give out my number, but give me a call sometime."

She turned and walked back to her car.

How many times had I heard that one? What she really meant was, I don't want you to think I'm a slapper because I'm giving you my number so easily.

There was something about Denise, apart from her sexy voice. She had that invisible stuff I've tried to describe.

Stretch put his foot to the metal, heading in the direction of his house. He looked at me. "I can't believe that. You were just talking about us finding a rich woman only five minutes ago."

US! "I told you I had a feeling about a rich woman!"

Later that night, Stretch asked me to copy down Denise's number for him. Yeah right! I had been waiting for someone like her since my release from prison. I pretended to search for her business card. I said, "I can't believe this, I can't find it. Sh*t…"

He laughed. He knew me too well. "Don't give me that bullsh*t."

Bullsh*t or not, I kept my face dead serious. "Listen, I'm not joking! Trust me!"

****

The phrases 'Trust me!' or 'Would I lie to you?' are common for womanisers. In my experience, whenever I have used them, it's either been in a situation where I'm trying to pull the wool over someone's eyes, or when I have been just generally unsure about an issue. So my tip to you is: be cautious whenever you hear these words! Whenever I hear them, I think, who are you trying to convince? Me? Yourself? Of course, there is always the odd exception that proves the rule. But I'd say nine times out of ten, beware!

****

He didn't buy it. "I don't believe you. If that's how you want to play it…"

After that, Stretch started to act funny with me. Did I care? Of course I didn't. I had one focus and one focus only. I told him to drop me home. He drove back to my place in silence.

That night, there was a heavy storm, so I decided to stay in. The Monday night following the weekend storm, I got up enough courage to phone Denise. I couldn't remember the last time I'd felt nervous phoning a girl. But Denise was no girl – she was a woman. She looked about thirty, and she sounded posh. All weekend I had wanted to call her, but I was worried about screwing up. I knew I was an expert when it came to young girls, but the older, classier women I had yet to master.

I guessed Denise would want more than a handsome face. I mean, I would have to lie about my age, my career, everything if I wanted to pull this one. Basically, I knew I would lose out if she suspected me to be the real womaniser I was.

I dialled her mobile number, and the call connected.

"Hello. Can I speak to Denise, please?"

"Yes, this is Denise. To whom am I speaking?"

I paused. I was nervous. For the first time I was lost. My balls had gone for a walk. Jay Johnson, Mr Absolute Confidence, was nervous! Where the hell had this come from? I didn't like it one bit. In fact, it completely stumped me. A womaniser who gets nervous when talking to a woman? The two didn't go together! I made a mental note – I would have to fix that issue, fast.

****

It was so different this time.

I could still talk a lot of bullsh*t to a lot of young girls, because they hadn't had enough life experience to have learned how to see what was going on right under their nose. I was young, but built into my DNA I seemed to have a higher awareness than the people around my age when it came to anything surrounding women - I also had good looks and on top of that I was intuitive, and I could see their blind spots. Those things coupled together gave me a huge advantage.

But on this occasion my intuition was prodding me that Denise was a cut above all of that. And all of a sudden I wasn't sure how to tackle her. She was what I now like to call 'seasoned' - in other words, she was astute, wise, experienced, and she rarely missed a trick. I'd met my match!

****

Fix yourself up, I thought.

The telephone call went something like this:

I put on a more subtle voice than my usually gruff tone. "Denise, it's Jay."

"Hi. You're one of those guys I met on the street, right?" she sounded as if she was ashamed.

"Yes I am, but do you remember which one I am?"

"Well, if I remember correctly you're the one who was in the passenger seat. Correct?"

"That's me. Denise, how old are you?"

There was a long pause before she said, "I'm twenty-nine, but more to the point, how old are you?"

"I'm twenty-five," I replied, liberally adding six years to my actual age.

"So how do you spend your time, Mr Jay?"

"Well, I'm at university, studying information technology." Lies, lies, lies. Now it was my turn. "What do you do?" I asked, holding my breath. As soon as I asked it, I thought, *Duhhh! It was on her business card.* But she still told me.

"I'm a property developer."

I had already thought about whether she could sort out a flat for me in some way. I paused. I didn't know what else to say. I made a mental note: I would have to brush up on my communication skills for talking to classy women. Then I remembered my friend's mother was having her thirty-fifth birthday party at the weekend. Well, I couldn't exactly take her to the clubs I was going to.

"Anyway, Denise, this was just a quick call to see what you're doing this Saturday?"

"I'm not sure. What do you have in mind?"

Some great sex maybe! "My friend is having her thirty-fifth birthday party this weekend. It should be quite nice. In any case, it will give us a good opportunity to get to know one another a bit better."

She paused. Then she said, "I'll give you a call on Wednesday and let you know. It was nice to hear from you, Mr Jay. I'll speak to you soon."

I gave her my number and hung up.

I didn't usually take girls out. I preferred to take them to bed! But I knew Denise was in a different league. I would have to deal with her differently for now, until I had her heart. Then I would change things. I knew her type: they didn't like to jump in bed on the first date. I would have to ask to see her the next day, which automatically made it a second date. *Yes, I thought, that's exactly what I'll do if she accepts the invitation.*

That night when I hit the sack I thought of a scam to run on Denise if I got her where I wanted her. I would tell her some guys were out to kill me and that they were demanding ten thousand pounds from me for fucking up their business. I guessed she would need more convincing than that. So I thought of the next step: I would get some guys to chase me down in front of her, and let off a couple of blank shots in my direction. I wondered all at once if Denise would fall for it. I wasn't to know that later on that very same scam would be the last thing on my mind! But for now, I couldn't stop thinking about her.

She called me on the Wednesday afternoon from her office. I explained to her I wasn't driving. She agreed to pick me up on Saturday. Half eleven on Saturday night I put on my Moschino suit – the one that Sandra had bought for me – and I finished it off with a splash of Versace cologne. Boy was I ready to woo this woman! Soon I heard a car horn outside. I looked at my watch – it was half past midnight. I looked out of the window, and there was the shiny black BMW convertible with Denise sat inside. I couldn't help but smile. For good measure, I waited ten minutes before I went out to the car.

****

I heard somewhere that Mohammed Ali always kept people waiting on purpose. His reasoning was that it conveyed his importance to their minds. I wasn't Mohammed Ali, but for sure my intention was to be great, like him.

I was still wet behind the ears, but I was starting to try to look through other people's eyes. It doesn't take a mathematical genius to work out that if you want to be successful or great, you must adopt the attitudes of the successful and the great.

However, it wasn't until some years later that I really started to learn to put those things into practice.

****

When I got out to the car, that sexy purring voice of hers called out to me. "Hi, Jayyy! I was beginning to think you may have fallen asleep. Meet my friend Kristy. Kristy, meet Jay."

I politely greeted them, and stepped into the car. Kristy! What the hell was that all about? There had been no talk of friends coming!

I don't know what excited me more as I sat there – her raw sensuality or the beamer! Here I was, sitting in the car that was a big part of my plans for the future. I directed her to the party as we gunned away from the curb.

The party had barely started when we arrived, but it wasn't long before people started to arrive in mobs. There were a lot of familiar faces, and Denise seemed to know a lot of people. I had assumed she wouldn't have known or associated with anyone in that circle, because of the way she carried herself. She looked posh – I thought, *Perhaps she's the kind of girl who's always washing her hands, but filthy in the bedroom!* She had caramel skin and long black relaxed hair. Her hips were to die for – she was as sexy as hell – but most of all she had bucket loads of that invisible stuff; I could feel it.

She was like a magnet – all the men were hanging around her like flies around sh*t, and it pissed me off. One man in particular – where he sprang from, I don't know. He put his arms around her and said, "Oh my God, where have you been, darling? You look amazing!"

"I can't believe it, Larry! I haven't seen you in… You look wonderful… terrific!" Denise replied with a whopping great smile on her face that she had not yet given to me.

"Come on! Let's have a dance," he motioned.

She linked her arm in his, turned round to look at me, and said, "Would you excuse me for a moment, Jay? I'll be back shortly."

Shortly my fucking arse! I felt small, humiliated, and stupid. I was known as a womaniser, and because of that I began to get paranoid. I started to think people were noticing. It probably wasn't true, but that's how I felt, and my ego was taking a bruising. I stood there trying to look at my phone as if I were reading the most fascinating text message. This was the first and *last* time in my entire life I can recall feeling the pangs of jealousy. To make things worse, she wasn't back shortly like she had promised. Her and that prick clung to each other the whole fucking night and I mean the whole night!

I was furious. I couldn't believe what was going on right in front of my very eyes. *You're going to pay for that, you silly woman,* I thought. Every half hour or so she would come back and ask me if I was all right. *All right indeed! Do I look fucking all right?* I wanted to shout back at her. I felt embarrassed. I had never been treated like that before – not ever. It was ridiculous. I take a woman out, and some 'Rico Suarve' looking motherfucker comes along and says thank you very much! That was usually my move, but here I was having the tables turned on me!

Some girl I had previously boned came up to me and asked who I had come with. Reluctantly, I pointed to Denise. "That woman over there, dancing with that man." The look she gave me said it all.

Later on, she came back to rub it in. I could tell she was delighting in my misery. Grinning, she added, "They've been dancing non-stop!"

I wanted to walk over to them and smash a bottle over his head. I didn't want that bastard to get away with stealing one of my women – and my investment! But there was nothing I could do. I knew it would only make me look even more foolish.

Just as daylight started to force its way through the windows, Denise had the cheek to ask me if I was ready to leave, and if I wanted a lift home. *I had been bloody ready after the first half hour!* I was too proud to say yes, so I said

I wasn't ready and that I was okay to get home on my own. She gave me a peck on the cheek, which I really wanted to return with a slap! Then she said, very casually, "Thanks for the night out. Give me a call sometime."

I ran upstairs to watch her leave out of the front window. I wanted to make sure she was going home alone. I saw her and Kristy get into the BMW and bolt off. I got a lift home from someone else twenty minutes later.

I wasn't feeling well and I couldn't work out why. The feeling was brand new to me. I was a kinaesthetic person. I went with how I felt about situations much more so than what I actually thought about them. And here I was feeling stuff I had never felt before. I was trying to work out what was going on. Why did it get to me so much? Why did I feel a drain on my strength and energy? Why had she clung to him and not to me? Why did I feel so jealous? It wasn't like me! How had I lost out at the end of the night? I fell asleep with all these questions on my mind, and no answers in sight.

It wasn't until the Monday afternoon that I found out I was still in with a chance with Denise. I had borrowed Stretch's car and I was heading to Sandra's place. As I passed the police station en route, I saw Denise standing at the bus stop with two kids. I wondered what she was doing and where the BMW was! I spun around and pulled up in front of her and the kids.

I said, "Where are you off to?"

"Hi, Jayyy! I'm off to my mother's," her voice purred.

"Where does your mother live?"

"Sandown Road..."

"Do you want a lift?"

"That would be very nice of you."

Damn right after the way you treated me at the party! I thought.

I opened the back door and let the children in. Denise got into the passenger seat. She introduced me to the kids, Steven and Holly. They turned out to be really cool kids, well-spoken and very friendly. There's nothing worse than dating a woman with rude kids!

As I pulled out, I asked her what had happened to her car. It led into a deep conversation through marriage–husband–divorce. She explained to me she was married and that she was currently going through a divorce, but that her husband was giving her tremendous grief. She also explained that one hour ago she had been in her car with a male friend when her husband had pulled up and caused a scene... She couldn't stand embarrassments so had she left the two of them arguing and jumped on the bus. For a second I wondered whether the male she was referring to was that 'Rico Suave' motherfucker from the party – but I didn't ask.

When we arrived at her mother's, she asked me if I wanted to go out later that evening. Of course I didn't refuse. Maybe I was getting a second chance – to teach her a lesson.

I said, "What time are you talking here?"

"How's eight o'clock with you?" she asked.

"Eight is fine by me."

"Then I'll pick you up at eight."

I said goodbye to the kids and drove to Sandra's, then I drove Sandra straight round to the bank. She gave me two hundred pounds. I drove back to her place, gave her a fifteen-minuter, and then headed straight back home to get ready.

Denise picked me up bang on time. *Of course I kept her waiting!* She took me to a nice little plush Italian restaurant in Hampstead. It was way above what I was used to. When we arrived, the first thing I noticed was that everybody greeted her by name. When we had been ushered to what the waiter referred to as her usual table I began to take in the whole ambiance. The place was first class all the way: marble floor, sculptures neatly paced in just the right places, grand mirrors the size of my hostel room. As for the service, well they treated me like royalty – I was taken aback by the whole set-up. It was a far cry from the world I knew.

Halfway through our meal, she said, "People must think you're my son."

I shot her a look that said, *Don't you dare go there.*

"Well, you don't look… you still have a baby face."

I said, "I think you're getting paranoid. If anything, they might think I'm your brother. You don't look a day over twenty-five."

"Arrr! You're very sweet."

We carried on with our general chit-chat and finished our meal at around nine forty-five. I started to wonder what was coming next, whether she would drop me home or…! I badly wanted to bone her. After all, it was the second date.

As if reading my mind she said, "Would you like to come back to mine for a drink?"

Yes, I bloody would... "That would be nice, Denise. I feel very comfortable around you," I replied. The truth was, I felt extremely comfortable around her. She definitely had some of that invisible stuff going on.

Her house was a major. It was too much! I later found it was just one of a few she owned. We settled down in her living room. The stereo was Bang & Olufsen; I'd never even heard of them before. It was full of all the expensive stuff. I was fascinated by the whole crazy set-up. I doubt I hid my excitement either.

As I was taking in what I presumed would soon be my new wonderful surroundings, my phone rang. Damn, I had thought I'd turned it off. It was Naomi; she wanted me to come around. I told Naomi I'd call her back in an hour. I hung up.

"Was that your girlfriend?" Denise asked.

By what she said next, I knew I had paused a second too long.

"Go on, you can tell me."

"No, it was just a friend," I said.

Denise poured us both a glass of champagne. This was the part I hated! She wanted long conversation. I felt no need for it myself; I wanted to bone first and maybe talk later. She was full of questions. She wanted to know all about me. A woman's formality was what it really boiled down to. I mean, I liked to know as much as I could about my women, but that was second to the sex. I figured women want it just as much as we do! But they are programmed to act as if they don't. *Cut it out, will you, ladies! You're not fooling us!*

"What course did you say you were studying?" she asked.

"Information technology."

"Why did you choose computers?"

"I guess I enjoy using computers."

"Are you there full time?"

"Part time." I continued the lie.

"So what do you do in your spare time?"

"Well, most of time I'm studying; when I'm not, I'm playing football."

"So tell me, Jay, do you have a girlfriend?"

****

Why was she asking me that again? I wondered. My instinct told me she didn't believe much of what I was saying. In fact, Denise had this way of looking right through me at times, and very often it made me feel uncomfortable. The look always came when I was lying. She was very astute and aware. Whenever she asked me a question and I got that look, she would change the subject and then ask me the same question as soon as I was comfortable again. I didn't know what she was doing then, but I do now - she was paying attention to my body language.

I saw she shared traits with me: she paid attention, and she could read whether a person meant A or B. It was an ability I had picked up by default. It's quite simple really - it just takes some discipline until it becomes habit. When anyone talks to you, it's important to be aware that there are always two forces at play - what they are saying, and what they are thinking: the outer and the inner. The inner motivates the outer.

Here's a small example: there was a woman who I haven't mentioned until now (for good reason); her name was Emma, and she was probably one of the sexiest women I ever went with. One day we were sitting in the car and some guys walked past and were looking in the car. She turned around to me and said, "Do you know those guys? Why are they looking in the car?" Now here's the point – it was the outer force saying that, but the inner force, the force that motivated her to say what she said, meant, "I want him to know how hot I am and that men are watching me." I read from that comment that she was very insecure. She wanted me to think B when she actually meant A.

The rule of thumb is to listen out for the inner force as well as the outer. Question everything. Ask yourself, if that were me, why would I say that? You'll find humans are not so different from each other. Once you practise, it becomes a habit and works on auto-pilot with no effort.

Denise could do it too! These kinds of characters have a high awareness, follow their instincts, and are very difficult to trick. They have the ability to see patterns early on, and when they see too many, they call it a day before they get too emotionally involved. Your aim should be to be an 'Astute Ruth' – this is what this whole book is about!

****

"No, not at the moment."

"No girlfriend? A good-looking guy like you?" There it was again, that sarcasm, and that look. It was as if she could read my damn brain.

"Nope." This was a lie. Two lies. In fact, they were all lies.

"Jay, I'd like you to kiss me," she said as if she were asking me to pass her a drink.

I kissed her at once. I kissed her the moment she asked, and I kept kissing her all the way up the stairs. I knew I would have to give her my best performance.

She clutched at me impatiently, twisting the pillow, tossing her head and hips as I licked first one nipple then the other. I clenched both breasts in my hands, bringing them together. The nipples almost touching, taking both nipples in my mouth simultaneously I sucked and licked them slowly. Then, as deliberately as I worked her stiffened nipples, I began to work between her thighs, my tongue moving mercilessly back and forth, then circular motions, never actually going too close. She said, "Oh God, please... please stop." That's always a sign to take the tempo up some more.

I continued to tease her, moving back up to the breasts and on to her ears, and then back down in between her thighs, my finger circling her passion button. She grabbed my baton and I said, "No, don't." I gave her no time to register her uncertainty. I grabbed her hands and held them, firmly.

"Fuck me, fuck me, damn it!" she screamed. I grabbed her two legs, pushing them above her head and lowering myself between her thighs where she was dripping wet. "Yes, do it, do it for fuck's sake!" she shouted. I gave it to her.

Later as I lay sweating beside her, I thought to myself, *Yes! The womaniser does it again!* I murmured, "I love you, Denise." *I love you indeed!*

****

I had used those words a lot, with a lot of different women. I thought the words 'I love you' were the cheapest in the English dictionary. Ladies, remember the words 'I love you' are just words. It's the action behind these words that demonstrates real love.

****

Now it was time to talk! I fired a few questions her way. Some ten minutes later, she burst into tears and spilled out her life story. She was a very unhappy lady. The man she was divorcing after eleven years of marriage was making her life hell. He was turning everybody they knew against her, telling lies and bringing her to the brink of suicide. He was also beating up on her every time their paths crossed. An Aware Claire, but a vulnerable one.

Well, she was my woman now, as far as I was concerned. I wasn't going to let any more of that nonsense go on, and I told her so. The part of the story that really got to me was the bit when she told me he had got some fraudsters to transfer tens of thousands of pounds from her bank account. When she told me, I felt as if I'd been robbed! But I also felt sorry for her.

I hugged her tightly, and I let her weep on my shoulder until we fell asleep.

CHAPTER 13
BANG IN LOVE

Two months later I turned twenty, and I felt like the happiest man on earth. I had thrown all my personal beliefs out of the window and fallen head over heels in love with Denise. How or when exactly it happened I wasn't quite sure. But by the time I realised and tried to halt my feelings, it was too late. I was in too deep!

As a womaniser I had always made sure my feelings for any woman never went too deep, making sure I was in full command. But with Denise it was beyond my control. She had an amazing hold over me; she was begging to alter my whole way of thinking.

****

I say it was beyond my control and it really was. Love can creep up on you and it's so powerful once you're in it. However, don't start thinking for one minute it is impossible to use your brain before the heart takes over because I assure you, you can.

At this stage of my life I wasn't aware of how powerful it was to temporarily remove the emotions and to pay attention to patterns in people to get an accurate overview of someone's character, an idea of who the person really is, before the love process kicks in.

Let's face it - right at the beginning of a new relationship, no one's going to highlight their negatives! But if you're hell-bent on detecting patterns when they appear, I assure you it will bring the true person to light, no matter how much they try to hide it.

However, in Denise's case I wasn't looking for any negatives. And to tell you the truth, with hindsight she was a beautiful catch – real 'wifey' material – I just didn't appreciate it at the time.

****

As my feelings progressed I decided to come clean as I felt Denise deserved to know the truth. To my surprise, I confessed everything to her: my age, university, the girls, and anything else I had lied about. Obviously, she wasn't too happy at first, but she later calmed down. I terminated all ties with my old girls. And I mean all.

I was so happy I wanted to share it with someone. When I saw Ms Carlton she was as happy as I was. She told me this was my opportunity for a fresh start and to leave my old life behind, and I agreed.

Denise and I never left each other's side, except when she went to work. Sometimes when she returned she'd have a little present for me. We would head straight to bed to make love. The chemistry between us was truly amazing. She would then take me out to some fancy restaurant for a meal. When we returned we would hit the bed for rounds two and three, sometimes even four.

It had been a long time since I had been out partying. One day I decided to call Denise at work at five p.m. Her secretary said she was in a meeting. She would get her to call me back.

She called back in ten minutes and I could tell she was in a good mood. She said, "What's up, are you missing me?"

It so happened that I always missed her when she wasn't around. Hearing her sexy purring voice made me feel horny. I said, "Yeah I'm missing you, but that's not why I called. I was wondering if you knew a nice night club we could go to?"

She said, "I'm really tired, Jay, can't we just, you know...?"

"I wanted to go out tonight, but as you're tired I suppose we can go out another time."

"I'll tell you what, how about we go to the movies?"

"That's fine with me."

"Okay, you're driving – I'll see you later when I've tied up everything back here."

I hung up. My baton was throbbing. It was amazing how she had such an effect on me. Jesus – she was good. She was five miles away!

I lay back on the peach sofa. Picking up the remote control, I pressed the button that made the TV swivel round to face me, and changed the channel to BBC1. I was just settling down to watch *Neighbours* when my mobile rang. It was Sandra.

"It's me, JJ. I want to see you. I'm missing you."

I was vexed now, because I had already politely told her that it was over, that I wanted to get on with my life, and that she should do the same.

"But Jay..."

I hung up. Straight away the phone rang, and again, and again. I didn't answer. I had no time for any girls except Denise, and as far as I was concerned she was no longer any kind of girl – she was my woman.

After watching several programmes, Denise came home at six thirty p.m. Briefly, she gave me a rundown on how tiring her day had been. When she was finished I grabbed her by the hand and led her into the dining area where I had put on a lavish dinner. I could see the surprise on her face. After our romantic dinner I gave her a massage to help her relax. Then we both took a bath and washed each other. Then we got ready to go to the movies.

I drove us to the UCI cinema in Edmonton. The lobby was packed; I had a good mind to turn back. It took us half an hour just to get the popcorn. Finally, we got settled in screen room eight. The film was *Four Weddings and a Funeral*. After twenty minutes we were in hysterics; it was hilarious. But ten minutes later we got distracted; discreetly, Denise started fondling me. I was getting excited. My hands were all over her and her hands were all over me, feeling me through my jeans. We both decided it was best we left.

I tore through the traffic all the way back to the house. Denise was all over me on the way back. We rushed out of the car, and she fumbled with the key in the door. When we got inside I was on her, she was on me, and in a matter of seconds we were on the hall floor having crazy sex.

Later that night Denise told me she was taking the kids to the United States for a holiday, and that she would leave me the car. She then gave me a grilling.

She said, "Jay, what do you want out of life?"

"I'm not quite sure any more. Just to be happy, I suppose."

Snuggling up to me and caressing the back of neck, she said, "Do you ever want to have kids?"

"Yes, of course I do, when the time's right."

"And how exactly do you intend to look after them? I mean, you're not working or anything."

Sh*t! She wants me to find a job. I was right. "I haven't thought about it," I replied weakly.

"Well, I suggest you find a job. I'm taking the kids to America next week, which will leave you plenty of time. You'll have the car so you can get around."

"How long are you going for?" I asked.

"One month."

"Why so damn long? I can't be away from you for one month!"

"I need time to think."

Think! What the hell am I supposed to do for sex?

A week later everything was set. I drove Denise and the kids to the airport. I was driving down Forest Road when Denise jolted in the seat. "There he is, Jay," she said, trembling.

"There's who?" I replied, totally lost.

"Cameron. My husband."

I was turning into a side road, but I turned to look and I just about caught a glimpse of him.

"Okay, it's all right."

She looked scared stiff. I asked her if she was okay, and she told me she was fine. I kept driving; as I passed Turnpike Lane Station I looked in the rear-view mirror and I noticed a similar BMW behind us, tail-gating us, right up against our bumper. The man driving was flagging me to pull over.

"Denise, is that him behind us…?"

She turned around to have a look. I saw the panic on her face, before she said, "Don't stop, don't stop, Jay! It's him!"

I thought, *I'm not having this rubbish.* "I'm stopping to see what he wants…"

"No, Jay, please don't, please, please!"

At this point I noticed he was parallel to us, on the other side of the road. He swerved into us. I tried to pull over, scraping a parked car in the process. He pulled over and jumped out of his car, and opened the passenger door to where Denise was seated.

"Why aren't the fucking kids at school?" he shouted.

Denise didn't answer. He repeated himself; she still kept mute. He began to pull her out of the car.

I said, "Listen, what the fuck you doing?" My blood was starting to boil.

"Keep your fucking mouth shut and keep out of my business."

I jumped out of the car and ran in between them. "Don't think for one minute that shit is happening with me here, you better understand that." My hand went in my pocket for you know what.

At that point Holly jumped out and said, "Please, Daddy, we're just going on holiday."

He turned to Denise and said, "How the fuck can you just fly off with them without informing me?" Then he turned to me. "You just fucking watch yourself." With that, he walked away.

We got back in the car and resumed our journey. Denise looked relieved. "I'm so glad I'm going away."

I wasn't relieved – I was pissed off that I hadn't punched him on the chin and sent him for a kip.

We got to the airport just in time. I kissed Denise and the kids and wished them a safe flight. Then, with the roof of the BMW down, I made way back into town. I thought about what I was going to do for a whole month with Denise gone.

Well, what do you think I did?

CHAPTER **14**
WHAT GOES AROUND COMES AROUND

During the first week Denise was away, I missed her so badly it hurt. By the second week, I was back to womanising. But I still loved her and everything. I phoned her every day.

One day she rang me to tell me she was pregnant. She said I should keep it quiet for now. *Quiet my arse! I was ecstatic - over the moon!* I pulled the car over. It was the last thing I'd been expecting her to say. I wanted a kid, and who better than Denise to have it! It's not like she was Lakisha Noel!

I phoned Stretch and my mother to tell them the great news. Stretch seemed happy for me, but my mother wasn't as enthusiastic about it. I was too happy to quiz her.

As I drove off I wondered if maybe that was why she had kicked off when she'd asked me if I wanted kids. Maybe she had already known then that she was pregnant? I put those thoughts to the back of my mind; I was too overwhelmed with joy... All I could think was, *I'm going to be a dad - a little Jay is going to come into the world and I'm going to bring him up better than how I was dragged up.*

But even with this surprise, it didn't stop me from catching up on all those lost months. The only way I can justify why I went back to womanising when I was in love with Denise is this: I cared too much about what other people thought about me. Deep down, I didn't really want to do it, but I felt I had to still show the world I was a womaniser – the male ego is a dark, complicated beast, and it was driving me hard.

****

Here is a huge tip – in fact, it's so important I'll rephrase: it's a humongous tip. This has more to do with life in general and covers all areas. If you are not already aware of it, it may very well change your life forever. I personally didn't have the awareness to see it at the time. Only through hindsight am I able to see it very clearly now.

At this stage of my life many of my actions were based on what I thought other people expected of me (in other words, I cared too much about what people thought of me and my image). Although I thought it was not possible for me to be influenced by others, I was still shackled by other people's expectations without actually realising.

Until you are able to free yourself from that bind, you will never know who you really are. I was caught up in my reputation – but your reputation is not who you are; it's who you think you are! Until you have enough courage to free yourself from that bondage you will never be able to make your own independent plans. Believe me when I say this – it can be the difference between living the life you want to live and never living it.

Of course, there are still other factors involved in living the ideal life, but understanding this one on its own will get you closer to those other character flaws that we all have to iron out in order to get where we want or that need to be corrected.

This will all make more sense later. Just keep reading.

****

Whilst out womanising with Stretch I came across one of my old girls. Her name was Leona Clarke. She was only seventeen but she was a little stunner. She came back with me to my hostel and we got drunk and boned just like old times.

It was later that night that I got the shock of my life. When she got into the car she said, casually, "This looks like my cousin Denise's car."

Obviously, I lost my breath for a second, and when I caught it back I said, "*Trust me*. It isn't."

I could see it was playing on her mind and that she wasn't a hundred per cent sure what the registration was. Curiosity got the better of her and she rang her sister, who did know the number plate. She ranted and raved about it, but to be honest I wasn't so worried about what Leona thought, I was more worried about Denise finding out. I made a mental note to make it the very last time – after we had sex again, of course.

I womanised non-stop for the next two weeks. Stretch and me, we nearly covered the whole of London, posing in the beamer. The women were breaking their necks to get my attention. As much as I had the good looks, the beamer was the icing on the cake. I felt very dapper – women were literally waving at me to stop, and the kind of person I was, I stopped for all of them.

Within three weeks I'd boned fourteen women. I was fast slipping back into my old ways. I kept reminding myself that it would have to stop when my baby came home, and I felt guilty that I was sleeping around. I could see the good side and the bad side to what I was playing at: they were having a table-tennis match, and it'd be fair to say that the bad side kept winning. But it didn't stop me.

The week Denise was due back, I stayed at my mum's. She was happy to see me; I hadn't seen her in three months. But the first night back, she started on one of her grillings.

First she banged on about Sandra: "You don't know a good thing when it's staring you in your face. You've hurt that poor girl too much. One day a girl is going to do the same to you, and the hurt you'll feel will be ten times worse. You've heard the saying, what goes around comes around? Well, if you haven't, you will eventually; nobody on this earth escapes it."

"Don't worry, Mother. I'll just send it back around," I said, half-joking. *How wrong I was!*

Then she started asking me if I thought I was ready to have a child. I told her that I was, but I could feel she didn't think it was a good idea.

On the Thursday, Denise was due back. I picked up Stretch and drove to the airport to meet her. Her flight was late. When it finally arrived and the passengers started coming through, I saw her straight away. I couldn't mistake that figure anywhere. She and the kids looked refreshed with their suntans. Denise came over and gave me a hug and a kiss on the lips.

"Hi, Jayyy. How are you? I hope you've been behaving yourself?"

"Of course! I've missed you like crazy," I replied.

And then came that look again!

The second bit was the truth; I had missed her.

I talked to the kids; they were telling me all about their holiday. Stretch and Denise fell into conversation as we all made our way back to the car. I wanted so badly to talk about my baby in her stomach, but I couldn't because it was still meant to be hush-hush. On the way back home I dropped off Stretch and then we continued to Denise's house. As I took her stuff inside all I could think about was fucking her.

Denise had other plans. Collapsing down into the sofa, she said, "So, Jay, what have you got to tell me?"

"What do you mean?" I replied, totally at a loss.

She shot me a strange look.

I thought, *She can't know about Leona already.* Whatever she was going on about, I had a feeling I wasn't going to like it.

She said, "Aren't you going to tell me you've found a job?"

Sh*t! I had forgotten all about that. I said, "Do we have to go into that right now?"

"Yes, we do. Do you understand I'm pregnant?"

I wondered what that had to do with a job – she was loaded.

"I understand all right," I replied.

"Well, if you're going to take that kind of attitude..." she said coldly.

This was the very first time I had seen Denise lose her cool. I was in shock.

"If you think I'm going to have your child whilst you sit on your arse doing nothing, you've got another thing coming!" she blasted.

What started out as a difference of opinion rapidly turned into a full-scale argument. It ended with no conversation at all. The last thing I heard her say was, "I'm not having your child, and that's final."

I left without so much as a good-bye.

It was ten p.m. when I called her cousin Leona and told her to meet me at the hostel. When she arrived, I took my anger out on her vagina. *That'll teach you, Denise: fuck with me and I'll fuck your cousin*, I thought.

I had no intention of phoning her. I decided she would have to say sorry before I would go back. *I'm Jay Johnson! She'll be running back to me in a couple of days*, I thought. I was wrong, very wrong. It was heading my way, and I couldn't even see it: *Mr Retribution!*

A week went past and in that time I fucked around with many women. All of them turned out to be very poor substitutes. It was no good. I was missing Denise like crazy, and she hadn't called. Two weeks passed and still nothing. I was literally cracking up, and I couldn't bear it any longer. I called her; she wasn't in so I left a message.

My mobile rang two hours later. I let it ring several times, and then I answered. It was her.

She said, "Hi, Jay, I've just received your message. It's funny that you called me today as I was going to call you tonight. I'm going to a private clinic on Wednesday. I have to be accompanied. I was wondering if you would drive me there?"

She couldn't be, I thought. I felt sick.

I said, "What are you going to the clinic for?"

"Come on, Jay, don't play silly with me now. You know exactly why I'm going," she replied.

"Denise, please don't go through with this…"

"I'm sorry. I have no choice…"

I hung up.

It was at this point that I realised how deeply I loved her. To my own astonishment I started to get tearful. *Why me, why me, why me, why fucking me?* My mother's words rang in my ears: "The hurt you'll feel will be ten times worse."

The day before Denise was due at the clinic I decided to write her a letter. It took me two hours to perfect it. I hand-posted it through her door. It was my last chance. I expected her to call me that night, but she didn't. I couldn't sleep a wink. Twenty times I had attempted to dial her number, cutting off the call before it connected. I held out, refusing to believe she would actually go through with it.

At five o'clock the next day, Denise called me. She said, "Jay, I've just come back from the clinic. Everything went fine."

I couldn't believe my ears. She had the nerve to tell me everything had gone fine. "So what happens between us from here?" I muttered.

"We'll just be friends, Jay. Please don't let us become enemies."

"Don't do this, Denise. Didn't I mean anything to you?" I pleaded, at the same time remembering all the times women had said those same words to me.

"Jay, don't, please. I don't need it," she said coldly.

I hung up.

I cried again. I felt used. For the first time in my life I knew exactly how all those girls had felt when I fucked them and abused them. I felt so sad. I knew this wasn't womanising behaviour, but it was as if I had no control over my feelings. And no matter how hard I tried to shake it off, it didn't work.

For two weeks I didn't leave home. The only outside communication was by phone, and even then I didn't make good conversation. Everyone was constantly asking me what was wrong. I kept telling them everything was great, my pride stopping me from telling the truth, apart from Ms Carlton. Ms Carlton tried her best to console me, telling me I was just like her son, looking for love, and a good-looking man like me wouldn't have any trouble finding it so long as I treated the lucky woman well and didn't return to my old ways… Her words couldn't penetrate the hurt I felt.

It wasn't until the third week that I received a late-night call. Stirring from my sleep, I answered it. It was Denise.

She said, "Jay, have I caught you at a bad time?"

"No, I'm up watching TV," I lied.

"Can I come round?"

Yes, Yes, Yes! I bolted out of bed and took a shower for the first time in two days. As I was in the shower I thought,

She's coming back! My baby's coming back! My depression vanished in the blink of an eye.

When she arrived, we talked for a little while. Then we hit the bed for some old-time chemistry, leaving me with the impression everything was back to normal. It wasn't until the next morning that she dropped the bombshell.

As she put on her coat to leave, she said, "Jay, I hope you haven't got the wrong impression about last night?"

"What are you talking about?" I asked weakly.

She said, "Just because I came here, it doesn't mean things have changed between us."

I was devastated. She walked out, and I followed her, begging, my tail between my legs like a punk.

As she got into her car, disgusted, she said, "Oh please, Jay, get a grip of yourself."

It was like she was wiping me off her shoe. I said, "Denise, please don't go – I love you…"

She roared off.

I crept back into my hostel, and I started weeping. I knelt down on my knees. I spoke out loud. "Dear God, why are you doing this to me? I know I've messed up a lot of women's heads, but please forgive me. I can't handle this situation. Give me strength, I beg you, Lord. Amen."

I crawled back into bed. I thought to myself, *God, I know you sent Denise to teach me a lesson that I must stop treating girls the way I do.* Five minutes later I received a text message from Denise. The text had one word – LEONA!!

CHAPTER 15
THOUSANDS ON TOP

Well, if God did send Denise to teach me a lesson - it didn't bloody work! By the end of the year, the womaniser was back! They say a leopard never changes his spots; I guess the same goes for womanisers.

Finally, I got Denise out of my system. I took the whole affair as a lesson. Women are not here to stay. She dumped me just like my mother did, I concluded. From that moment on I promised myself I would never get so involved again. There was no way on earth I was going to let any woman have me the way Denise had – not ever.

I was now more determined than ever to womanise the rich sprats. I wanted to show Denise I could do better than her.

A week after I got my strength back I called Sandra and told her I wanted her back. Roughly five days later she took me to Kriscross and spent five hundred on me.

Stretch had taken up fraud for a living, which appeared to be paying him a generous wage. I was tempted to join him, but that wasn't my kind of thing. I didn't fancy seeing a prison cell again. I knew that I had what it takes to make it off women. I had heard somewhere that you must play to your strengths. I decided I was going to do exactly that! All I needed was one rich woman – or even a few average women – giving me a few hundred each a week and I would be fine.

Stretch printed me up some business cards that claimed that I had my own mobile phone business. I womanised constantly for the next three months. I made certain that at least fifteen women got that card every day. I would later separate the non-prospects from the gems.

It was while we were partying one night that I had a brainwave. I couldn't understand why I hadn't thought of it before. *Hampstead! That's where all the rich women are.*

"Stretch," I said, after an exhausting day's female-hunting, "we're looking in all the wrong places!"

"What are you going on about now?"

"Chicks! What else could I be talking about?"

"You're right. Maybe we should go over to south London."

South London my foot! Stretch had no ambition.

"I'm talking about Hampstead…"

"Hampstead? That's nothing but yuppies. They're not interested in men like us."

I looked at him in amazement. My mind flashed forward to the future. The picture was vivid. There he was in the same place. Where was I? Monte Carlo! I had an obsession with Monte Carlo. I'm not 100 per cent sure why; I'd never been there. But I loved the name: it sounded so classy. And it was the place I believed I should be – with the rich.

Stretch shot me a look back; I could tell he thought I was crazy. "You really mean it, don't you?"

I nodded my head; I was dead serious.

"When it comes to women, you never cease to amaze me. I think you're taking this *galist* thing a bit too far. The next thing you'll be telling me we have to wear tuxedos…"

My mind drifted again; I could no longer hear him. I was wearing a tuxedo; I liked it; in fact, I loved it! I was seeing myself in a different light. My mind came back into focus.

"I know what you're saying," he continued, "but there are other ways."

"Name me one," I asked.

"Working?" he joked.

"You're damned right, working! *This is* my work!"

Pointing at me, he said, "I bet it's because of Denise you're thinking like this."

I suppose he was right. In fact, he had put his finger on it. She had taught me a valuable lesson – I had been aiming too low!

"It's nothing to do with her."

"Are you sure?"

"Forget about that. Are you in or not?"

"I doubt it. We're not going to get any women up there."

Dumb arse, I thought. I stood up and slid onto the dance floor.

It was ten days later that I hit the jackpot.

I persuaded Stretch to take a trip up to Hampstead, just to check it out. No suits, no tuxedos; just plain old us. Secretly,

I was wondering if it was going to be my lucky day. For some time, it didn't seem so. For an hour or two we scoured the streets, looking for rich women, but really it seemed like an impossible task – they were all stuck-up yuppies. That was until the eleventh hour, just as we were about to throw in the towel, when I saw my dream.

My eyes lit up like electric light-bulbs as I honed in for a closer inspection. It looked classy, with a big bumper all leathered up in white – what a head turner. As for the woman behind the wheel of the Mercedes, she looked just as good, and to top it off she looked young!

I turned to Stretch. His eyes were fixed on the woman. *No way, this one is mine.* "Follow her," I said.

Stretch put on his hazard lights and did a U-turn. As we made chase, I felt excitement flood through my body. I knew this woman had to be rich. It wasn't until later I found out she wasn't rich. *She was wealthy!*

We watched her pull into the petrol station, and we pulled up alongside her. I watched her every movement as she got out of the vehicle and inserted the petrol nozzle in her car. Close up, she looked young – maybe twenty-five – definitely a stunner. *The younger the better!*

For a brief second there, I wasn't sure if I wanted to manipulate her – she was one hell of a looker. I remembered Denise and the heartache she had given me. Then I blew that thought into oblivion.

I got out of the car and walked into the shop. I shuffled around a bit before buying a carton of juice and leaving. I timed it precisely so that our paths would cross as she was coming in and I was going out. Just as she was about to walk past me, I stopped her dead in her tracks.

"Excuse me, I can't believe I'm doing this, but you actually took my breath away when I saw you at the pump. Nobody has ever stopped me in my tracks like that. I have to introduce myself. I'm very sorry if I've put you on the spot but I had to compliment you on how beautiful you look."

"Why, thank you, thank you very much."

"My name's Jay; and what's yours?"

"My name is Olivia."

Even the bloody name sounds wealthy!

"Well, it's been a pleasure bumping into you, Olivia. I have to go now as I'm running late for a meeting… Hope I bump into you again sometime."

"Maybe. It's a small world, they say."

I smiled and walked off. *This is the fucking one.* I got back in the car.

"Did you get the number?" asked Stretch.

"No."

"Did you give her your number?"

"No."

"Are you mad? She looks stunning!"

"Just cool it a minute," I said, peeping at the woman through the window. I could see she was looking in my direction.

I didn't want to seem too eager. Previous observation of women – not girls – had revealed that they don't like eager men. I was probably the only man who hadn't asked for her number. That, I was sure, would play on her ego a little bit, even if she wasn't vain.

I waited for her to get back into her car and then I wound down the window. "Olivia, sorry to bother you again but can I ask you a question?"

"Yes, you can."

"If you were me and you'd just bumped into somebody who grabbed your attention like nobody you'd met before, and you really wanted to know the character of that person, what would you do?… Be honest."

She paused, and then replied, "Well, I suppose I would ask to see if it was possible to get to know them."

BINGO! She did the work for me. I smiled and she smiled back. I gave her my business card and said it would be nice to go for a coffee sometime. *Coffee!* Damn, it was amazing how quickly I could adapt! *Please God let her call me.* The truth was, I actually fancied her too.

Later that evening, while lying down watching some nonsense on TV, my mind kept drifting to Olivia. Either I was telepathic or I was also on her mind, because she called shortly afterwards. We were on the phone for hours. To be honest it was rare for me to be on the phone with any woman for that long. It's a good sign when that happens. Communication is everything.

We discussed most things. I was ninety-eight per cent deceitful as usual, but she was very easy to talk to; she had that natural ability to fill in the gap when a silence pops up. Eventually, we agreed that we would take in a movie together. I hung up.

I couldn't believe my luck. But for a split second, I wondered if it was luck, or God sending me another lesson; I certainly hadn't learned the last one.

When Olivia picked me up, I switched off my phone; I wanted to ensure there were no distractions as I was determined not to fuck this one up. When we arrived at the cinema we both agreed on what movie to watch. Throughout the whole film, all my thoughts were on her; I could barely tell you what happened in the movie. I wanted to kiss her, caress her, and most of all, fuck her brains out, but I didn't attempt anything. I was growing and learning; I changed the script for Olivia. I was playing it cool, as if those were the last things on my mind.

****

Ladies, the key to being a good womaniser is their ability to adapt to the character they are dealing with. Womanisers know that to bone those kinds of women, you first have to bone their brains! Once they have fucked their brains, everything else comes automatically.

****

I could tell that Olivia fancied me physically, but she was an 'Aware Claire'. So I played it really cool and acted as if I was only interested in her as a sort of friend. I made no movements or suggestions of anything, which I knew would make her want me even more. I decided I would wait until she was literally giving me cues.

So when the film ended, she invited me back to her place for a drink. Of course I told her I couldn't, and that maybe some other time would be nice. I knew that would puzzle her.

As soon as I got in and turned on my phone I had a missed call from one of my old girls, one of my fly-by-night relationships. I was puzzled that she was ringing me – technically, she was no longer speaking to me because I had slept with one of her friends and she had found out. Before I fell asleep I returned the call, but it rang out.

I met Olivia twice more before I actually agreed to go back to her house. *The house!* I couldn't believe my eyes! It was just – wow! It had the works: jacuzzi, sauna, gym – you know, just the like the places you see in the movies.

I've fucking done it! If I were a woman, I would have screamed with excitement! I was ecstatic, but I was good – I never let it show. Would you?

After a tour of the house, as if reading my mind she said, "My grandfather died and left me a lot of money."

She was actually twenty-three, younger than I had originally thought. She didn't work, but then again I didn't blame her – she had no need to. She was well-educated and appeared very wise. She suggested we watch another movie. She led me into the TV room. The TV was enormous. I wondered why she had bothered to go to the movies – it beat me. She poured me a drink of brandy, and we relaxed back to watch a film.

As the movie progressed I could sense Olivia wanting to move closer to me. Before long, I could feel her breathing down my neck. I got a baton stand instantly. I wanted her as I had done in the cinema. I cursed myself for getting excited so easily. I felt her soft lips touch my neck, working together with the tongue up and down my neck, then into my ear.

Then all of a sudden she said, "Jay, you seemed to have changed. You don't fancy me, do you?"

I played dumb. "What do you mean?"

"Oh, it's nothing."

I was shocked at myself. I've always obliged when women wanted it, whether it be the first, second, or third night. Well, not this time. I was learning. I wanted her to fall head over heels for me first. I knew I had to leave before I burst a blood vessel!

I said, "I have to get going now. Thanks for a nice evening. I have to get up early in the morning."

"Jay, are you not attracted to me?"

Was she sick? Didn't she know I was almost coming in my pants just being near her?

"Yes, I am," I replied.

"Then why don't you stay here for a while?"

I have every intention of staying here with you, and for a lot longer than you think!

"I wish I could, but not tonight, babe."

Olivia slipped on her coat and guided me through the kitchen door, and then through another. It led to the garage, and sitting there was a silver beamer convertible. My mind jumped back to Denise and her beamer for a split second. If she was trying to impress me it was bloody working.

On the way home I wondered if I had done the right thing by not fucking her there and then. I decided it was the best move. When she pulled up outside my hostel she asked if she was going to see me again.

I couldn't understand it; she was acting as if she were the lucky one.

****

When the young girls fell head over heels with me straight away, I understood it, because they knew no better; they were still wet behind the ears. A handsome man with a bit of ego: they thought that's what it's all about.

But I knew Olivia was sensible, and intellectual. I couldn't work it out. She was well rounded. With more thought I came to the conclusion she was insecure, for whatever reason. I didn't know why. But it was her weakness... Ladies, be very careful: womanisers will exploit this vulnerability.

****

"Of course you'll see me again. I'll phone you tomorrow."

As I got out of the car I could feel her eyes penetrating me; I opened my door and went inside.

I jumped up and touched the ceiling. Yes... fucking yes! I was happy, really happy. I switched on my phone to call Stretch. I wanted to tell him that I'd finally done it, and my life was about to change forever!

It was about to change all right.

CHAPTER **16**
PLEASE GOD! NOT AGAIN!

It wasn't to last. Just as I felt things were on the up for me, in a matter of two weeks it all changed; I found myself back staring at the inside of a cell. In the blink of a rich girl's eye, my life had suddenly come tumbling down again.

I was arrested on suspicion of one count of possession of a firearm and one count of aggravated burglary with a firearm. To make it worse, I was actually arrested on the runway, inside a plane destined for Kingston, Jamaica. They said I was fleeing to evade capture. It didn't look good.

The police laid it all out like this: me and a woman named Marsha, another girl called Kasey, and a second man had allegedly gone to a man's house with a gun and roughed him up, stealing some of his personal belongings and a case of money. They claimed all this happened because the man had attempted to rape Marsha, who was allegedly one of my women. Now, I couldn't *possibly* comment on all this, you understand. That's what my solicitor advised me, anyway, so that's what I kept saying. *No comment.*

The next day I was put in an ID parade. The rapist picked me out. An hour later, they charged me. I hung my head in the palms of my hands and muttered, "Please God! Not again! I don't deserve this."

So there I was, lying down on my top bunk inside my cell. I'd just had a conversation with my cellmate, Mark Smith, who claimed he was more of a womaniser than me! Silly boy! I had to let him know he was living in fantasy land about that one. He had the cheek to say to me, "We'll see when we're back on the streets." *Dumb arse*!! Mark was below me on the bottom bunk, writing a letter to one of his so-called women. He didn't know that I was lying there confused and extremely unhappy.

I was wondering how the hell it was that Jay Johnson, reformed criminal, had once again turned prisoner. My number was MD318. I was also reflecting on my life in quite some depth – all there is to do in a place like that is to think – and writing it all down. I was constantly asking myself why it was that my life had turned out the way it had. Was it something to do with my childhood? Although I had always thought of my father as the Monster, I was aware I had picked up some of his less flattering character traits, the ones I'd always hated.

My thoughts took me back to Ms Carlton my old neighbour, and I began to question the things she used to say to me. I was starting to wonder if what she had been saying was that what happens to you in childhood has a major impact on your adult life. Whether it was true or not, it seemed I had now run my course. My ears were constantly ringing with the prediction my mother had made all those years ago – she would say, "Women will be the death of you one day!" It seemed she was right.

My barrister had informed me that my trial was to be at the Old Bailey. If I was found guilty of the charges I faced, the judge would probably throw the bench at me as well as the book.

My mother was sticking by me. And Sandra was still there for me, along with some other women.

****

The story of my life so far indicates that I was a womaniser, but the purpose of sharing this with you is not to focus on my womanising. Throughout my story, I have told you my life story in a way so that I could highlight the blind spots of good, decent women.

The truth is, all human beings have blind spots. If you were paying attention, it's obvious that I have quite a few of my own. How many blind spots you have is a direct result of how well you can see them. You cannot change something you cannot see!!! We will always have some; they are inescapable. They are what help us grow and learn.

Now here's my most important point – you don't have a chance in hell of seeing the blind spots unless the rational and emotional sides of your brain are working in sync. The signs that should tell you he's a womaniser are always there and apparent if you pay attention to the patterns on a rational level. Remember: patterns don't lie. A womaniser can only pretend to be someone he's not for a short period of time before his true self is revealed. You must find out who someone really is, not who he pretends to be or who he thinks he is.

Intuition and instinct play a huge role in overcoming your blind spots, but you need to listen to them!

I can only see these things through reflection, and increased awareness and understanding. At this

point in my story, my opinions on life and what
I wanted were changing dramatically.

****

A screw opened my door and told me I had ten minutes before
he would come back and unlock me for my judgement.

There is one thing I thought you might like to know before
I sign off: if I did get off this damn case, I'd decided to
settle down and start a family with Sandra. It had taken
me a long time to realise that she was a good woman, and
no matter what I did, she was there for me. Why would I
need anyone else? In any case, she didn't deserve to be on
the Misery Ride!

How about it? Womaniser turns family man?

WISH ME LUCK!

INTERLUDE

My guess is – you thought my time was up, didn't you? Well, you and me both! In fact we couldn't have been more wrong. I thought Mother Nature was paying me back for all my past actions. Turns out her sister, Lady Luck, paid me a visit instead!

Now here's the bizarre bit. I wrote everything you just read, apart from the sections that have been *separated with the stars* (*****), well over ten years ago in that very same prison cell.

So you have just been on a journey through part one of my crazy life… Now you are about to move into part two, adulthood, where my road takes some very interesting, exciting, and strange turns!

Are you ready? Fasten your seat belt – Part II is about to get really bumpy!

Part II
THE EPIPHANY

FOREWORD

Imagine this: a man, dressed in a perfectly tailored Gucci suit steps off a plane at Nice Airport. This man has an air of confidence about him; it's as if he doesn't have a care in the world. Confidently, he makes his way to the heliport and climbs into a helicopter. The engine and the propellers engage into a fast spin as the helicopter lifts off into the air.

When the helicopter arrives at its destination, the man jumps down onto the Monaco heliport tarmac. He slides into the back of a waiting limousine and makes his way to Monte Carlo Casino Square. There, he exits the car and walks nonchalantly towards the entrance of a luxurious hotel, passing by Bentleys, Ferraris, and many of the finest cars ever made without a glance.

It's as if he's been here a million times before.

He checks in at the hotel front desk. He flirts with the lady behind the desk as he gives her his details. The lady blushes; she is unable to take her eyes off him. As she gives him his room key, the man gives her a slow wink before heading in the direction of the rooms. The woman's face lights up; with her eyes she trails him until he vanishes inside a lift.

The man arrives at his room, the concierge close behind. He opens the room to the suite, turns around, and tips the concierge a hundred euros. He carefully places his luggage in the corner of the room, then he takes off his jacket and lies down on the bed. He doesn't even look around the room; it's a familiar place to him. He takes out his mobile phone and makes a call.

"Hi, hun. What time will you be arriving?"

The lady at the other end of the phone replies, "Hello, my darling. I'll be arriving at around eight. Do you fancy going to Jimmy's tonight?"

"Actually, Jimmy's sounds good," he replies.

"Okay, I'll catch up with you later, my darling..."

It is only after the conversation that a glowing smile appears on his face. The look that says, *Bingo!* The look that says he has just solved a problem, one that has been plaguing him for a long time.

Now imagine this – that very same man I just described is the same man you have just being reading about in Part I. *Yes, it's me again!*

I suppose you are wondering how the hell I jumped from looking down the end of a fifteen-year prison sentence to luxurious Monte Carlo. Judging from my previous patterns, you're probably thinking that it came about like...?! You may be right.

CHAPTER 17
JUDGEMENT

DAY 1

Judgement Week at the Old Bailey was terrifying: it was the most anxiety-ridden week of my whole life.

I was looking at a very long stretch – fifteen years. If I got a guilty verdict, I was dead. Prison life isn't for guys like me. When I was inside for the first time, the worst part of it had been that there were no bloody women! Obvious, I know! But believe me, the reality is worse than the imagining.

I was in the dock with Marsha; Kasey and the other guy had escaped charges. I turned to look at her. She didn't look as worried as I was. It occurred to me that maybe her barrister had told her to blame everything on me. When it came to people saving their own necks, I trusted no one.

The entire courtroom was preparing for Judge Walters to surface from his chambers. I wondered what my mother was thinking. I knew she was in the courtroom with one of my women, Gina, who I didn't really care much for, and some of my family members. But the way the courtroom was laid out, the gallery was above my head, so it was impossible for me to see any of them.

My mind jumped about. I started thinking about that book I had written while I was in my cell awaiting this trial. I had named it Galist Exposed (and you've just read it). That morning I asked my barrister to give it to Gina, with specific instructions:

1: To send it recorded delivery in my name from me to mum's address.

2: To send a copy to Xpress Publishers.

I had really wanted to give it to Sandra to post, but I couldn't bear the idea of her leaving me because of the confessions within it. Gina was nothing to me really; she just happened to be one of the women I saw once in a while. So I could risk her. When she found out I was in jail, she started visiting me regularly and sending me money.

I wondered if my book would make it past the slush pile…

Just before the judge entered the courtroom, my mind drifted again, this time back to my arrest on the plane. I had been on board for ten minutes when the pilot announced that there was an oil leak, and that if we looked to the right we would be able to see the engineers attending to the problem. I just happened to be sitting in the middle aisle and couldn't see anything. But half an hour later, some men in suits boarded the plane and headed in my direction. I had a hunch that they were coming to me. Why? Because three hours before, my auntie had rung to tell me that armed police had raided my mother's house. They asked to see my passport and then led me off the plane onto the tarmac where they arrested me and put me in handcuffs.

Later on, I found out how close it had been. The police had come to the airport for me earlier and had been informed that the plane had already left – which, by rights, it should have done. But there really *had* been an oil leak – it wasn't a stalling tactic, just my bad luck. When the front desk found out the plane hadn't left, they called the police back! I would have made it to Jamaica and been sipping martinis under palm trees if there hadn't been an oil leak.

****

It makes me ask myself the question, was I meant to get arrested? When I say meant to, I mean destined to - were the Forces Above driving the situation?

Now, you may think I have turned into one of those weird spiritual guys, and you may be right, but don't make a call yet, because what you're going to read in the upcoming chapters is going to get a whole lot weirder. Mark my words!!!

****

In the courtroom, again my mind drifted. How the hell had the police known I was on the plane? It was nowhere to be seen in the disclosure of prosecution statements. The only people who had known I was on that plane were my mother and Stretch – he had also been arrested, solely on the basis that he fitted the description of this other guy the police was connecting to me.

When I had told my mother I was going to Jamaica, she had begged me not to go. She was terrified of the place where I was going, Tivoli Gardens, and was convinced it would surely be the death of me. She knew I had an attitude and a short fuse at the best of times, and that I didn't take any nonsense. She also knew that in Tivoli Gardens they really didn't play about like they do in England; they squeezed triggers and asked questions later.

Surely it hadn't been Stretch who had informed the police? Why would he have done that? He didn't really have a good reason to tell them. He knew he hadn't done anything, and eventually he would get off because the rapist man would fail to pick him out in the ID parade and the case against him would be dropped.

No matter how hard I tried, I just couldn't work it out.

It took me a long time before I figured out who had actually grassed me up. In the end, I worked it out by following my intuition, but I kept it to myself for years until I could confront her – because I didn't blame her: if I had been in her shoes I would have done the same thing. Can you guess who that informant was? It was Stretch's mother! Because Stretch had been arrested before me she had assumed I was running off, leaving her son in the shit… I couldn't blame her. If it was my kid, I'd have done the same.

But back to the courtroom. My mind shifted again back to that lovely rich lady Olivia I had met just before I got arrested. Now I had lost her number, and I knew I probably couldn't find her house again.

"Can the court please stand? Your honourable Judge Walters is now presiding."

Here we go again!

At this point it was all about swearing in the jury, which to my joy consisted of a fair amount of women. As if you didn't know by now! Women were just drawn to me like a magnet: why would it be any different just because they were on the jury? *That's exactly right – it wouldn't! Once a magnet, always a magnet!*

Once the jury was sworn in, it was down to business. Mr Prosecutor rolled up his metaphorical sleeves and set about attacking Marsha and me. I listened intently to every scrap of detail; I wasn't about to rely on my barrister to win this case

– I'd done that the last time and look what had happened… six bloody years.

One of the things that amazed me when Mr Prosecutor was presenting evidence was that he never brought up that I was actually arrested on a plane and that the police had claimed I was fleeing the country. I had been worrying for months about how that would look, but it never came up; it was inadmissible for that very reason – that it could prejudice the jury. Apparently, they could have used it if I'd been arrested on the same day as the incident; but because I'd been arrested weeks later, they could not prove I was running from anything. That was Round One to me, I guess.

The only real evidence against me was that the so-called *victim*, the rapist man, had picked me out in the ID parade, which on its own has probably convicted many a man before now. The prosecution then made their case by trying to link Marsha and me.

Now, my defence was that I had never seen any of these people before in my entire life. Marsha had denied the fact that she had ever seen this man again after he had tried to rape her. So it made sense for the prosecution to try to get some link between me and her, which would validate a reason for me being at Mr Akpu–nku's house.

I suppose you're wondering how I got fingered with all this in the first place. Me too. I found out later on that Marsha had a Jamaican babysitter – name unknown – who was an illegal immigrant. When the police stormed Marsha's house, and they found out the babysitter was illegal, they pressured her: in the end she caved in and, *for some strange reason*, gave them my name in return for a stay in the country. Nice.

But because of that unconventional tactic, the police were unable to use her as a witness. *Aren't the police just...!*

So the prosecution had no fingerprints, could not prove that I knew Marsha, and couldn't describe the manner of my arrest. All they could say was that the victim had picked me out in an ID parade. To my mind, that was a huge advantage! Why? In Stretch's ID parade, the victim rapist dude had sworn *blind* that a random volunteer had been the second man. The way I looked at it, his vision and judgement were obviously therefore pretty unreliable – how could they find me guilty beyond all reasonable doubt?

That first day, I felt fairly confident if I kept all this in my mind, but despite it all, the prosecutor was doing little things to undermine me enough to be worried. The prosecutor was very good, but I think he underestimated me.

At the end of Day One, I went back to my prison cell and studied the witness statements and the rest of the paperwork.

That night, I was restless. Fifteen years hanging over your head is no easy prospect, especially when you know you don't deserve it.

Day Two

Day Two started out just like the day before. This Marsha woman and I sat in the dock, just paying full attention. I barely spoke to her. I really didn't trust her. Anything I did say to her was really about squeezing information indirectly. I could tell she wasn't the smartest of women, and this was my area of expertise, remember.

But at around three p.m. I got a massive shock. The prosecution presented another piece of evidence – my jacket, which they claimed I had left at the scene of the crime.

My mind was going ten to the dozen. "That's not my fucking jacket! It must be a replica!" I wanted to scream. But if it was mine, how the hell was it in their possession? Then I remembered how the airline had said they'd 'lost my luggage' and the police had said they 'didn't take it off'... how convenient!

All of sudden, my head felt twice its normal size. It seemed they were prepared to go to any lengths to secure a conviction. At that point it really wasn't looking good for me.

Then the 'victim', Mr Akpu-nku, took the stand. I felt the immediate shift in Marsha's body language so I turned to look at her. She was tense, with a look of pure hatred in her eyes as she leaned forward to stare at him. I looked at this man wearing his high-class two-piece black suit with a crisp white shirt. His hair was cut very short, and he had a hard face with a self-righteous grin.

It was during his questioning from Mr Prosecutor that things took a turn in my direction. I wasn't sure if everyone noticed, but I definitely did!

During the examination the prosecutor asked him if the jacket he was wearing was similar to the one I was supposed to have worn on the night in question. What the prosecutor hoped was that Mr Akpu-nku would say, "No, sir, he was wearing a jacket that looked like *yada-yada*," with a full description. But I guess he had no idea how arrogant his star witness was.

"No! My jacket does not look like the one he was wearing! I don't wear *poor people's stuff!*" He then proceeded to tell the court about all the wealth he had accumulated. It turned out he was quite a rich man.

It was when he said that sh*t about poor people's stuff that I saw the jurors' faces all express righteous disgust. I could feel their energy and it was full of contempt – all aimed in his direction, not mine!

Another factor that went in my favour – as much as I don't like to say this – was that he was black.

Up until this point I had been trying not to pay any attention to the jury – my barrister had advised me not to. But all of sudden I was thinking that the ladies on the jury looked quite nice. I know, it's amazing: there I was sitting in the dock, fighting for my life, and I still found time to eye up some women on the jury. *Well, I guess that's just womanisers for you!*

I remember looking at them and one in particular caught my eye. She looked as if she was smiling at me. I wasn't sure so I turned away, but curiosity got the better of me in the end. *She really was smiling!* I couldn't believe it… I was a thousand per cent sure from that moment on that this particular juror was on my side!

The prosecutor quickly finished his questioning of Mr Akpu-nku – as I would have done if I were in his shoes, because he was hurting their case so much! Before my barrister cross-examined Mr Akpu-nku, I ushered him over and I said to him, "Do everything you can to upset this man; he's arrogant – he won't be able to hold it in."

My barrister knew exactly what I meant. "Don't worry," he replied, "I've noticed."

On cross-examination, it was as if my barrister had smelled blood! He asked Mr Akpu-nku to tell the court what he believed had occurred on the night in question. Mr Akpu-nku began to relay his version of events. And what came next was music to my ears.

"What makes you think this incident went the way you say it did?" My barrister's sarcasm was barely in check.

"What do you mean?"

"I'll rephrase. Why are you so sure that the events unfolded exactly the way you say they did, or that they even happened at all?"

"What do you mean, what makes me sure? I've got eyes, haven't I?"

"Pardon me, can you speak up, please."

"I said, I have got eyes! I'm not blind!" he replied, clearly agitated and raising his voice.

"Are you sure what you saw is exactly a hundred per cent accurate?"

"Yes."

"I'll ask you again: are you sure?"

"Yes! I am sure! Do I look stupid?"

"No, you don't. That is why I cannot understand why you made such a critical error in your account of what happened on the night. Can you explain to the court why, if your account of events is so accurate, you managed to pick out an innocent man in the ID parade? You *swore* that the man had attacked you at your house when it could not have been possible."

"What is this? *I'm* not on trial here! I don't care about him! I know that man over there was at my house attacking me!" Now he was shouting and pointing at me.

"You don't care? About putting an innocent man in the frame for something he has not and could not have done?"

My barrister tore him apart! He did everything in his power to upset him and it worked! Mr Akpu-nku came across as someone who thought he was above average people, someone very capable of raping a woman.

That evening, when I got back to the prison, I called my mother. As soon as she answered she went on about how arrogant Mr Akpu-nku had been on the witness stand. In her opinion, it wasn't looking too bad for me. I told her I loved her and hung up.

I worried about my mum sometimes for the simple fact that deep down I knew that she was aware that if she'd been a little bit stronger when I was younger, things might have been different, and she blamed herself. I loved my mum to bits, and didn't really blame her at all. She had never said it to me but I could tell: it was written all over her face sometimes.

That night I slept a little better than the night before, but I was still worrying about what the final outcome would be.

Day Three

It was my turn to take the witness stand.

I was unaware that the prosecutor had what he thought was an ace up his sleeve, and he was intending to go for my jugular. What he didn't know was that I had a talent for calculating where someone was headed before they got there.

After asking me some routine questions – Where were you on the night in question? Have you ever met Marsha before? et cetera et cetera – he threw his ace at me. He lifted up Exhibit 125 – my jacket – and then lowered his voice. My instinct warned me straight away that he was up to something; just a moment before his tone had been rough and he'd been trying to antagonise me, but he had suddenly changed gear. I wasn't sure where he was going with his questioning, but my instinct put me on guard.

He said, "Mr Johnson, could you put on *your* jacket, please?"

Yeah, right! He was underestimating me if he thought I would say yes and imply that it was my jacket!

"That's not *my* jacket, sir, but I'll put it on if it helps me to prove my innocence and aids you with your questioning."

"Yes, I would like that."

The court usher brought over the jacket and asked me to put it on. I put the jacket on.

"Does your jacket feel comfortable?"

"No, it doesn't feel comfortable, sir, but even if it did it makes no difference because this jacket is not mine."

"Can you just answer my questions with a yes or no please."

I knew that he wanted a yes or no answers, but I wasn't about to let him twist things around on me and misguide the jury to his advantage.

"Mr Johnson, could you kindly put your hands into your pockets, please?" I put my hands in the pockets.

As soon I did, he threw down his trump card. "Mr Johnson, could you please now put it in the other remaining pocket?"

Wow... you're good, I thought!

The jacket had one more pocket that was ninety-nine per cent concealed; the only people who would know this pocket existed were the person who'd made it and the person who owned it.

But I was one step ahead of him. "I'm afraid there are no other pockets, sir."

I looked him right in the eye. I could see his disappointment.

He made one last-ditch attempt. "Are you sure?"

I looked down and around the jacket and said, "I'm sure."

His ace had turned into a joker right before his very eyes. He turned to the judge. "I have no further questions."

When the court had recessed for the day, I was taken down to the cells to await my transfer back to the prison. My barrister paid me a visit and told me that the following morning he would be going for acquittal on technical grounds. It was something to do with the man picking out an innocent victim in the ID parade. I was over the moon; if he managed to achieve that I would be out the next day. On top of that, they would probably have to compensate me!

That night, when I got back to the prison, I spoke to Sandra and told her the news. She had wanted to come to my trial but she was currently doing her degree exams and I insisted she didn't miss any. *That was more important as far as I was concerned; if she passed, it meant a better job* – and *more loot for us!* I also knew that Gina was at court every day with my mother: the last thing I needed was them bumping into each other.

I told her not to get her hopes up, even though mine were sky high. I told her that if I didn't get acquitted, the jury would be going out on Friday for a verdict. She wished me luck and told me how much she loved me. To be honest, I was starting to feel that I loved her.

That night I prayed to God. I begged Him for my freedom and said that I wanted to be a better person if only He'd help me.

Day Four

In the morning, the first thing Judge Walters did was announce to the jury that they could have a break as there were some technical issues to be resolved. From that point on, my barrister was thrashing it out with the judge as to why I should be acquitted.

The whole time my eyes were fixed on the judge, as it was his decision at the end of the day. I could tell from the very beginning by his body language that he didn't want to let me go, even though my barrister was making some valid points.

In the end, the judge rejected the acquittal and reconvened with the jury. I was devastated, as I knew at the very end of this trial the judge would sum up the whole case and that summary could have a huge influence on the jury's decision. Right then he didn't appear to be leaning in my favour!

When the jury came back, I saw that the lady who had smiled at me previously was talking to the woman next to her. Then the woman next to her looked at me and winked – I couldn't believe it! If a woman anywhere else in the world had done that, I would have taken it my stride. But on my jury? Well, I couldn't believe it!! But I still had ten other jurors to think about, so it wasn't over yet by a long shot – or was it? Maybe the woman was trying to tell me with her wink that all the jurors were leaning towards a not-guilty verdict! I just couldn't be sure.

The rest of that afternoon was given over to the closing arguments from the prosecution, my barrister, and Marsha's barrister. Just before it began, I summoned my barrister over. I wasn't taking any chances, like last time. I told him I wanted him to make sure in his closing statement that he mentioned reasonable doubt, and to ask them how I could be found guilty beyond reasonable doubt when the 'victim' rapist man had already made such a big mistake in the other line-up. He reassured me that he had everything in hand.

True to his word, he summed up beautifully, even throwing in some joke about OJ that made all the jurors laugh. In my view he couldn't have done any better.

Finally, the judge summed up the whole case for the jurors, and to be fair to him it was not one-sided as I had feared it would be; if anything, it was very accurate. After his summing-up, the judge told the jurors the court would reconvene at ten a.m., when he would send them out to deliberate.

When I arrived back at the prison I phoned Sandra and told her the bad news: that I hadn't been acquitted and that my fate would be decided the following day. *I wished I hadn't told her the last bit!*

She wished me luck and told me how much she loved me. I told her how much I loved her.

That night I couldn't sleep a wink. I knew the next day was either bringing fifteen years or freedom. I really didn't know which way it would swing even with the winks!

Day Five

I was so on edge when I walked into the courtroom. Even Marsha, who had looked so calm up until now, looked tense.

When the judge came up from his chambers he spoke briefly to the jury about what to do if they were unable to reach a unanimous verdict. Suddenly, I heard somebody from the gallery shout, "You little shit! Give him life!"

What the hell, hold up! That's Sandra! I thought. I looked at the jurors; their eyes were all turned up towards the gallery. But she was supposed be doing her exam? Reality sank in; there was no doubt in my mind it was her. *What bloody timing!* My mind jumped straight back to the jury. What were they thinking now?

The judge ordered her out of court, and then he told the jury to ignore such remarks and sent them out to deliberate.

I was then taken back down to the court cells. When I got down there who should I meet but Carlo, a man I knew from my Feltham days. He looked sad. I asked him what he was doing there and he told me he was waiting for his verdict on a murder charge; that he and some other guys had been on trial for robbing some jewellery shop and that the owner had been shot in the back and had eventually died. I ran down why I was there myself, and then lapsed into silence.

I picked up a copy of the *Daily Mirror* newspaper, which happened to be lying right beside me on the bench. It was open on the star signs page. Although I was not into all that kind of prediction stuff, the current situation I was in made me feel curious as to what it said about Capricorns for that day. *Today is your lucky day, but remember – you cannot be in both places at the same time.* I remember thinking, *Lucky day?* Well, obviously I hoped that meant I'd be getting a not-guilty verdict, but the second half? What was that all about?

My mind drifted to Sandra, and quickly jumped to the jury and what they might be thinking. I was left in agony for two hours, after which the jailor opened the cell and told me it was time to go back up as the verdict was in.

My stomach was all over the place.

I wished Carlo the best for his murder verdict, and quickly left the cell.

It seemed to take forever for the jury to come back into the courtroom. When they did, one of the women smiled at me again. Was it a sign? When they were all seated, the usher passed an envelope to the judge – the verdict. My eyes were glued on him, but he gave nothing away. The usher then asked the foreman of the jury to take the stand.

"Do you find the defendant, Ms Brown, guilty or not guilty?"

The foreman took his time, then responded, "We, the jury, find Ms Brown not guilty on all counts."

I didn't look at Marsha, but I could feel the excitement rush through her body. My eyes were still glued on the foreman.

The judge asked him, "Do you find the defendant, Mr Johnson, guilty or not guilty?

Now my stomach was in my mouth.

It seemed that the foreman took even longer this time, and then he replied, "We, the jury, find Mr Johnson not guilty on all counts."

Bingo!

When I had been arrested on that plane ten months before, it had been my worst feeling to date. Now I was experiencing my best feeling to date.

The judge looked at me and gave me a very small smile. I think all along he had wanted that outcome. But that's just my opinion; I guess I'll never know what he really thought.

Now all the jury were smiling at me. And I remember thinking for a moment, *Damn, those women are coming to my aid in every direction!*

When I went back down to the cells to get my stuff and sign my release papers, I was jumping for joy.

I saw Carlo. "I got a fucking not-guilty, son!"

There was no emotion at all from him. I asked him what the matter was, and I got no response. He was going down. I didn't know what to say. What do you say to a person who has just been given life? "Be strong," I mumbled. "You can make it," and I shot out of the door as fast as my legs could carry me.

Upstairs, my mum hugged me. I could see the relief on her face. I asked where Gina was; she told me she had gone to get the car. I asked about Sandra; she explained Sandra had arrived first thing in the morning and sat beside her; Gina had been on the other side. It had taken some time for Sandra to clock Gina, but after a while she had said, "Hold on a minute, Mum, who is the girl sitting on the other side of you?" My mum said she hadn't responded because she didn't like to get involved with my shenanigans, but Sandra had clicked and lost the plot, screaming at the top of her voice.

At that precise moment I was upset for her, but I was too overjoyed with my new-found freedom for it to really sink in. I phoned Gina to ask her why she was taking so long coming back with the car, but the phone was switched off. *Switched off!* Then it dawned on me – she wasn't coming back with the car. She was gone!

And in my mind I saw and understood that horoscope, still lying down in that cell where I'd been not that long ago: … *but remember - you cannot be in both places at the same time!*

CHAPTER 18
THE BEGINNING OF THE END

It was the beginning of a horrible end.

I was free again, free like a bird with my whole life ahead of me. To begin with, I didn't have much of a plan, but I consciously decided to stop the womanising and settle down with Sandra.

The time I spent on remand had got me thinking. First of all, I started asking myself where all this womanising stuff was taking me, and every time I asked the question I couldn't come up with anything positive. There was something inside me that surfaced very subtly every now and again, a little voice that kept tugging at me, saying this womanising stuff was wrong. On this particular occasion I decided to follow it, which led me to think about Sandra: when I put her under the microscope I couldn't find anything wrong with her. The more I thought about her, the more I realised she was a really good catch and that I would be lucky to have her. I weighed it up in my mind. She attracted me physically, made me laugh, loved me to the core of my being, and she would have my back no matter what the scenario. On top of that, my mother was very fond of her – motherly instinct is powerful, I concluded. With all that in mind I came to a firm decision: I was going to settle down with Sandra and only her.

That afternoon, when I left the court and got back to my mother's house, the Monster was there to greet me. He wasted no time in letting me know what was on his mind. "You listen to me, boy. If you think you're coming to live back under my roof, you got another thing coming. You have the police coming in my house, pointing guns at me, rolling around the walls, climbing on the roof, and marching me outside in my pants. 'Let me tell you, boy, I'm giving you one week to find somewhere to live and that's final'

Wow, same old, same old, I thought. He did have a point, though. But I just remember thinking, *Fuck you, I'm going to go and live with Sandra so I don't need this sh*t.*

Sandra had got her own place since I had been arrested and I was sure she would be only too happy to have me after I had apologised about what happened at the court and told her I now wanted to get serious. I didn't need any of the Monster's lectures; what I really needed was to lie down with Sandra, hug her, and tell her how sorry I was for using her and what a fool I'd been for not appreciating her – followed by some good sex!

So I picked up the phone and called her, but it rang out. I left a message for her to call me back. My second call was to Gina, to find out what had happened when she left the court, but it also rang out. *What the hell is going on?* I thought. *Hello! I'm out! Are you lot dumb?*

It wasn't long before Stretch turned up with some alcohol. We had a drink and a chat. When I told him I'd had enough of this womanising stuff and that I was going to settle down with Sandra, he hissed through his teeth and rolled his eyes. "You? Settle down? Give me a break! That's not in your make-up!"

I let his response go over my head because, as far as I was concerned, I had had enough of womanising. But we continued to chat about what had happened since I had been away. It turned out nothing much had changed in those ten months; I hadn't missed that much.

By the time he left, sometime around two a.m., neither Sandra nor Gina had called me back. Well, I wasn't having any of that! I couldn't have cared less that Gina hadn't called back, but the fact that Sandra hadn't called worried me a lot. So I dug out one of the letters Sandra had sent me whilst I was in prison. I scribbled down her new address and asked my mum for some money for a cab fare.

When I arrived at Sandra's and pressed the bell, I glimpsed her looking out of the window. I expected her to open the door straight away, but she didn't. It took me around ten minutes with my finger constantly on the bell before she actually opened the door. When she did, she welcomed me in as if nothing had happened.

****

Right there and then, my instinct prodded me. When it does that, it is telling me something is not right and, more often than not, something bad is going to happen. It makes me pay attention to see what it is that I can avoid, what it is that's going wrong.

****

Once I was inside I started to give her the sob story, explaining why Gina was at the court. I knew from speaking to my mother that she had no real proof of anything; all she had seen was the reaction on my mother's face. So I told her Gina had found out through a friend that I was up for sentencing and had come up on her own accord.

Although Sandra tried to pretend she was lapping up my story, my instincts told me she wasn't buying it – she was ultra calm! It didn't fit with the Sandra who'd exploded in court.

I decided to tell Sandra how I really felt: "Sandra, I've been thinking whilst I was in prison. I'm really sorry for the way I've treated you in the past and I can't explain why I've been such a jerk. But if you accept my apology I promise I'll be everything you want and more. I can see that my future is with you. I love you for being so good to me."

After all the talk we went to bed and had sex. Just before I fell asleep in her arms I had an uneasy feeling. I knew something wasn't right; I just couldn't put my finger on it.

In the morning I found out what my intuition was trying to tell me.

She woke me at ten a.m. "JJ, you have to go now. I have to go out."

"What do you mean, I have to go now?" I said, shocked.

"I have things to do. Thanks for a lovely night. I needed that, but from now on it's over. Erase my number and erase me out of your mind."

Thanks for a lovely night...? Erase my number?

I couldn't believe what I was hearing. If there was anything I could say for sure about my women it was that I knew them inside out. After all, it had been part of my job description! But there and then I could tell this was a different Sandra, and I could tell she was serious – she was too calm!

I tried the sweet talk, the anger talk, the sympathy talk, and every other kind of talk I could think of – none of it worked. Her decision was set in stone. Just as I left, I noticed a picture of me on the side; it had my eyes and my heart poked out.

I left Sandra's feeing totally lost, sad, and bewildered. *Now, imagine that!* Just when I make a firm decision to engage in some kind of meaningful relationship with her, settle down and treat her like a queen, she goes and dumps me. *Wow, isn't life funny!*

****

With hindsight, I now know it would never have worked out with me and Sandra. She wasn't the right woman for me. Settling with someone just for settling-down's sake just doesn't work.

****

So the Sandra episode came to a sharp end and there was nothing I could do about it. What was I to do? I was dumbstruck. My mind drifted back to my mother and Denise, and I convinced myself that it wasn't meant to be. Maybe Stretch was right after all – maybe I wasn't cut out for this settling down palaver! You're probably thinking the same, given my previous patterns!

So I fell right back in line with what I knew best. This time my intentions were to take it up a few notches. If only I had known what was waiting for me a few years away, I might not have chosen that path. But then again, maybe I would have. I'm not sure – I'll let you make that decision when you get there!

When I left Sandra's, I went straight back to my mother's house and phoned Gina. This time she answered. I spun her a web and everything went back to normal.

Gina wasn't a woman I would have settled down with under any circumstances. I just didn't fancy her and the way I looked at it there was no point committing to a woman if you couldn't wake up in the morning, turn over, and smile! She was currently living in between her mother's house and a hostel in South London awaiting her flat. We quickly came to an agreement that I could live at the hostel until she got her flat and then we could move in there together – which I had no intention of doing.

****

Ladies, one of the key things you must clarify to yourself is what his <u>intentions</u> are. I have seen this one pattern so often. The man's and the woman's intentions are not in line with each other. If you don't question his intentions you could end up wasting years of your life planning for the both of you when he is only planning for himself or even himself and some other woman!

****

So once again I said farewell to my mother and left the family home, but not before I received a letter from Xpress Publishers, who were showing an interest in the book I'd written in prison! They felt it needed some more work in certain places, but they were prepared to give me a helping hand. What did I do about it? Can you guess? I threw it down somewhere. As far as I was concerned I was free now, so I didn't have any time to be writing. *With hindsight, what a dumb move!*

When I moved into the hostel, for a while I felt sad. It felt like a real regression. It was a dump concealed in a three-storey house. It looked nice from the outside, but the second I walked in, my energy was zapped. The carpet needed incinerating and the walls looked as though they hadn't seen a paintbrush since the 1800s. The kitchen was nasty, with dirty pots and pans in places they shouldn't be. The cooker was lined with years of grime; I wouldn't be using it. Finally, when Gina showed me her room, the corners of my mouth drooped. Of all the places in the world, it reminded me of my prison cell. I could tell by the way she was showing me around and by the way she had never thought to tell me how disgusting it was that she was accustomed to this kind of living. I knew I couldn't stay there for long. I had to do something, and fast.

Later that evening, when Gina had left, I bumped into a character named Lewis who lived in the room beneath ours. We ended up having a long chat that night; we were destined to become good friends and he was to get me in with his crew.

Lewis was four years older than me, dark-skinned, and built like a horse. He laughed a lot, for good reason – he was genuinely funny. He tended to live in the past; he had once had status and money until he hit unfortunate times. Sometimes I got the impression he still felt he had status; he couldn't see that most people don't care about what you had – they care about what you've got now. He was a bit delusional like that. He loved nasty girls; he always wanted to be on the sidelines when other people were boning women. Women did love to be around him, mostly as a friend – he made them laugh, and that was his way into getting sex. He was very knowledgeable but somehow failed to use it to his advantage. Couldn't work out his path in life, I guess. He was shackled at the ankles by what other people thought of him.

****

Lewis also made a huge mistake that most men make when it comes to women. He would approach a woman and talk about himself; in other words, he would try to convince the woman how wonderful he was!

Women, you know the kind of guy who makes you want to run a mile. But, ladies, be careful of the opposite guy, the one who is just out to stroke your ego. Remember, depending on how good he makes you feel about yourself, if he really makes you feel good, guess what? You will perceive him as having… yes, it's that magic word CHARISMA! That's when your emotions kick in – but this is when you should be temporarily removing your emotions and using the rational side of your brain instead.

****

Within a week of being in that dump, I came to a quick but firm decision that I needed my own place. I knew the council had a long waiting list, so I spent a whole day figuring out how I could jump the queue. Then it came to me: I had perennial rhinitis (I was allergic to house dust-mites). I knew if I went to the council and said I was homeless, they would put me in a hostel. I didn't want a hostel – I wanted my own place. Now I guessed, and I guessed correctly, that if my doctor wrote a letter about my condition then if the council put me in a hostel they would have to go to all the trouble of ripping up the carpet and giving me special bedding and curtains. I figured they wouldn't want to bother with all that hassle and would just jump me to the front of the queue and give me a flat. So I went to see my family doctor – she loved me like a son. When she gave me the letter, I made my way down to the council, who put it into action immediately.

I had to wait two months, which, to be honest, was very quick.

While I was waiting, I bumped into an old acquaintance, a girl I hadn't seen in some time. She had been one of those nameless encounters of my past who passed you by in the whirlwind of Part I, but she was about to play a much more central role in my life. Her name was Bianca; I had met her not long after I served my six-year sentence. She used to throw me some chump change every now and again. She was far from my usual type looks-wise; she was dark-skinned with black coolie hair, a small head, and small features. Not that she was ugly, but she just didn't do it for me personally.

Now she definitely had blind spots! Bianca left me aghast sometimes for the way she would always put other people down. She would tell me stories about her friends and people she knew – "Yeah, my friend's so stupid and naïve, she can't even see that her boyfriend isn't even into her. He just uses her for money. She's so blind!"

Fucking incredible! I couldn't believe my ears whenever she used to say stuff like that! I used to laugh to myself and think, *Well, what the hell do you think I'm doing to you, dumb-dumb! Blind spot or what?*

****

As I'm typing I can't help thinking that many women will actually be going through similar situations I write about. But I can already see many women making this one major mistake – _denial_. They will start looking at everyone else apart from themselves. Just like Bianca, they will still be on the Misery Ride and not even realise it.

Now, here is a good way to find out if you're in denial. First of all you need to understand when anyone is in denial it is a matter of the ego. The ego is very fragile indeed. Look at the ego like this: it protects the image you have in your mind of how you want the world to see you. However, at the best of times that image can be inaccurate. In other words, if somebody says something that tarnishes the image of how you would like the world to see you, your ego begins to scream. Your ego likes consistency: anything out of the norm and the barrier goes up and the defences kick in. Your ego wants to protect the way you want the world to see you!! Your job is to always go beyond the ego. Why? The reason is simple: so you can see the reality – the truth of the situation.

****

Another thing I found quite bizarre about Bianca was that she didn't really like sex. This happened to be great for me, because I didn't particularly like giving her any. It was almost as if she just liked being with me so that she could say to her friends that I was her boyfriend. I know how that sounds, but I couldn't find any other explanation.

She couldn't have picked a better time to resurface; I was fresh out of jail again and broke.

Back when I'd first met her she hadn't worked; I don't know where she'd found the money that she gave me and I didn't bother to ask. On a few occasions Stretch would ask me, "Have you ever asked Bianca where she gets her money from?"

I would always reply, "No."

He would then continue, "Aren't you curious, though?"

"No, I'm not. I don't care where it's coming from. My only concern is that it's coming."

Every time he'd asked, Stretch had seemed to be fascinated by the fact I wasn't bothered where she was getting her money from. The truth was, I hadn't given a damn.

But here and now, she was telling me that she was working in a bank, and all of a sudden what she did was of the utmost importance! *Cha-ching! The bank!!* My mind started working overtime. Are you thinking what I was thinking?! Well, if you're not, here's a tip – *major turning point!*

We exchanged numbers and I made a mental note to pay her a visit very soon. The rest of those two months consisted of me boning loads of women back at Gina's hostel: needless to say I had them there when Gina least expected.

Lewis couldn't believe how many fit ladies I had coming and going. I could tell he was in awe of me and my accomplishments. One after the other he would say, "Damn, you got some skills – can I watch?" At first I used to think he was joking, but I soon found out he was deadly serious. That kind of stuff did nothing for me.

Eventually, the council gave me a one-bedroom flat on the ground floor of a house, and I was very happy. For me, there was nothing worse than living under a woman's roof.

I did the rounds on a few women and got it kitted out superbly. I went to town – ice-colour leather suite with thick cream shagpile carpet, long white blinds to cover the bay windows, VCRs and TVs in each room, plush lime green carpet in the bedroom. You would never have believed it was a council flat. I remember when the council guy came to look around to give me my one hundred and fifty pounds decorating allowance, he stood there for twenty seconds in shock and then said, "This is a very nice place you got here!" I was tempted to say, "Courtesy of my women."

It wasn't long after I had finished doing up my flat that I was walking past a petrol station when I saw a woman. The first thing I noticed was how pretty she looked. I knew straight away I wanted her, but I had no idea her intentions were to put her foot under my table!

CHAPTER 19
MY LITTLE ANGEL

I don't know how the hell it happened. I was just getting back into the swing of things when in next to no time this woman moved into my flat.

I couldn't quite work it out myself. It all started when I was walking past a petrol station. I saw this lady pulling up to get petrol. It was one of those hot days in the middle of a heat wave and she was in the car with a whole load of kids. I remember thinking, *She's a good girl. She should be out looking for some hot men, but there she is looking after kids.*

I waited until she got out of the car to put the petrol in. Then I approached her and asked if I could talk to her for a minute. I noticed her hand shaking on the pump throughout the whole conversation. The kind of astute guy I was, it was fair to say I already had her in the bag. She told me her name was Destiny and that she was on vacation from Washington DC. I asked her how long she had left and when we could go out. She told me she had one week left to spend time with her family. Eventually, we arranged to go out that night. *Go out my arse! Go to bed more like!*

That evening I phoned her and changed the plan. I said I was tired but she was welcome to come over to my place

– where I had the condoms tucked under my pillow! She agreed.

When she arrived she was dressed up to the nines. When I had first seen her at the gas station she had looked pretty, but now she looked absolutely stunning. I couldn't believe my eyes. She looked like Stacey Dash. My baton agreed with me. How did I know? Because it started twitching, of course! I could tell she thought she had a winner on her hands, and I must have been thinking that too; not in a financial sense, but someone who could be wifey – the one who sits at home, looks pretty, and cooks the bloody food! *Damn, didn't that sound like the Monster!*

After a long conversation during which I told her she must be my Destiny, she confessed to me that wasn't her real name – that it was Azaria. That night we boned like there was no tomorrow; in fact, we boned right into tomorrow. It was a marathon; there was definitely some chemistry there.

Before I knew what was going on, her return to Washington DC was out of the window and she was living with me in my flat. It happened really quickly. She fell for me and I actually fell for her. I remember having some reservations at first, as it became apparent very quickly to me that she had a feisty side, an argumentative side. On top of that, the whole Denise affair was still very fresh in my mind. But she still managed to make me feel good and it clouded my rational thinking! When she moved in it gave me a sense of achievement. I had done it – I had settled down.

Shortly after she moved in, she got a top PA job in the City, and she begged me to get a job on the buses. Considering I had never had a job before and had never had any intention of having one, this was very uncomfortable for me. There were some back-and-forth discussions and some tone-raising moments before I reluctantly agreed. The decision was more to make her happy, but I still had every intention of only doing it for a while.

When I went to the interview I felt as nervous as hell, because it seemed I had to lie in response to every question I was asked.

I found out that I hadn't got the job. I should have been happy but, to my surprise, I wasn't. I actually felt worthless over the fact I couldn't even get a bus-driving job.

When I told Azaria, she was as calm as anything. "Don't worry. My cousin works for the management department there. I'll give her a call."

One week later, I had a position.

After the initial training, I had my first day out with the public, and it wasn't as bad as I had expected. In fact, I quite liked it; I could tell that many women were shocked when they saw me driving a bus. Many of them made it clear they fancied me in their own little ways. Although I had no intention of taking their advances further, it felt good to be acknowledged!

But the good feeling didn't last too long. The passengers in general really started to get on my nerves; it began to feel as though they just came out of their houses to take their problems out on me. And being the person I was didn't help; I guess I only fuelled things even more by telling them where the hell to go! So within in a matter of months, driving the buses felt like being on a treadmill.

Around this period I began to wake in the mornings feeling sick. On many occasions I actually wanted to vomit. I couldn't work out what was wrong with me. It eventually stopped after three months. You may not believe this, but I had Azaria's morning sickness, because she was pregnant! I was ecstatic as one can be, and I was keen to tell Ms Carlton. She insisted that I let her know when the baby had arrived.

Following that, Azaria's boss made up some rubbish and fired her from her job. I insisted she sue them. At first she didn't want to, because she didn't believe she had a case, but I wouldn't let it drop. Eventually, she contacted a lawyer, who informed her that she definitely had a case.

I'll never forget the day my little angel was born. How could I? I was there at the birth. Azaria gave birth to a five-pound fourteen-ounce little girl – and guess what we named her? Fate, of course! Everybody (apart from the Monster, of course) came to the hospital: her family, my family, Ms Carlton, Lewis, Stretch. It was a very special moment for me. I was a dad and everybody seemed pleased for me – especially my mother and Ms Carlton. When I was alone with Ms Carlton she stressed how important it was for me not to follow in the footsteps of my father. I explained to her that could never happen, and that I would do everything the right way.

Although I had explained things to Azaria about the Monster's ways, she wasn't pleased he hadn't showed up at the hospital. She told me that she was going to have words with him as soon as she came out. I wished her luck, as I knew she would need it. None of my previous women had even got close to him as much as batting an eyelid in their direction, let alone accepting them.

The next time Azaria saw him, she walked right up to his face and said, "Excuse me, Mr Johnson, I would like to talk to you. I don't know what women Jay has had in his life and, to be frank, I don't really care. But let me assure you, I am nothing like them – and I won't tolerate your rudeness. How dare you not come and see your grandchild? Whatever you and your son have, don't involve my daughter in it." She walked off before he could say anything.

I was shocked, and I guess he was too. I'm not sure how he dissected that outburst, but one thing's for sure: he listened to her, and they have been friends ever since. Did it have an impact on his relationship with me? Not an inch!

After the birth, I told Azaria I wanted a blood test. Was she happy about it? Of course she wasn't. But after the stunt Lakisha had pulled on me all those years ago when I was at West London College, I didn't really care what Azaria thought. It was all right for her – she knew without a shadow of a doubt that Fate was hers; she had come out of her body. I wanted that peace of mind too.

The same day Azaria gave birth, her Uncle Patrick, who was married to her aunt, took me back to Azaria's mum's house to celebrate – you know, the whole champagne thing. I really liked her Uncle Patrick – he was one of those characters who everybody loved, with exceptional people skills. He was a Capricorn like me, and a womaniser – I could tell – regardless of him being married. The champagne was flowing constantly. It was unfortunate for Azaria that she had to stay in hospital overnight because she missed out on the celebration! But it was later that evening that I got a big shock.

We were all in the kitchen drinking – me, Patrick, his wife, Azaria's mum, and the next-door neighbour. At some point, Patrick and his wife went to bed in the spare room. That left me, Azaria's mum, and the neighbour to continue the celebration.

Not long after Patrick and his wife had left, Azaria's mother said to the neighbour, "Look at my gorgeous son-in-law!" Then she turned to me, dragged me onto her lap, and kissed me on the cheek.

By this stage I was drunk, and I said it: "I'm drunk."

Azaria's mum then told me that I could have her bed for the night. I never gave it a second thought as I was feeling giddy-headed – all I thought was, *A bed is exactly what I need.*

Ten minutes later I heard the front door shut. Then the mum came into the room, and without a word she jumped on me, her hand going straight under my boxer shorts and grabbing my baton. *Boing, boing, boingggg!* She started to force her tongue into my mouth. Was I turned on? Enormously! But as excited as I was, I felt disgusted by the fact that her daughter had just had a baby, my baby, that very same day and she was trying to bone me.

"What the hell are you doing?" I gasped.

"Don't worry, nobody will find out," she replied casually.

I threw her off me immediately and stomped out of the room swiftly, making my exit.

The next day, when Azaria came out of hospital, I told her everything that had happened. She wasn't happy. Pretty soon I wished I hadn't told her, because she started blaming me! *Dumb arse!*

Eventually, I got rid of all the women I had. When I called them, it was clear some were really upset and some were furious. One even had the cheek to say to me, "I'm going to get you fucked-up, you using mother-fucker... you opportunist... wanker!"

"If I was you I wouldn't embarrass the man!" I replied, and hung up. Of course she phoned me back, but I just ignored the calls until she gave up.

There was just one woman I held on to: Bianca. The fact that she lived on the other side of the river and she didn't like sex made it seem to me that it wasn't really cheating. So every once in a while I would go and spend an hour or two with her and get paid for time well spent... *Okay, maybe I was lying to myself that it wasn't cheating!*

But I had my family now, and I was trying to break old habits. And to be honest, I didn't really have the time: I spent any spare moment I could with my little angel. I adored her and I felt I had to be there to protect her at all times. I was a very hands-on dad and I did everything for her: I changed her nappies, I fed her through the night, and she always slept on my stomach.

Whenever I looked at her, I promised her I would give her a better upbringing than the one I had received. The birth of Fate managed to summon up real feelings that I'd never felt before. I wanted to be better person, for her sake.

Even so, I felt happy with Azaria. For the first time I felt fulfilled and normal; everything felt right. But I still wasn't shot of some old bad habits.

Around that time, I paid Bianca one of my usual visits. Our conversation went like this:

She said, "Jay, I heard you fucked Jenny. Why do you fuck them little tramps?"

I had boned the woman she was referring to, but it had been a long time ago; all the same, I denied it.

I said, "Stop chatting rubbish, and if you're going to start, I'm leaving."

"No I won't bloody stop. You have fucked almost every girl around here. Why do you have to fuck the ones on my doorstep?"

"Fuck this, I'm going," I replied as I started to walk to the front door.

I knew she was going to follow me and stand in front of the door; it was a regular pattern of hers. As expected, she stood in front of the door, begging me not to leave. "Why do you do it? I'm a perfect package!" she whined, bigging herself up as usual. This was something she did regularly – put everyone else down and big herself up. I suspected she did it because she felt inadequate around me. Whatever the reason, it pissed me off.

"You can't tempt me with a package unless it involves dollars and pounds!" I said blatantly. "In fact, I don't want anything from you. I just want this relationship to be over."

****

Generally, womanisers tend to be very calculated. Now, with me saying to her, "You can't tempt me unless the package involves dollars and pounds," you're probably thinking, You dumb woman, are you blind? But that's not the case!! She was already on the Misery Ride! In her case it was too late; I knew I could say that and get away with it.

Saying, "I don't want anything from you. I just want this to be over," straight after was even more calculated – it was a lie and no accident. I had no intention whatsoever of ending it. I just knew what her emotional side was going to come up with next or shortly after...!

****

"Jay, let's go on holiday and sort this out. Please?"

Bingo! I needed a holiday. I was feeling a bit stressed and I secretly had dreams of travelling to every country in the world before my time was up.

"Okay. Give me the money and I'll book it," I said.

Bianca went upstairs and came back with four hundred pounds. Then we went to the cash point and she gave me another three hundred. At that point I felt content because I'd got what I came for, so I relaxed with her for a few hours before I caught a cab home, but not before telling her I needed a video camera to go on this holiday. She assured me she would have it before we left.

The next day, I booked an all-inclusive holiday to Majorca, due to leave in two weeks. I told the boss at work I was going on holiday; he tried to tell me it wasn't due. So I looked him in the eye. "I'm going anyway. Make sure my job is here when I get back." I walked out of his office before he could answer.

I didn't really care about driving buses anyway. When I'd started I'd said to some of the veteran drivers I would only be there for a maximum of one year, and they had all laughed and said that's what they'd said thirty years ago. I'd laughed at the time, but inside I knew there was no way on God's earth I was going to settle for being a bus driver... no fucking way. I'd have rather been dead, that's how I felt about it – I thought too highly of myself. And it wasn't just the buses – I couldn't see myself working for anyone for too long. I hated people telling me what to do. Even in school and prison they had wanted me to see a psychologist because they said I was so anti-authority. I simply didn't like being told what to do. Perhaps that stemmed from being bossed about by the Monster.

Two days before the flight, I paid Bianca a visit so that I could collect the camcorder she told me she had already bought. When I arrived, her mother was there. She was helping her pack stuff in her suit case. *What for, I'll never know!!* After a bit of nagging she gave me the camcorder and I made a speedy exit as I didn't feel comfortable with her mother being around.

****

There was never a moment I really felt totally comfortable around sprats' parents. I used to try my best to avoid them at all costs!

Take heed... I didn't know why at the time but I know now. The reason was that the parents weren't emotionally involved with me, so they could see what their daughters couldn't. Bianca's mother was no exception - she had told Bianca and I to leave each other alone more than once. But as per usual!! Bianca didn't heed the patterns!!!

****

The day of the flight I made my way to the airport with the camcorder flung over my shoulder. From the moment I got there my phone kept ringing and I ignored it! It wasn't until I reached the departure lounge that my companion turned round and said, "Why don't you just answer the bloody phone?"

I looked at the screen and replied, "It's Lewis. I can't be bothered."

The tannoy announced it was time to board the flight. I switched off my phone and made my way onto the plane –

one arm over Azaria's shoulder, the other arm holding Fate to my chest as we boarded flight 345 to Majorca!

So long, Bianca! You're probably thinking, damn, Jay, that was cold, and with hindsight I agree with you one hundred and fifty per cent.

When I got back, I told my mother what I'd had done. She wasn't pleased. Although I didn't see my mother as often as I would have liked, when I did see her I always told her everything. And when it came to women she would always say the same things:

"Jay, women will be the death of you if you don't change."

"Jay, life pays you back exactly what you pay it."

"Jay, sometimes you see bad people and they appear to get away with stuff, but let me assure you that the universe doesn't sleep. Everyone always gets what they deserve."

"Please, Jay, change your outlook."

"Somebody will come along one day and treat you exactly the same way, and it'll hurt ten times more."

I would always reply, "Mum, I will try for you. Okay?"

But as I said it, I was thinking the total opposite! *Treat me the same, my foot! It's impossible for any woman to treat me like that!* I was absolutely sure: how the hell could a woman hurt me?

After the whole Denise affair I had promised myself I would never let my guard down again. My view was, it was better for a woman to love me than the other way round. *Hurt me! I found that hilarious, I really did.*

I was unaware of what lay ahead of me. Neither you nor I could ever have predicted, not in a million years, how things were going to unfold!

CHAPTER 20
HAD ENOUGH

For the next two years or so you could say I went through a quiet period. I left my job not long after I came back from holiday in Majorca. I couldn't hack it even though I had it easier than all the other drivers. Let's just say when I came back from holiday and my job was still there for me I realised I had my boss in my pocket, so I pushed all boundaries. Even so, I still hated the job so I left. Most of the time I stayed at home with Azaria and my daughter Fate, who I totally adored. Every now and again I would go out with Lewis and some of the crew, and every once in a while I'd pay Bianca a visit.

How did I live financially with no job and Azaria not working? Off Bianca of course! She had been furious when she never got to go Majorca, but the person I was, I came up with some story about getting arrested.

****

Now, as I have explained before, I was aware Bianca was emotionally involved and how blinded a person can get once they are in the love process – I already knew before I even left for that holiday that as long as I came up with some half-baked excuse that could sound like it was true, I would win her over.

When a woman is in that state, it's not about it being believable - it's more about just giving her a good enough explanation, a seed of doubt; just a little one is enough - something for her to hang on to. As long as I gave her a story that was even half good, she would start to make excuses in her own mind that would tell her it was true. In other words, she would do whatever was necessary to block out the pain of the truth!

****

When I came back from Majorca, I got hold of a friend of mine's charge sheet and swiftly doctored the name and date so it looked as though that I had been arrested instead of him. Deep down, I believe she knew it wasn't true – but it was enough for her to tell herself it was! Her mother was going loopy! She didn't buy my story one bit. But while Bianca believed she kept paying, and that was enough for me.

It was at some point during the third year that things started to go wrong between me and Azaria. It wasn't easy, bringing up Fate in a one-bedroom flat. The stress came out in ways I would have never expected. Azaria and I started taking it out on each other.

Roughly a year after Fate was born Azaria had been awarded four thousand pounds in court for unfair dismissal. So she had bought herself a new car and I got the old one. It wasn't until maybe a year or so later whilst looking in a drawer that I stumbled across her bank book. I found out she had not been awarded four thousand pounds like she had said – it was seven thousand! *Slick move!* Did I say anything? Of course not; I just made a mental note. Over the years I have come to the conclusion that most women have a secret bank account, including my mother! *Smart one, ladies!*

But the real problems began when she developed thyroid problems which affected her behaviour – she became extremely argumentative and difficult to deal with. Now, as much as I liked her, I believed then that a woman should know her damn place – which was in the kitchen, doing the cooking and cleaning and all the other womanly stuff, with no feisty behaviour to her man – especially not in public. The man would have the last say, and that was final. There was no way on earth I was going to allow a woman to overpower me with any nonsense.

****

Take heed, ladies – this kind of cave-man mental attitude should serve as a red light.

****

I know! I know! It sounds like the Monster! As time passed, I began to see my father's traits emerging in me. I can honestly say I never had them to the degree he had them (or so my ego informed me!), but nevertheless there they were. *Incredible!* Some of the things I hated most about him – in particular the way he treated my mother – I actually started doing myself, such as, "The woman should cook the food!" and, "No backchat!" I made a mental note to change it – I was disgusted with myself.

The arguments between Azaria and I were steadily getting worse and worse. I could see it was starting to affect Fate, but I wasn't quite sure how or what to do.

As it turned out, nature was going to intervene. *I mean the nature down below!*

One evening, during one of our humble periods, she told me she was going to stay over with her vertically-challenged family. It so happened that the next day I was going to sell my car, because Bianca had given me a huge pay rise! I asked Azaria if she could come back at ten in the morning so she could follow me in her car when I went to sell it. She agreed and then took off with Fate.

When she had gone I decided to go to the club with a guy named Aaron who I had met through Lewis. We had become good friends; Aaron was one of those mixed-raced pretty boys, I could tell by the way women responded to him. He couldn't dress to save his life, though. I guess he made up for the lack of dress sense with the amount of raw cash he had. He was loaded but it wasn't apparent. He sold drugs but didn't like flamboyance. He had a live-in girlfriend and her name was Kelly. I half-suspected she was only with him for his loot. Kelly and Azaria were close friends at the time.

That night, whilst we were out in the club, Aaron chatted up this woman and asked me if he could use my flat to bone her. I told him that he could; it wasn't a problem as Azaria was at her mum's. But it was only then he told me that she was with a friend and that the friend was coming along too, because she was staying at her house for the weekend. So after a long night of drinking we made our way back to mine.

To be honest, I didn't have any intention of sleeping with the friend. But the way things played out, I only had a one-bedroom flat so I gave Aaron the living room and, obviously, the friend had to stay in the bedroom with me! Well, you can guess what happened? She got in my bed and… *boing, boing, boingggg!*

But what happened afterwards was nothing but reckless. As soon as I had climaxed, I went and double-locked the front door from the inside. Then I went back to bed, reminding myself that I would have to be up around eight at the latest as I had to sell the car, and that Azaria would be back at ten.

Well, ten a.m. came around all right, and when it did, guess where I was? Yep! Fast asleep with that woman in my arms. I woke up to the sound of Aaron shouting at me, "Azaria's banging on the door!"

I jumped up in a state of panic. *Not again.*

As I got to the door I heard Azaria shouting, "If you don't open the door, I'm going to smash the window."

I stood there motionless for some time until I heard the window smash. I knew at that point there was no way to get around the situation; I was caught bang to rights!

I finally decided to open the door, and Azaria predictably went mental. She lunged for the women. I grabbed her and held her tight so Aaron and the women could make their escape.

Azaria cried and cried. I tried to concoct some story to explain why the women were in the flat. But she didn't buy any of it. When she was all cried out, she walked out. I tried to stop her but she was not listening to me.

In all honesty I was kind of devastated; we had been arguing so much, I thought I wouldn't care, but when I saw how distraught she actually was, it changed things.

That evening she came back with her mother and started packing her stuff. As much as I begged her not to go, and as much as I told her that I hadn't slept with anyone, she wouldn't listen. Then, right on cue, the mum came in and had the cheek to tell me that I was no good! I couldn't believe my ears! I mean, I knew I hadn't been a good boy, but compared to her shoving her hands down my shorts on the day our daughter was born, well, that was the lowest of the low even by my standards! I wanted to shout out what I really thought of her, but I decided against it.

When Azaria had finished packing she turned to me and said, "Can I have my car key?"

My car key? Are you out of your mind? "What car key?" I replied, knowing exactly what key she was talking about.

"My fucking car key," she shouted.

"It's my car! What the fuck are you talking about?"

"Your car? I lent it to you, and now I want it back."

Azaria knew that she had given me the car because she was happy I had pressured her to take her employers to court. But now she wanted to be spiteful. All the same, I had no intention of giving it back. After an hour of back and forth arguing, she called the police. In the end I had to give it back to her, even though it was registered in my name.

But the car wasn't such an issue – Bianca had given me three thousand pounds the week before to buy a car. The real issue was my daughter. My daughter would no longer be with me; she wouldn't be there to greet me whenever I came through the door. I wouldn't be able to ask her how much she loved Daddy and she wouldn't be able to reply, "I love you the whole world." I always looked forward to that little routine when I came home. I didn't feel the need to say anything to Azaria at the time, as in my mind there was nobody on earth who could stop me from seeing my little angel.

So that was that; they were gone, and in the blink of an eye I was free and single again.

Two odd things happened in the next two weeks. *Talk about coincidences!*

Exactly one week to the day after Azaria and Fate left, a friend who lived on my road called me and asked if I wanted to go to a club called EC1. I had never been there before so I agreed. I couldn't have been there for more than twenty minutes when I saw Azaria, and it took another three seconds for it to register that she was with some coolie-looking man.

I felt the rage building up inside me. Who was this prick, and where the hell had he come from? I was unable to contain my anger. I charged towards them, but as I was in motion Azaria saw me and I guess she could tell from the look on my face that I was not about to do any talking. They ran through the exit doors, and fortunately for them they were able to jump into a taxi before I could unleash my rage.

My mind was working overtime. Where the fuck had this guy come from? He must have been around before the morning when she had caught me with those women. I mean, I had lived with her for a few years and I had never seen him before. So that made me feel a little more justified.

Imagine – I had never been to that club in my life, was I missing something? Or was I supposed to be there? I tried to make sense of it all. Of all the places I could have gone to, it just happened to be there, where she was entertaining this man.

Okay, so that was weird happening number one. It didn't stop there, though.

A few days later, Bianca called me and said she was going shopping at Brent Cross and asked me if I wanted to come.

Of course I said yes; I knew I would get treated to more or less everything I wanted. I had never been to Brent Cross in my life.

Un-fucking-believable! I could not believe what I was seeing. There they were, Azaria and that man again, on the floor below. But this time they were with Fate, and guess who was holding her hand? I froze instantly – my whole body suspended in time. The only thing functioning was my thoughts. How can this be? Is life playing some kind of joke on me? How can she do that to me? Is she fucking crazy having some man holding my daughter's hand? I'm going to kill them!

That was my last thought before I saw the devil. Right there and then, I lost the plot. Steam was coming out of my ears. I quickly told Bianca to meet me back at the car. As angry as I was, I wasn't about to let Bianca know what was going on. She had no idea about Azaria or my daughter. When Bianca was out of sight I made tracks towards Azaria. My knife was in my pocket, and to be honest I was ready to stab him there and then, cameras or no cameras. When I was approximately thirty meters away Azaria saw me coming, and I could see the panic on her face.

I grabbed her and said, "Who the fuck is this prick?"

"He's a friend of the family…"

"I really am…" the man butted in.

I could smell the fear emanating from both of them, which as you know now gave me more strength. In between my rage I glimpsed Fate; she looked confused and then instantly began crying. At point I wanted to rescue my daughter from this whole scene, but I couldn't! My anger was getting the better of me. In a second I went for him and I don't remember anything else apart from being swarmed by security. As they wrestled to get me out of the centre I spat at them.

That evening, when I got home, I couldn't get my head around how I had managed to bump into her in two places that I had never been before with another man within the space of a few days. I found it very difficult to believe in those kinds of coincidences. It was just too much. And how was it possible for her to meet someone so quickly and to let him be so close to my daughter that he could be holding her hand? Who was this man who was around my four-year-old angel? I had to find out; the whole thing was hurting me.

So I went out and looked for a woman to take it out on. For the next two months I went hunting; it was time to rebuild the stocks. My time living with Azaria had reduced my database of women to zero, except for Bianca. That same week I met a woman called Bonnie in a nightclub. She was one hell of a character: beautiful and sexy, and I mean Catherine Zeta Jones sexy; visibly, she was every man's dream, but unfortunately for me she swung both ways.

****

I'm not sure why I've never been a fan of bisexual women. I always have a picture in my head of me saying to her, "That woman on TV looks sexy," and over my shoulder she says, "Hmmm, hmmm, yes, she doessss, doesn't she!" Eugh. It's just never sat right with me, personally.

****

Apart from her bisexuality, there was one other thing that stood out a mile – she was spoilt rotten! She didn't like to be told no. I guess it all stemmed from the fact that her parents were filthy rich.

The first time she came back to my place I remember she stood in my hallway and stuck her two fingers inside herself and licked them. *Boing, boing, boingggg! It bloody went through the roof!*

For weeks we were at it. You could say she lived at my flat with me for a while, as she was there more often than not. Her freakiness would drive me absolutely wild; she certainly knew how to get a man fired up. She would do all these moves I hadn't experienced before, like the corkscrew motion she favoured rather than the old up-and-down – she would spin three-hundred-and-sixty degrees on my baton. It would drive me bloody crazy. Or she'd tie up my hands and blindfold me and put ice in her mouth and blow the hell out of me. At times she would start playing with herself in the middle of a conversation or movie, or in the car, knowing damn well it was giving me a brain haemorrhage.

But then, from nowhere, she started being possessive. And I started hearing on the grapevine that she was a bit of slapper – which, to be honest, didn't surprise me; but all the same, suspecting and knowing are two different things. So it wasn't long before I gave her the boot. So maybe you're wondering, rich parents – why didn't I hold on to her and get some loot? Well, a womaniser's ego is a funny old thing… it's quite a paradox, but although I was slapper myself, my ego wouldn't and couldn't take the fact that she was one too, and that everybody knew it. *Bizarre.*

She didn't take very kindly to being dumped, and she made it quite clear. On a few occasions she turned up at my place demanding to come in, and I told her where to go. Then one day she got her way – and I never saw it coming.

Azaria and I somehow reconciled our differences – even though I hadn't been too keen on getting back with her. After some time it transpired that the coolie-looking guy who had been hanging around my daughter really was a long-term family friend. However, I was convinced something was happening or had happened in the past: why else would he pop up just at the time we separated? She came back easily; I got the feeling she felt we were equals now. If it weren't for my daughter Fate, I would definitely not have let the whole situation slide back. But I missed her too much, and wanted her back home; it swayed me immensely.

One night after midnight, when I was in bed with Azaria, the doorbell rang. I wondered who the hell it was, and then remembered that crazy woman Bonnie and it flickered across my mind that it could be her. As I made my way to the door I prayed it wasn't her. Whoever was there was leaning on the doorbell. Eventually, I opened the door, and there she stood.

Now, my flat was the ground floor of a house; there was a main door to the street, then a small hallway that led to the internal front door of the flat.

When I saw her, I knew she was about to start her usual crap.

"Hiya! Can I come in?" she said, all casual, as if we were still together.

"No, you can't. Azaria is here," I whispered.

I saw her face change in a split second. She said, "What? I thought you were finished?"

"We were, but we're back together now."

I saw the rage building up. She had finally found her angle! "I want to suck your cock right now."

"Shhhhhh! Don't start," I said, wondering if Azaria was out of bed and could hear her.

"Listen, you either let me suck your cock right now, or I'm going to start a commotion and tell her exactly what we've been up to in there. You know what I'm like, you know I will!"

I looked her in the eye and I could tell she was deadly serious; she was holding me to ransom. I had no choice! If she created a fuss until Azaria came out, and told her, Azaria would have left me there and then. To be honest, it wasn't so much her I was worried about – it was losing Fate all over again.

"Okay, hold on a minute, let me just check if she's sleeping."

"I don't care if she's sleeping", she replied, raising her voice.

"Just give me a fucking second!" I replied, squeezing the words out quietly.

"Go on then, hurry up. But if you think you're going to close the door, don't bother because I will bang this door down all night."

"Okay, all right."

I was in a catch-twenty-two situation. Really, I wanted to show her who was boss, but it was impossible for me to do anything because if Azaria even knew she was at the door it would have been chaos. Azaria had already asked me point blank if I had had any women in the flat during our separation. I had lied, of course.

I sneaked back in and checked on Azaria. She was half asleep.

"Who was that?" she muttered.

"It's Lewis. I'm just talking to him about something. I'll be in soon," I replied.

When I went back into the hallway, Bonnie had a look of triumph on her face; you know the look – the *I've got you, you little fuckerr!* kind of look. She really did, but I planned to sort that all out; not right now, but soon.

I took it out and let the nutcase do her stuff; it was crazy. I hated her for having me like that, but at the same time it didn't stop it from going *boing, boing, boingggg!* As she was doing her stuff, the situation with Azaria and that guy popped into my head. It was still hurting me. A part of me was thinking, *Good, you bitch,* as Bonnie took down every last drop.

As she was leaving, Bonnie said four words: "Get rid of her," and walked off with a smug grin on her face. I didn't answer. I just wanted her off my doorstep.

****

Imagine that: Bonnie had actually manipulated the manipulator. I was actually aware of it but I really couldn't do anything at that point. Bonnie had used <u>fear</u> to manipulate me. In fact, ladies, take note: if you are being manipulated in any way, shape, or form, the manipulator is coming from one of these angles: fear, intimidation, guilt, stroking your ego, curiosity, or playing to your desire. Read that sentence over and over again until it is ingrained and you will hear it whenever someone is doing it to you. Pay attention; I have constantly used these angles, to manipulate all the women in this book.

Here is another reason why many people get blinded by strong manipulators – they underestimate how far the manipulator will go to win the argument or simply to get what they want. The harsh truth is, everyone is manipulating each other!!! Yes, I didn't say that incorrectly. People are motivated by self-interest – it's human nature and not a bad thing. It is only a bad thing when used selfishly! And that is commonplace with womanisers.

In fact, the same manipulation is even being done at the top. Everyday companies manipulate us with their advertising. Parents manipulate us by saying this is what we should do, when in fact that's because it fits in with them and their belief system and what they want. Friends tell friends they should behave this way and so on. The truth is, if situations don't fit in with the way they see the world – it's wrong. That's their ego.

Now, I'm not trying to justify my behaviour. I'm just saying you need to make sure you're not being manipulated by hidden motives.

****

It wasn't long at all before I was able to get rid of Bonnie once and for all. Azaria got her own two-bedroom flat, so we moved in to it as it was more spacious. I rented my flat to two Polish women. Bonnie must have been pulling her hair out when she came back and found I had moved.

So that was the end of Bonnie.

The new flat was hell for me. After about a month, whenever we got into an argument (which seemed to be more often than not), Azaria would order me to get out of her place.

Now, for me the worst feeling I could have was not being comfortable in what should have been my home. The very first time she ordered me out I warned her, "Don't ever say it again." But did she listen? Of course not! She thought she had one up on me.

The second time she said it, I sat down and thought about the whole set-up. I came to the conclusion that as much as I wanted to live under the same roof as my daughter, her living in such a tense environment was not doing her any good. I noticed that whenever we were arguing she cowered in a corner. So I went back to my flat and gave the Polish women four weeks' notice. They weren't happy, and I felt sorry for them, but there was no other option available.

I bided my time and I didn't say anything to Azaria. When the notice period was up, I called a friend with a van and went to move my stuff. During the removal Azaria came home and was obviously in shock that I was leaving without any warning. She started crying and begging me to stay. But I really didn't care. I had made up my mind and was not going to change it.

****

To stay in a relationship when you are no longer happy is one of the greatest wastes of time in life – period. Although I was unaware of it at that point, it still sits true today and I suspect it always will!

****

But I was sad to leave my daughter behind.

I was on the move once again!

****

Before I continue, let me make something clear. From here on, at times it's going to get weird and I mean really weird.

Something can happen in one person's life, but because it doesn't happen in yours, that doesn't mean it's not true. We are each unique and have unique life experiences – the history books prove it!!

Let me put it another way: if somebody had told me what you're about to read before it had actually happened to me, I'm fairly sure I would have thought it was make-believe. I would have probably said to the storyteller, "Hold up one minute, I'll be right back!", and they wouldn't have seen me for dust.

But the fact remains, it did all happen to me, and it's entirely up to you how you take it.

Buckle up: you are about to enter the Matrix!

****

CHAPTER 21
MYSTERY 101 – THE BEGINNING

I couldn't have been back in my flat more than a month when it happened.

That night I fell asleep on the sofa in my living room. When I awoke, I looked at the time on the VCR and it read 1:01 on the digital display. I got up, brushed my teeth, and went to bed as normal.

The next night I went to bed around nine p.m. Sometime during the night I woke up and turned to look at the time on the digital clock – it read 1:01. What a coincidence, I thought. I turned over and went back to sleep.

The next evening I went to a nightclub in the West End with some friends. I was doing what I did best, seeking out the cream of the crop! I remember I was at the bar, about to buy this woman a drink, when I took out my phone to check the time, and I couldn't believe my eyes: it read 1:01 again.

I had to sit down. I thought, *What the hell is going on?* I mean, I knew I was intuitive but this was some real freaky sh*t.

It didn't stop; every night without fail for about six months, I saw 1:01. If I was in bed sleeping I would wake up at 1:01. If I was out and I just happened to check the time, it would be exactly 1:01. Now I don't know what you're thinking about this 1:01 thing, but believe you me, at that point I thought I was going crazy, just wondering if I was going crazy!

Eventually, I told my mother, who came up with some wacky explanation that my angels were taking snapshots of my thoughts. *Yeah, that's what I thought too – angels, snapshots, my arse! I'm not even sure how she could come up with such madness!*

I told Stretch too; if anyone understood me, it was him. Although I didn't see him often any more (he still lived in North London), we still spoke regularly on the phone. When I told him, I got the impression that he was very sympathetic to the whole thing. He knew I was intuitive and he was always telling me how blessed I was. But I was wrong – he confessed to me later, after he'd witnessed something himself, that at this time he'd thought I was chatting out of my rear end.

I didn't dare tell anyone else; I mean, it does sound crazy, doesn't it? I was worried someone might cart me off to a mental institution.

Now, as suddenly as it started happening, it stopped. Just like that. And when it stopped, eventually it went to the back of my mind as most things normally do, in time. But I had no idea this 1:01 thing had not finished with me yet!

Not long afterwards, I went to see Bianca. I hadn't seen her for a while but I'd kept the relationship on the boil by speaking with her regularly; I knew that, in her mind, the whole time I hadn't seen her I was still her boyfriend. I'd come up with a plan at one point which I'd then put on a back burner; now it was fresh and alive again. I knew if I could pull it off it would stand me in good stead. It was time to see how much Bianca really loved me!

When I got to her house, I wasted no time. "Babe, I've had enough. I want us to leave this country; I want us to be somewhere nice, so we can be together." Which wasn't far from the truth: I wanted to leave England, just not with her.

"Where are you thinking of?"

"Maybe America. I'm fed up with England. I just feel I'm not meant to be here" Funnily enough, my mother has told me that. From fifteen years old, I was always saying exactly that! I don't know why, I've just always felt it.

"So how are we going to make that transition, Jay?"

WE! "I'm not sure yet, but I just know we need to get away from all the bullsh*t where these idiot girls are always saying to you that I boned them; I know it makes you unhappy. We just need a fresh start."

"I know what you mean…"

****

I knew wherever she went there was always talk about me sleeping with some woman or other, and I knew it upset her. I was using this angle (stroking her desire, and fear) to play on her emotional side, to win her over with what I was to spring on her shortly. I knew exactly where I was going with this conversation.

****

I let the conversation die, on purpose. I wanted it to look as though I was deep in thought about how we could really make it happen. Then I sprang it on her as if it had just popped into my mind. "Maybe you could get some money from the bank?"

"What do you mean?"

What do I mean indeed! "I mean, there must be a way to get some money out of the bank without them knowing it's you who took it?"

"Jay, are you serious?"

Serious! I couldn't have been more serious about anything. "Babe, don't you want us to get away from this bullsh*t?"

"Of course I do, but…"

At this point, I put my arm around her. "Baby, I have to leave. I can't take it here any more. I really have to go, and I want you to come with me."

****

Now, I had already worked out that this whole love thing is selfless. I was fairly sure, because she was in love with me, that she would put the solution to my pain before her own pain, which was the thought of what would happen to her if she actually got caught.

To be honest, I had already made the assumption that she was going to play ball as soon as she'd said, "Of course I do, but…" I could just feel it! It was just a matter of applying pressure indirectly, and playing on how much I was miserable here and that life would be great for us somewhere else.

****

In the end, she agreed to look for some kind of loophole in the system.

What did I do from that day onwards? I spent most days and nights with her, giving her the love and affection she craved from me!

****

Bianca had blind spots shooting out of her arse. I mean... I had never even spent a whole night with her in all the time I had known her. But all of a sudden, there I was spending enormous amounts of time with her.

You may be thinking, "Yeah, but that couldn't happen to me! She's just young and stupid!" Well, firstly, she wasn't that young. And secondly, age plays only a small part when it comes to blind spots. Yes, wisdom does come with age, but how much wisdom depends on your experiences and how hell-bent you are on learning from them. Once that love process kicks in, you're blind.

As my life story unfolds, you will see why I say love is the strongest force on the planet, and if you don't get to know the person and take heed of the patterns before you go and fall in love, it's too late!

****

I bided my time. I think it took her about a month to find it: she had discovered a way to get the money out. When she did, she was determined she was going to steal the money, but it was going to come at the cost of one of her colleagues. One of the guys at the bank fancied her and was always trying to chat her up. I convinced her he should take the fall – it would teach him a lesson to be messing with one of my women.

The plan was simple: steal the money and then let it appear as if he had stolen it, through some sort of ID system. When she told me, I was smiling all the way to the bank! My plan was working.

There was just one little matter to clear up – how much should be taken. I don't know why I said it – but twenty grand sounded like a good round figure at the time. Bianca told me she planned to take it the following Friday. Damn, I couldn't believe it! I mean, loads of girls and women in the past had given me money in drips and drabs; probably if I added it all up It would have been more than that figure from them all. But never before had a woman given me so much in one go. You can imagine how excited I was getting. *Twenty grand!*

The following Friday morning I woke up like a child on Christmas Day. We ran through the details again. I was to be in close proximity to the bank at around two o'clock when she would give me a call and I would go around to the back of the bank. I would stay there until she went into the toilet, where there were no cameras, and slipped the money in between the iron bars at the window. Then I would run away, smiling my arse off!

After Bianca set off to work, I couldn't sit still. My thoughts jumped back and forth at a huge pace. *Is this going to work? Twenty grand? America? Hilton Hotel?* And so on. I just couldn't take it. The suspense was killing me. At half past one I made my way down towards the bank. When I was close, I went into a McDonald's and grabbed a drink to wait for my phone call. It came dead on two.

"I can't do it today," she said.

Can't do it today?! I was enraged. Steam was coming out of my nostrils; I suspected she was getting cold feet.

"Just do it and stop thinking about it, will you?" I was finding it difficult not to shout.

"I can't. I'll speak to you about it later. I have to go. My boss is here now." And she hung up.

My blood was boiling. But there was more to come: that afternoon, as I waited for her to get off, I got some bad news: my brother Paul had been remanded in custody for some kind of robbery with six other guys. I knew that was not my brother's style and he had been influenced somehow – and it angered me.

So I was just one great big seething ball of fire when she made it through the door. I made it clear to her that if she didn't get that money, it was over between us (using the angle of fear again) – indirectly of course – and then I went back to my flat. The next week, whenever she tried to call, I ignored her. I knew that would have her pulling her hair out.

During that very same week I got the shock of my life. *Talk about a blow to a womaniser's ego!*

My daughter had a party; when I arrived, my mother and the Monster were already there. I said hi, and kissed my mother on the cheek. I didn't say anything to him.

From there, I went into the kitchen and gave my daughter a big hug. I was talking now with Azaria: at this stage we were getting on fairly well. As I was talking to her, her phone rang, and as soon as it did I could feel a sudden shift in her energy. She told me that her boyfriend was coming.

To be honest, I was glad he was; I wanted to see what kind of character was hanging around my daughter. I wasn't jealous in the slightest: she could have been sleeping with ten different guys; I really didn't care any more. But the phone started to ring again, and straight away I felt her unease. Then I connected the two: her unease was at the phone ringing. I grabbed it off the side and looked at it.

The caller ID read 'Mark Smith'. I knew two Mark Smiths; both of them were well-known in our circles. One was in Lewis's crew, someone I was currently hanging around with. The other was a guy I had been banged up with in jail. I already knew it was one of them; her unease gave it away. The question was – which one? I hoped it wasn't the one I had been banged up with.

"Which Mark Smith is this?" I asked.

I could now see the unease on her face. "That's my boyfriend," she replied, trying to stay calm.

I saw right through it. "Where is he from?"

"He's from Hackney."

My fears were confirmed. It was the one from jail. You remember that Mark Smith. We had shared a cell together and we'd got into a debate about women. Now I'm sure you can guess why I really didn't want it to be him!

So here I was, in the present, and he was with my daughter's mother. My ego was blown to smithereens. Although I knew he really wasn't up to par compared to me, it didn't matter because I knew in his mind that as far as he was concerned, he had now proved it.

I turned to Azaria and said, "Do you know that I know him?" I paid close attention to her body language as I asked her; she looked tense.

"Do you know him? From where?"

I wasn't sure whether she was telling the truth so I quickly changed the subject to my daughter. When I saw she was comfortable I quickly asked her again if she knew that I knew him. As I thought, she went tense again. She had confirmed she was lying without even knowing it. I suddenly hated her with a passion.

I knew Mark Smith and his crew never left home without a gun. While I waited for him to arrive, I thought about how to deal with this situation. It was obvious that they had already slept together; the only thing I was concerned about was my daughter.

As soon as he arrived, he asked if he could speak to me in private. We went into Azaria's bedroom.

"Jay, I never knew, man. I only found out one day when she showed me the picture of Fate's dad. I really didn't know."

I was right! She did already know that I knew him - bitch!

"I'm not concerned with that, Mark. There's nothing I can do about that. All I care about is my daughter. I don't want none of that shit around her, you feel me?"

"I wouldn't bring anything like that around her, come on."

"Good. That's all I care about. She's all yours."

The truth was, there was nothing I could do about it; they had already done the deed. The only thing I hoped for was that he wouldn't bring any of the street stuff to their home. *That very same fear became a massive reality one year later!* As for him being with Azaria, I really did think, *Poor him* – he had no idea how argumentative she was.

I stayed for the rest of my daughter's party and then made a swift exit.

The following Thursday, Bianca called me again. This time I decided to answer her, assuming Friday could well be the next golden moment of opportunity.

When I answered, she said, "Jay, I'm going to do it tomorrow. I promise."

"Are you sure?"

"Yes, I'm sure…"

"Babe, I don't mean to be so harsh with you. It's just that I've made so many plans for us, that's all. I'm coming down now, okay?"

"Okay."

I hung up. *I was at her house in a flash!*

The next morning we went through the whole thing again.

****

This time I prepared her mentally! "Bianca, do you know what I love about you most? That you always follow through with what you say you're going to do, no matter what. I really admire that about you!!" Indirect pressure: her ego would not want to shatter that image!

****

She called me at two o'clock, just like the last time. But this time she was quiet and quick: "Come round the back. I've got it."

I didn't have time to think. I bolted round to the back of the bank and arrived in an alleyway that led up to what looked like a car park and, in front, the bank window.

I paused to make sure no one was around. It was all clear.

I looked to see if I could see Bianca at the window. I could just make her out behind the iron bars. I rushed up to the window.

"Where is it?"

She lifted up a pouch with a padlock. Before she could even attempt to squeeze it through the bars, my hands were on it. I pulled at it, but it got wedged between the bars. I could see the panic on her face.

"It won't go through."

Won't go through indeed! There was no way on this earth that bag wasn't coming through. I started to struggle.

"Jay, leave it. It's not going to work."

The idea of it not working must have given me some extra strength, because with one mighty tug, I had it. I looked at Bianca; she looked terrified.

"Don't worry, babe. It will be okay."

I didn't wait for an answer; I was off.

I couldn't believe my luck. There I was with twenty thousand pounds in cash, in my hands. My next thought was – where the hell should I put it? Where was going to be safe? I considered my mum's, but as quick as I had that thought I changed my mind: if it turned pear-shaped and Bianca gave my name to the police, that's one of the first places they would look for it; and my mother would ask too many questions. So I decided to pay my godmother a visit; she loved the socks off me and if there was anybody I could trust a thousand per cent it was her.

I jumped in a cab and made my way over to West London. During the journey I couldn't help smiling, I remember the cab man commenting on how happy I looked. I also remember thinking, *So would you be if you had this bag*! When I arrived in West London I asked the cabbie to drop me half a mile from her house; I was taking no chances.

When I arrived her son opened the door and let me in. She was in bed; she wasn't well. She was getting old, I guess, but she still had all her faculties.

"Aggie, I want you to hold something for me and don't let anyone touch it."

"What is it, Jay?"

I sat down on the bed, cut the bag open, and tipped the money out. I began counting it.

"Where did you get all this money from, Jay… what have you done now?" she asked in a shocked tone.

"Don't worry, Aggie, it's totally legal."

"Legal my foot!"

"Please don't start; I'm telling you it's legal. A girl gave it to me."

When I finished counting the money, I was a little disappointed: it wasn't twenty thousand as I expected – it was nineteen and a half. You would have thought I would have been grateful for that, but I wasn't – there was five hundred missing!

I told my godmother how much there was, and asked her where she thought I should put it.

"Put it under the wardrobe, Jay."

She had one of those old-fashioned wardrobes with an arch at the front. I stuffed the money all the way to the back and placed some of her stuff in front of it.

Then she started to lecture me. "Jay, why do you do all these things? Since the day you were born I have had the minister burn a candle every day in church for you. He told me you were special because you were born on St Anthony's day. Why do you have to behave like this...?"

She went on for half an hour. Did I listen? Vaguely; my mind was working overtime thinking about what I would actually do with *my* money. I had no idea something was brewing behind the scenes. One of my childhood fears was soon to become a reality!

Eventually, I kissed her and said my goodbyes. I loved my godmother to bits; I didn't show it to her as much as I would have liked.

I headed back to my flat to pick up some money. I decided I was going to book a room in the Hilton Hotel, get some champagne, and celebrate my windfall! I called Stretch and told him to meet me later, but I didn't tell him what had happened.

When I got home I fell into a chair and reflected on the whole situation. I decided I would give Bianca two thousand for her cooperation. I wasn't sure what I was going to do with the rest of the money, but I knew for sure I was going to go away for a bit to New York.

When Stretch and I were on our way to the Park Lane Hilton Hotel, I told him what had happened that day. He started laughing. "Stop chatting shit!" When he realised I was deadly serious, he laughed again. "Only you, Jay! Only you can pull off shit like that!"

Amid all the hubbub in the lobby there was a happy man grinning from ear to ear – me! I pulled a fat wad of money out of my pocket and peeled back some notes to pay for the room. I could tell the man at reception was intrigued. I guess we didn't fit the look of their regular clientele, as I was dressed in blue jeans and a blue-and-white shirt with a hood on it – it was the style back then. Stretch was wearing almost the same.

As the man booked me in I asked him where I could get a bottle of champagne from; he pointed to the bar.

Stretch said, "Just get them to send it to the room!"

"Good idea!"

So that's exactly what I did – I ordered a Dom P and we headed to our room. I could see people were giving us strange looks, but did I care? Of course I didn't! My pocket was heavy!

When we got to the room, the first thing I did was sit on the glass table that was right in front of the window. I looked out at the view; it was awesome to me at the time. I could see a lot of greenery; above that, the London skyline. I smiled. I felt on top of the world.

Room service arrived with my bottle of champagne. Stretch cranked it open and poured out two glasses.

I saluted him. "Looks like we made it."

"To the L-O-O-T," he replied with a wide grin.

I swigged down the whole glass and poured another, then I lay back on the bed, hands behind my head. In my mind I said, *Thank you, God.*

Just then my phone rang, and I had a sick feeling in my stomach; I knew it was going to be bad news. I contemplated not answering it at first, but curiosity got the better of me. It was Bianca.

"Jay, I've been arrested. You have to bring the money back."

Bring back the money indeed! "Where are you?" I had to know.

"I'm at the police station…"

"What money are you talking about? I haven't got any money."

"Jay, don't play about. I'm serious. I got arrested. They had a camera in the skylight."

"Listen, I don't know what money you're talking about. I'm busy at the moment. I'll call you back."

I hung up the phone. At that point I didn't feel good, but I knew no matter what happened I wasn't giving back any money – none.

I turned to Stretch and told him.

"What are you going to do?"

"Carry on drinking of course!"

Before I could even get another drink down me, my phone rang again. This time it was a number I didn't recognise. I answered the phone. Some woman was shouting down the phone; it was Bianca's mother.

"You better bring that money back… you hear me, you little piece of scum!"

"I'm sorry, I only speak English."

Nobody on this planet ever got anything from me by ordering me about (apart from Bonnie…). The only thing they did was put my back up.

"I'm going to get some guys to deal with you… I promise you, you're a dead man walking."

"Okay… Be sure to tell them who they're coming after, yeah."

I hung up. The phone rang straight away. This time it was Bianca's number. I didn't answer.

As the evening progressed there were a few more calls. One in particular had me nervous to say the least. My mum told me the police had called and had asked if I could come down to the police station. But that wasn't the call that worried me; if the police had a solid case, they would not have been asking me to come down to the station; they would have come and got me. So I continued drinking. No, it was the next one that sobered me up. It was from Rocky. I hadn't heard from him in a long time.

"What have you done?"

My mind scrambled for connections. How the hell did he know? I played dumb.

"What do you mean, what have I done?"

"I just got a call from a friend saying that Kain's looking for you." My knees wobbled at the mention of that name. Kain had grown in stature since I was younger; now he was notorious as a murderer: even the police knew it, although they'd never been able to put his arse behind bars for it. He'd even had books written about him. What was once a childhood fear was now right out in the open and on my doorstep. *FUCK!*

"Why is he looking for me?"

"I don't know. But just be careful, okay?" He hung up.

I turned to Stretch; I could see the fear in his face and Kain wasn't even looking for him. I guess he knew it was only a matter of time before Kain would come looking for my best friend. The next call, on Stretch's phone this time, came from Greece; it was some Greek guy who used to live on his road calling to warn Stretch that Kain was looking for us.

I couldn't believe it: news travelled fast!

I phoned Bianca. I guessed her mother had something to do with it. "Why the fuck is Kain looking for me?"

"I don't know! It's nothing to do with me. I just need you to bring back the money, please!"

I hung up. It wasn't making sense. How the hell did Kain know what happened?

Then it all clicked into place... all the connections came into focus. I remembered telling Bianca once in pillow talk that I had never wanted to get into any problems with Kain. Then I remembered that one of her friends was the sister of one his friends. It all made sense now; they were setting me up. I called back Rocky and asked him to get me Kain's number. He got it for me. When I had it, I rang him and

I remember the conversation went exactly like this; I will never forget it.

"Yeah, Kain, it's Jay; I heard you're looking for me?"

"You see that money you took? It's mine. Bring it back and the argument is finished."

Bring it back my arse! I mean, I did fear him but not to the point that I would hand over twenty grand.

"I haven't got the money. I spent most of it."

"What did you spend it on?"

"Guns," I replied, out of fear I guess.

He paused briefly and then, very calmly, said, "Okay, let's meet up."

"What for?" I asked.

"Let's just meet up and talk."

"I'm busy right now."

"Okay, listen, you can run, but I'll find you." He was as calm as anything. Then he hung up.

His calmness spooked the fuck out of me. It wasn't normal. I had never experienced that kind of behaviour. He should have been shouting something like "If I don't get the fucking money I'm going to put two bullets in your brain!", but he wasn't. My conclusion was this: he was a man of action, not words.

It was only when I got off the phone with him that it registered he was saying it was *his* money. Maybe Bianca and her mother hadn't called him? But then, how did he know? It didn't make any sense. But I didn't have time to figure it out.

I needed somewhere to stay for a while. I knew that staying in my flat would be too dangerous. I called one of my young girls, Brook, who lived at home with her mother. I hadn't been with her that long, but all the same I liked her and I knew she was head-over-heels for me. So the next day I moved in there; when I briefed her on what had happened, it turned out she knew all about Kain – he had been behind the shooting of her cousin. I needed to get out of this mire; all of a sudden America seemed to be calling me that much harder than before.

I made some arrangements with Stretch. I decided to take him with me, as I knew he was also in danger. I called my mother and told her to call her brother in Orlando to say we were coming over. Then I booked two open tickets. I made one final stop before I left: I went to see Ms Carlton, but she wasn't home. So I went to the corner shop to get some stationery. I wrote Ms Carlton a letter explaining that I was going away to start a fresh, and that I would stay in touch because she had been like a mother to me. I told her that I would miss her and that I had enclosed two thousand pounds, and that I would be in touch. I put it through the letter box and made tracks.

I was on the move again!

CHAPTER 22

AMERICA AND BACK TO MYSTERY 101

As the plane was about to take off, I remember I was singing an R Kelly special, 'Looks like we made it!', as we sipped our glasses of champagne.

Guess which way we turned as we boarded the plane? Yep, you got it – we were first class all the way. As soon as I got on the plane I felt super-great: I not only had the money, but I had another seven grand that I had accumulated from previous generosity from Bianca. All in all, I was about twenty-five grand up. Translate that into American dollars at that time and it was a handsome fifty grand. The whole business with Bianca and Kain disappeared into the back of my mind as soon as the plane was airborne.

The plane must have been in the air for about ten minutes when Stretch jumped out of his seat. He twisted around to me and muttered, "Do you know who that is, sitting in front of you?"

I peeked through the seats but I didn't recognise the man. "I don't know. Who?"

"You really don't know?"

"No, I bloody don't! Who is it?"

"That's Peter Mandelson." I racked my brain, but it meant nothing.

"Never heard of him."

"He's one of those government guys."

I changed the subject; the truth was, I wasn't that impressed, probably because I didn't know anything about the government or anything close to that nature at the time.

When we arrived at Orlando Airport we got a grilling from the authorities. Why did we have so much money between us, and what did we do for living back in England? I was so happy I nearly told the official, "Womanising is my profession, sir, and it pays very handsomely!" Instead, I told him the first thing that came into my head: that I was a bus driver and we had come for three months as our uncle was sick; we didn't even have that much money, just five grand. I guess he believed me because he let us through.

My uncle met us at arrivals. I had never met him before. He was bald with startling green eyes and he had a beer belly that bulged beneath his denim shirt and hung over his jeans, which were covered with specks of cement. We said our hellos and made our way back to his house in his rusty old truck that was full of tools.

On the way I couldn't believe how many people knew him. All we kept hearing was, Kojac this, Kojac that; he was very popular. As I got to know him better it became obvious why. He was hilarious, especially when he had a few drinks inside him – which he made sure he had most evenings, after work.

When we arrived at his house I was amazed at the neighbourhood; there were only blacks, and I mean only blacks. Even the postman was black!

When we got inside he introduced me to Banton, a lodger who worked on the construction site with him. Then he showed us to our rooms: obviously, I got the bigger one. The house was one of those bungalow-type houses with four bedrooms (and was also a house that could be literally moved around, I later found out).

That night Stretch and I hit the Caribbean Beach Club. It was full of Hispanic and black women… damn, I loved those Hispanics! We did the whole champagne thing in there, but my awareness alerted me that the American girls were not like English girls. In general I could see these women wanted men with money. I had guessed life was a lot harder over there than in England. But when I thought about it, I decided the real reason was that in America they are more blatant as opposed to in England, where they are more subtle. The bottom line is: most women want a man with money to look after them and many will go to great lengths, just like a womaniser, to secure a man with money – manisers! Damn, there were lots of them about!

That first night, when I was just observing the whole club set-up, I looked at my phone to check the time, and have a guess what time it was? 1:01. I wondered if it was just coincidence, as I hadn't seen it for a long time. It threw me off my game. I didn't even get one sprat's phone number that first night. I was so shocked; my ego took a bit of a beating.

The next day my uncle and Banton went to work. Stretch and I decided to explore Orlando. I was aware quite quickly that this was not the place for me; it was too rural as far as I was concerned. It was so spread out, and there were too many motorways; it was almost impossible to get about unless you had a car. To get to the corner shop you had to get a bus! It was ridiculous.

The people were rural in their attitudes too; at times I could barely make out what they were saying. It just wasn't for me. All my life I had been used to city life, where the houses have two floors. But I knew I wasn't going back to England any time soon, so I decided to make the best of it.

That night Stretch and I went back to the same club again. Once again I clocked 1:01, and I was freaking out again. I remember I turned to Stretch and showed him the time. "I bet it's something to do with someone's door number." Stretch wasn't really paying attention. As quickly as I'd said it, I dismissed it; I had noticed all the door numbers out here were crazy, all in their thousands. Whatever 101 was, it was on a roll again.

After about a week of staying with my uncle, we got to meet the neighbours, some middle-aged folks; it wasn't too long before I bumped into their daughter, Josephine. She was normal looking, but she had a smashing body. I wanted her and I made it clear; it took me one day before I had her giving me a polish in my uncle's house.

After I broke the skin, I don't know what happened but the women just started flooding in. I know my uncle thought I was running the place like a hotel, but he didn't really mind so much.

Eventually, I got to know Josephine's sons; they were only young but I was amazed at how advanced they were compared to English kids. One day, when I was out the front talking to them, they told me they wanted me to come back to their place. I told them to ask their mother: I knew she would say yes as she had been trying to get back in my pants for some time. She knew I had lots of women coming to the house. She said yes and we all jumped in the car and headed over to a part of town I hadn't been to before.

When we arrived in the complex, I got out of the car and followed them to their front door. *Wait for it!* I nearly fainted. The door number was 101.

I couldn't believe my eyes, and it showed because she started asking me, what's wrong? At first I said nothing, but when I finally composed myself I told her the whole thing: that I kept waking up at exactly 1:01. She didn't seem that surprised at all; in fact, she told me she'd had some sort of similar experience. Then she went on to tell me I should play the cash three on the lottery. In fact, she made me promise I would do it. So I did; I promised I would put one hundred dollars on it the next day, as money was no object at the time.

I called Stretch at my uncle's and told him. He seemed surprised, but deep down he still wasn't convinced of it all. Josephine and I made out in her bedroom, and later she dropped me back to my uncle Kojac's house.

Later that same night when I was in the kitchen, the phone rang. It was Josephine. "You're not going to believe this. I just picked up the phone to tell you to play the numbers straight [meaning play for 101 straight, not in any other format like 011 or 110], and the time on my phone was one-oh-one" Now I'm freaking out!

As soon as she said it, I turned my head to look at the old clock radio sitting on my uncle's table-top – it also read 1:01. Wow, I made a mental note that I would definitely put a hundred dollars on it in the morning.

I didn't sleep well that night. At five a.m. I was woken up by my uncle and Banton getting ready to go to work. The first thing on my mind was 1:01. I got up and went to the kitchen and made a drink. They were both about to leave when I sprung the whole 1:01 madness on them.

Banton said straight away, "Make sure you play those numbers."

My uncle looked at me and said, "Don't be stupid, and go back to bed."

I did exactly that – I went back to bed. Around eleven a.m. a lady who I had previously met at one of the clubs came to pick me up. We went down to Daytona Beach for the day. I spent all day trying to get into her knickers but, unusually for me, she managed to hold out. Well, then at that point she did anyway! I didn't get back in until around two a.m. Everyone was asleep so I went straight to bed.

It was around five a.m. when I heard my uncle banging on my door and calling my name. As soon as I heard him, my heart sank. He had never banged on my door or woken me up when he was going to work. In a split second I knew he had seen the news as he was getting ready for work; it was his normal pattern.

"Yes, uncle?" I answered feebly.

"Jay! Did you play the cash three?"

I couldn't believe my ears – wasn't he the one who had told me to stop being stupid? My suspicion had been confirmed.

"Why, uncle?" I asked, but I already knew the answer.

"Mi just sees the news; one-oh-one come up last night!" He slipped into a Jamaican accent.

I felt sick; I couldn't believe it. I hadn't remembered to play the lottery.

"No, I forgot."

"Are you stupid or something?"

Stretch heard the commotion and came out of his room. "Jay, please don't tell me you forgot to play the number?"

"Yeah, I didn't remember…"

When my uncle left for work, Stretch confessed to me that he had thought until now that the whole 101 thing was nonsense.

"But what the hell was you thinking? Did you expect God to come down and play the numbers for you?"

After talking to Stretch for an hour or so I went back to bed. I really felt sick; I was gutted. The thing is, I'd been adamant that I would play 101 on the lottery, and yet I'd forgotten. I couldn't work out how I had happened to forget. The whole day when I was in Daytona with that lady it hadn't popped into my head once, and I mean not once.

When Josephine found out later that 101 had come in she found me instantly, and she was all excited. I had to tell her the bad news. She went on about me not getting that opportunity again, which made me feel ten times worse.

I went back to bed and thought about the seventy-five thousand dollars I had won but never won. Later that evening I went and put a hundred dollars on 101. I remember the cashier asking me if I didn't have anything better to do with my money. I went back to the house and prayed the number would come up again, but it didn't. I never did tell anyone I played it the next day – I felt stupid.

For two days I stayed in bed. I was so angry with myself. I mean, how much clearer did I need it? Something or someone was obviously helping me up there. Why or how was irrelevant at that moment. It was on this second day that I thought about everything in depth. I mean, I wasn't religious; I didn't even go to church. But I came to this conclusion: I wasn't meant to win that money, because if I was, I bloody would have. I believed whatever 101 was, it wanted me to pay attention to that number. I just guessed it wasn't to do with the money; it was something special and when the time was right I wouldn't be able to miss it even if I tried. *How right that thought turned out to be!*

I'll give you my reasoning for why I thought that at the time. Unless I was going crazy (and I didn't think I was, because Stretch, my uncle, Banton, and Josephine were all in on it now) it was fairly clear to me there was some higher force guiding me to something – exactly what, I didn't know. Now, let's say hypothetically I was that higher force over you, and I could see everything that you did, every day, all day; well, I would know the exact point that you would go for 101! There would be no mistakes! So that's how I summed it up in my head. From that day of missing the lottery, 101 disappeared again. There was no more waking up at 1:01 or even catching it. At times I would deliberately try and catch it, but even then was I unable to get it.

After a while Stretch and I started to work for my uncle; it was my suggestion, not because I had to, but I was aware that the money I had wouldn't last forever, especially at the rate I was spending it. I wanted to try and preserve it until I found a way to maximise it. The work consisted of us pouring cement into mixers and then into wheelbarrows and running it up to the plasterers, with other odd labouring duties. I didn't mind the work so much; I knew it was helping to preserve my stash. What I did mind was that Stretch quit after a week, saying he couldn't handle it. It pissed me off, because I was giving my uncle money out of my wages for our board and lodgings. So I'd return home from work, tired and dirty, to find the house in a mess and Stretch sitting on his arse, drinking brandy and watching MTV. And then I'd be giving him money to go to the clubs; in fact, I was giving him money for everything, because he had none.

I went to see my cousin in Miami at one point, and I didn't take Stretch. I don't remember why he didn't come now, but I think it was because I was pissed off with him sitting on his arse. Wow! Miami was heaven on earth! I nearly didn't come back. South Beach! I couldn't believe how many beautiful women there were down there. I was on the beach every day, drinking champagne and boning women. I loved it; this was where I was supposed to be, where I wanted to live. I stayed at my cousin's massive house in its gated complex for two weeks, and got used to the swimming pool and all the luxuries that came with it.

I hadn't known my cousin before I came to Miami but she remembered me from a time when she had visited England when I had been very young. She and her husband treated me like royalty. Her husband took me everywhere. One time he even took me to the gun range and let me bang out four hundred shells from his licensed 357 magnum. *A licensed gun? What the hell is going on?* I remember thinking. Miami was a whole different world to me, but one I had fallen in love with almost instantly. It planted a seed in me that it was the American cities I wanted to see; and the big daddy of them all was the Big Apple, New York. I wouldn't get there this time around, but that was for another time.

When I returned to Orlando, Stretch was really getting on my nerves. He was becoming a burden and I was finding it hard to hide it. So exactly three months to the day after our arrival, I booked his flight back to England. When he got home, he phoned me to let me know that Kain had phoned his dad, demanding to know where he was. I also found out he had called my mum's house, demanding that they pay for the money I had. *Big mistake*! He had got through to the Monster, who had told him where to go! The Monster was the last person a gangster should go to for anything – they would have to kill him first. It's not that he was looking out for my interests or anything; it was more to do with the culture of Jamaica regarding threats: they don't pay the money and they don't get told what to do.

After Stretch's departure, it took me about a month to get really bored of Orlando. It was too country for me, and that boredom got me thinking about my daughter. I was really missing her. I had been lucky that she and Azaria had not become mixed up in all the trouble; the fact that they lived on the other side of London was a huge bonus. It was thinking about them that made me decide to return to England and face the music. I guess I was hoping that all the trouble with Kain would have died down by then. So I said my goodbyes to my uncle and Banton and all the lovely women I had accumulated, and I promised I would be back soon.

When I arrived back in England, I went straight to my girl Brook's house and laid low; that's when I met her crazy cousin TY. TY was the gangster type – you know, the kind of guy who never goes anywhere without his gun, and I mean nowhere. He had a sleepy eye, which usually makes you look like a geek, but for some reason with TY it made him look serious. I guess the reason we became friends was because we had a common enemy – Kain was on my case and Kain had apparently murdered his cousin.

A few days after I got back, I went to see my daughter. I took TY's gun with me; I wasn't taking any chances. So far, so good. My daughter was as happy to see me as I was to see her. I'd really, really missed her. So I stayed with her until late that night, and then made my way back to Brook's house.

But in the second week, as I got settled in, things started to get out of hand. One night Brook, her cousin, and a friend went to this club in South London. TY and I agreed we would be down there a bit later; but when we were getting ready to leave I had this funny feeling: my intuition was prodding me. I wasn't sure exactly what was wrong, but I knew something was up.

Just as we were about to jump in my car, I stopped. "I'm not driving my car."

"Why?"

"They know what car I'm driving." I was referring to Kain and his soldiers.

"They won't be in that club."

"I'm not driving. I'll call my brother's friend Wayne to drop us up there."

"Okay."

We went back inside and I called Wayne, who came along promptly. When we arrived at the club everything seemed normal. We saw Brook and her cousin in the corner dancing to the R&B music that was blasting out from the speakers, so we joined them. Then all of a sudden I felt that feeling of dread that I had felt earlier when I was getting into the car. I knew something bad was going to happen; I just didn't know what. I was on edge, nervous. I told TY to pass me the gun. I took it and tucked it in my waistband. I was taking no chances with this Kain character. I had heard that he had told all the so-called gangsters in London that I had taken his money; he was smart – he knew that by doing that he had a much better chance of catching me.

It couldn't have been more than ten minutes before TY and I went to get drinks from the bar. I remember leaning over the bar, waiting for my drinks, when I felt a tap on my shoulder. I turned around, and before I could work out what was going on this person I didn't know was gun-butting me in the face. My reaction was instant; I grabbed TY's gun from my waistband and pulled the trigger.

For a second, it was as if everyone in the club had disappeared, including my attacker. As my eyes focused, the only person I could see was a bouncer at the exit; our eyes locked; he glared at me; I glared back as if to say, "Are you crazy enough to try to stop me?" I saw the submission in his body language, but then I heard gunshots and saw flashes of light on the other side of the club. There were a few guys shooting at me.

I froze for a split second, and then I ran towards the exit door of the club, which was blocked by the bouncer. He stepped aside and let me escape. As I turned around I saw TY running with me. When I got outside I returned some shots while trying to get the hell out of the grounds. I ran towards the exit, and TY for some reason ran to the right, into what I now know was the car park.

As soon as I was out on the street I flagged down a car with some girls in it and I asked them for a lift. One of them said, "That's the guy who started the shooting!" and the driver put her foot down and the car sped away. Then a cab driver randomly pulled up and asked me if I needed a cab. I jumped in, not even having time to register how lucky that was.

My phone was ringing; it was TY.

He whispered, "I'm lying under a car in the car park, and they're searching it."

I couldn't leave him there. "Okay, I'm coming."

I told the cab driver to pull up at the car park entrance. Just as he pulled up, TY ran out. Whoever had been hunting us down had just left the car park and gone back into the club grounds; that's when TY made his escape.

TY leapt into the open back door and the cab driver sped us away. All TY said was, "Fuck, that was close." The rest of our journey was silent: I put my finger to my lips; we couldn't trust anyone. I tried to get my head around how the fuck it was I was still alive.

We made it back to the house!

A half hour later, Brook came home with her friend. She was frantic; she had seen everything, and what she described was crazy. It happened so quickly for me that I had hardly seen anything. She told me that the gunmen had been so close to me it was impossible for them to have missed; it was as if the bullets went through me or they were firing blanks. She said they had held up every car coming out of the car park, sticking their guns in the windows. My intuition had saved me! If I had driven my car that night I would have parked in the car park! One way in and one way out! I probably would have been dead.

To this day, I can't tell you who the fuck those men were, but I made up my mind that night it had been too close a call, and that I was going to New York, and for good.

There was one little thing I had to attend to before I left: my brother's court case. He was about to be sentenced. On the morning of his case, I took the train to the Crown Court. I had thought about driving but decided it was too risky. When I arrived, I went straight upstairs where I knew my mum would be. It wasn't until I reached the top that I saw them. My knees buckled.

It was Kain's soldiers.

As soon as they saw me, one of them got on his phone. He was the one who was Bianca's friend's brother – he was known as Twigs. I guessed he was phoning Kain. At that point I saw my mum sitting on a sofa, so I went and sat beside her. My mind was ticking fast. If my mum was paying any attention, she would have known something was up, even with me trying to act normal. Panicking, I phoned TY.

He was asleep.

"TY, Kain's boys are here at the court."

"Whattttt?" he replied, yawning.

"I said, Kain's boys are here at the court."

I was trying not to raise my voice.

"What they doing there?" He was awake now.

"I don't know, but get down here with the machines, quickly."

"All right, I'm jumping in a cab now."

As I sat there I could feel their eyes on me, all six of them. I really wanted to just get the hell out of there. But if I tried to leave they would come after me anyway. So I sat it out while my mother talked to me about something – I couldn't concentrate on a word she was saying; I was too on edge.

Eventually, it was time to go into court, and believe me there was so much tension in there I'm sure the judge could feel it. It turned out that one of the guys up for sentence with my brother was one of Twigs' friends. When they all came up into the dock I saw my brother look at me, as if to say, "What the fuck are those guys doing here?" He knew something was likely to happen. Every now and again I could feel them staring at me.

Halfway through TY called me – he was outside. I left the courtroom and went downstairs. Security and its metal-detecting machine were going to cause me a problem. So I had to think on my feet.

I ran outside; as I passed through the arch of the metal detector, I said to the security man, "I'm just quickly getting my cousin, they're about to pass sentence."

TY was waiting just outside the door.

I said, "Quickly, come on."

As we rushed back through the metal detector went off. Before the security guard could say anything, I said, "Remember, I just went outside a second ago? They're just passing sentence!" And we kept going.

"Oh yes, go on," he replied.

It was a close shave and a stupid move. But to put it in perspective, I'd heard stories that Kain's soldiers were going to murder me because I had disrespected him and had not returned his money. I was in fear of my life, and people do all kinds of sh*t to protect their life; I was no different. I was pretty sure they weren't in court with their guns, as they hadn't been expecting to see me there. But I was also pretty sure their guns wouldn't be far away – probably in their car.

When we got into court they all turned around, stared at me, and screwed up their faces. What they didn't know was that I was now strapped, and my fear had gone; well, almost. My brother looked at me, worried. I tapped my two fingers on my shoulder, signalling to him that I was loaded.

Eventually, they all got sentenced; my brother got three years. When I came out of the courtroom my mother was talking with one of the other mothers. I could see she was distraught, but I was more focused on getting the hell out. I kissed her briefly on the cheek and said goodbye.

As TY and I descended the stairs we could see all of Kain's soldiers lined up along the banister rail. I could sense something was going to happen. As we passed them and continued on down, one of them spat in my direction. Then they all ran after us. We steamed outside – we wanted to draw them out because we had our weapons – but then we stopped. They came rushing out of the door, expecting to chase us, and pulled up abruptly, shocked.

I said calmly, "I'm here now. And what? I have been hearing how you're going to put some in me. Well, I'm here now."

I could see the shock on their faces; they must've known I was carrying, because of my confidence. I heard one of them say, "Is that the one...?", as if he didn't know.

Then Twigs said, "Don't worry, we know where he's at."

"You don't fucking know where I'm at," I said, raising my voice and sensing their weakness.

Twigs turned and said to the rest, "Come on…"

With that, they all left.

I was glad it had ended there, because looking back I'm sure I probably would have pulled the trigger, even though we were outside the court.

Later that day, I set my plan to leave into motion. I put my car up for sale, and I told Brook I was leaving for New York. She was devastated, but I explained to her that if I stayed in England, I could feel something bad was going to happen. I felt it in every muscle of my body: it wasn't going to stop until someone was dead. As much as feared Kain, I just wasn't the type to lie down and I wasn't giving up one cent of that money. On top of that I was genuinely happy about going to New York.

A week later, I kissed Brook goodbye and went to the airport with Azaria and my daughter. I kissed Fate goodbye, and promised her she would see me again soon. As much as it was hurting me to leave my daughter behind, I was excited again – it was goodbye little England, hello Big Apple!

CHAPTER 23
THE BRONX, NEWYORK

When I touched down at JFK Airport I was excited and anxious all at the same time. It was a new beginning for me, but I wondered how it would unfold.

I was putting the whole Bianca and Kain thing behind me. I hadn't spoken to Bianca since the last time she had told me to bring back the money. At the time that I took it, I had no idea that it would cause me so many problems. When I thought about it on the plane, I asked myself if it had been worth it. In the end I concluded – *Yes, it bloody was!*

For as long as I could remember, I had wanted to leave England. And now it had finally happened. I still had money. I didn't have any kind of plan, but I felt free. I didn't have to look over my shoulder and I could start all over again. Well, that's what I was thinking, anyway!

My aunt Grace picked me up at the airport, and took me back to her one-bedroom apartment in the Bronx. I had never met her before, and on first impressions she looked pretty miserable and ever so slightly malnourished. Her face told the story of a hard life. She wore a dated, faded floral dress that was out of whack with her age.

Her apartment was tiny. It was in a small tower block and on the fifth floor. Straight away, I wondered how long I could stay there. That evening we chatted about the family, and about general life stuff. I got the feeling she knew about the money, although she didn't say it directly. *News travels fast*, I thought.

Later that night, when she left for work, she told me I could have her bedroom as she always slept in the living room. I didn't believe her for a second: I assumed she was just being generous. And before she left, she gave me the spare key. On my own, I began thinking about how New York would turn out for me. Money wasn't an issue for me right now, and I knew I couldn't stay in these cramped conditions for long. I knew I had to find a woman, and fast – but I had no idea I'd find her within an hour!

I decided to go for a walk along White Plains Road, which was the high road behind the apartment. As I was passing a KFC I decided to get some chicken. A woman working there caught my attention; it turned out she was the manager. I thought she was quite cute. As I waited for my order, I thought about my aunt's apartment and the cramped conditions. So I wasted no time putting it on her. Her name was Cali, and I chatted her up for maybe five minutes until eventually she gave me her number. I could tell she was fascinated by my accent.

When I got back to the apartment I felt a deep loneliness. I thought about Fate and I longed for her. I planned to send for her regularly.

The next night, when my aunt Grace had gone to work, I called Cali and asked her to come over. She arrived and we talked for a while, and eventually we hit the sack. She seemed like a nice girl. The next morning when my aunt came in I told her I had met the manager from KFC. Straight away she told me that I should ask her to marry me so I would get my American papers and then I could get a job. *Get a job indeed*! If she thought I had travelled all the way over the Atlantic to find a job, she was mistaken.

She was right about one thing, though – I did need to get married so I could stay in America. So when I had spun my web and Cali fell head over heels into it – which didn't take long, mind you – I sprang the whole marriage thing on her and she agreed with no hesitation.

As time went on and she was sorting out the marriage papers, she brought me back to her home where she lived with her grandmother, her two sons, Cameron and Carson, and her brother, Fox. I didn't really take to Cameron – he was one of those rude kids who just don't listen and do the opposite of what you tell them to do. As for Carson, I began to love him like my own son – maybe because I could see he was going to be a ladies' man when he grew up! As for Fox, he was a loose cannon, the typical hoodie type: jeans hanging down under his pants and a gun fanatic. He was also a member of the notorious Bloods gang.

During that time I became friends with a guy named Zane, a drug dealer who didn't deal with dime bags – only the substantial amounts. He saw himself as a kind of womaniser, but he was of a different kind to me – he did get lots of women but it was because he flashed his cash around and used it as bait; they were just after his money. He didn't have that natural talent I, and other characters I had come across, shared. I suspected that if he lost his money, he would lose the women. All the same, we got along very well; we connected over women and money.

The first night out with him and his crew, I got a first-hand taste of what the Bronx is really like. They took me to a club on Boston Road. I had only been in there an hour when some guys burst into the club and shot three men. Two of them died. It was all over the news the next day.

One of his crew, Rikki, was identical to me. I don't mean in looks – more that he had that *invisible stuff*. He had women all over the place, and I was to find out later that they were giving him more money than his weekly wage. I guess that's why he and I became the closest. We understood each other.

Then there was Sham. He was a youngster who had come over from Jamaica and was trying to find his way; he was really struggling when I met him. I liked him. There was something genuine about him, but most of all I always saw myself in him – he reminded me of when I was fourteen and I had been kicked out; of that helplessness I felt in not knowing how I was going to survive. I sensed the same thing with him and I didn't want him to turn into a criminal or make the same mistakes I had. I guess that's why I couldn't help myself from giving him a helping hand financially whenever he needed it.

Then there was Rocco, a trigger-happy thief. He smoked weed all day and lived and breathed rap music. I could tell he was delusional; he couldn't separate the fantasy of rap and the reality. The one thing my instincts told me about him was to never trust his ass. In the end my instincts were proved right.

Then there was Lucas. He wasn't part of that crew but we all knew him very well – he was close; you know, one of those guys who keeps himself to himself and just concentrates on making money; and he did that very well, selling drugs. One of the big differences I noticed about New York compared to England was how much more money the drug dealers were making. Maybe the ones I knew in England were small-timers, but even so, this lot were making serious dough. But as tempting as it was, I didn't get into it.

One morning when Cali had left my aunt's apartment, my aunt came in from work. I had noticed for the last week or so she had been acting funny. But I didn't know why, so I had tried to stay there as little as possible.

She came out of the bedroom with a pair of knickers in her hand and said, "What the fuck is this?"

"Knickers," I replied, totally confused.

"Yes! That dirty girl's knickers! What the fuck are they doing under my bed?" she shouted, not waiting for my answer.

Why the hell would Cali leave her knickers there? I thought. I called her straight away and asked her. As I expected, she told me to stop being so silly.

So why was my aunt making this up? Had she planted the knickers there? It was obvious she wanted me out, but why? I called my mum and told her what was happening; we both came to the conclusion that my aunt Grace had only let me stay because she had heard I'd come into some money, and when she realised none of it was coming her way, she wanted me out.

Over the next few days she niggled at me about loads of different things, making it very clear that it was time to leave. So I left: I packed my stuff and moved into a motel. But I knew I couldn't stay there for long; it was too expensive. I called Cali and explained my circumstances. She assured me she would look for an apartment for us and her kids. But the problem was, I needed somewhere now.

On the third day in the motel I bumped into a woman named Cathy when I was coming back from the store. She lived around the corner in a big house with her family. It turned out her mother had two spare rooms in the basement. *Bingo! So what happened? I gave her some of the good stuff...*

I must have been living there for a month or so when Cali and I got married at a registry office. Her brother Fox was the witness. I remember when he turned up the first thing he said to me was, "What kind of bootleg wedding is this?"

I didn't answer him. I knew it was bootleg all right, but it wasn't meant to appear that way. The thing is, I did fancy Cali, but I'm sure I wouldn't have married her if I didn't need my papers. Although Cali knew I was getting married for that reason, I have a sneaky suspicion she was thinking it would eventually turn into a genuine marriage. But I guess it was more than obvious to Fox that I was marrying her for my stay. After all, there was no honeymoon or celebration; after the ceremony I went straight out with Zane and Rikki.

Two weeks later we got a three-bedroom apartment. Cathy didn't like that one little bit; she did everything possible to try to keep me at hers in the basement where she had me at her disposal and could jump on me when she liked. But I was out.

Once I was settled in the apartment, I felt relief... I was starting to feel like the Bronx was my home. And as soon as I felt comfortable, I went to work. *Womanising!* There was not one night I wasn't in the clubs. I became very popular in the Bronx, and everyone started calling me English. How was I living? Off women, and my wife, of course! I did treat my wife occasionally, but usually from some other woman's pocket. Life in the Big Apple was starting to taste sweet.

Then I got a call from home. It was Azaria. She was upset, frantic. "Mark is threatening to shoot me!"

To be honest, all I could think about was my daughter. I just wanted to know whether my angel was okay or in any danger. "Why?" I asked her.

"I don't know! Something's happened and he's going mental."

I was furious; I remembered the promise he had made to me that his sh*t wouldn't come near my daughter. As much as I couldn't stand Azaria, I knew whatever was happening would probably filter down to Fate somehow, and I had to protect her at all costs.

"Give me his number now."

She gave me the number and I hung up. I placed the call to his phone. "Mark, what the fuck is going on? What's this shit about your threatening to shoot Azaria? Are you mad? Didn't I tell you, 'Don't fuck about, don't get my kid involved'?"

"I know, but Azaria is crazy! She keeps threatening to shop me to the police, and it's serious!"

Straight away I knew this problem stemmed from Azaria. I knew her too well – that was exactly her aggressive style, never knowing when to shut it.

"Listen, I will deal with her and make sure her mouth is shut, but don't threaten her again – it's my daughter I'm talking about here."

"Okay, I hear you. Just get her to keep her mouth shut, please."

I hung up. I called Azaria only to tell her to keep her fucking mouth shut, and not to drag our daughter into her bullsh*t. She promised me she'd do as I said. I didn't even ask what it was she was keeping quiet about. I wasn't interested.

Sometime later I got a phone call from Azaria; Mark had been arrested for shooting three people and was all over the national news – one of them had died. I was speechless; this man had actually been living there with my daughter. I hung up on her. She made my blood boil.

Roughly one year later, I called Ms Carlton to see how she was doing. Straight away she started quizzing me about the money. I was evasive and switched the conversation. It was then she told me that she wasn't well. After the phone call I remember lying on my bed, staring at the ceiling, and reflecting on England. I started thinking about 101 and wondering whether it would come back or whether I had missed my one opportunity. Somewhere in between, my mind ran on to Bianca and the whole bank situation. I felt compelled to phone her. I wanted to know if she was okay and what had happened to her. I jumped off the bed, went to the corner store, and bought a phone card. I hesitated for a few seconds, and then I placed the call. She answered.

I paused, and then I heard her say, "Jay, is that you?"

"Yes, Bianca, it's me. How are you?"

"I'm cool. How are you?"

"I'm not doing too good," I lied.

"I bet you've spent all that money, haven't you?"

"How did you know?" I lied again.

"That's you all over…"

I couldn't believe it; she was as calm as anything. Eventually, we got down to what had happened. She told me she had got off with a fine and community service because her solicitor had said she had done it under duress. When she told me that, I felt much better in myself. Many times my conscience had pricked me about her. I didn't like the fact that I had left her in all that trouble, but I had justified it when I remembered that she had set Kain on me.

Then she started telling me she wanted to see me. At first I was sceptical, as I still wasn't a hundred per cent sure how Kain had found out. As if reading my mind, she told me, "I wasn't the one who told Kain, you know? I told my friend about it and she told her brother, Twigs, who told Kain."

If that was really what had happened, Bianca must've known her friend would tell Twigs, and that it would get back to Kain. My instinct also told me that she missed me.

She said, "Can we meet in Miami? I'll book the hotel and your flight?"

"Okay, you book it up and call me on my mobile."

I gave her the number and hung up. I couldn't believe it! Was she nuts?! Or was she setting me up? Really, I knew I shouldn't go, but I couldn't resist.

When Cali got in from work I told her I had to make a trip to Miami to meet my mother. I was glad she didn't ask to come, because I would have had to have come up with another lie.

So two weeks later I arrived at the strip in Miami and Bianca was there, waiting. I was as sceptical as hell. But after maybe a few hours I started to relax. I realised it was just *love*.

With all the things I had done to her, her eyes were still firmly shut!

Later that evening she took me to the mall and bought me some clothes. It was when we were leaving and heading for the taxi rank that I spotted two women walking by. One was giving me that look. *You know the one!* She was as sexy as hell. I can't even remember her name now but I sure remember what she looked like. She had lovely caramel-brown skin with long golden hair and long legs. When we got to the taxi rank I told Bianca to wait there while I went back and quickly checked how much a money clip I had seen earlier cost. I ran back inside the mall and quickly found the woman; I told her I was on vacation from New York (women always seem to like out-of-towners!), quickly gave her my number, and told her to call me.

When I got back to the taxi rank Bianca and I went back to the hotel. We had a long chat, and as we did it crossed my mind that the real reason she had come out to Miami was to see if I still had the money, which of course I had no intention of admitting. Later that evening, when I was by the pool, my phone rang. I knew it was that women from earlier; I could see it was a Miami number. The truth was, I hadn't stopped thinking about her since I'd met her. We had a little chat and we agreed to meet just outside my hotel at eleven p.m. At about ten o'clock I told Bianca I was tired and going to bed; I knew she would want to be in it with me. Then I put my phone on silent. At about quarter to eleven, when we were settled, I jumped out of the bed and told her I was going to walk on the beach as I had some thinking to do. Then I got dressed and left. I skipped all the way down the stairs, thinking about getting in between the sexy woman's long legs!

When Ms Sexy (whatever her name was – that's what happens when you've been around too much: you start forgetting their names) finally arrived at twelve (she'd rung, very politely, to tell me she was running late) we had a chat outside the front of the hotel. Then I went to reception and booked another room in the same hotel; it turned out the only room they had available was six doors down from the one I was booked into with Bianca. As the front-desk man was handing me the key he gave me a look as if to say, "Are you crazy?" I shot him a look back as if to say, "Mind your own fucking business."

When we got in the room we started drinking and talking – you know, the formality stuff. I remember we got quite drunk that night. I don't really recall all the stuff she was saying one bit; she was so sexy I couldn't concentrate. She had the longest legs I had ever seen, and legs had been my thing from a very young age. When we were plastered, I just went into *bold* mode. I just told her to strip, *and she did*. When she was naked I asked her to dance for me, *and she did*. There was something about American girls; it was as if they had no inhibitions – well, not this one; she wasn't shy at all. When she finished dancing, I told her to put her heels back on, *and she did*. My baton was going through the roof as I made my last request for her to put her big belt back on, *and she did!* I was up and naked in a flash. I kissed her all over, slowly, and finally, when I knew she was gagging, I worked the passion button, and worked it, and worked itttttttttttttt.

****

I had picked up a valuable observation that I would say goes over many men's heads. How I hadn't realised it younger is beyond me. What am I talking about? The passion button! Now, forgive some of us men, ladies, for not realising how important that button actually is. My ego had blocked me from seeing that one simple fact – it's more about working the outside as opposed to the inside!

****

When she started squirming, I quickly spun her around and entered her from behind. I started slowly then, picking up pace, I bent her forward and ringed the belt into my palm from behind, and then... I rode her like a damn horse! It was a fantastic night.

When I awoke it was eight a.m. I jumped up; she was still fast asleep. I quickly said my goodbyes to her and left. As I came out of the room and passed the next door, I saw Bianca coming out of her room.

"Where have you been?" she asked.

"I told you, I've had a lot of things on my mind. I was down on the beach all night."

"What's the matter with you?"

"Nothing, just got some problems."

"You haven't got any money, have you?"

"No... but it's not your problem."

"Are you going for breakfast now?"

"Yes, I am. I'll see you in a minute."

As soon as I got in the room I took a shower and thought about that sexy woman who was probably still six doors down.

For the next two days everything went smoothly. Bianca got the attention she wanted, and I got the holiday I wanted!

The few days after my night with the Ms Sexy we met two girls down at the bar – well, I met them and introduced them to Bianca. One of them had that hot Filipino look. I fancied her and I could tell she fancied me. We all had a few drinks and a chat. I said I was going to bed, but the truth was, I wanted to get Bianca to go to bed so I could whip back downstairs to the Filipino lady. So after twenty minutes of being upstairs I told Bianca I was going for a walk on the beach again. This time I promised her I wouldn't be too long.

When I got downstairs the ladies were still there. After a while I knew the Filipino lady and I were thinking the same thing – *Why doesn't her friend just go to bed!* It was that unspoken eye contact thing. I knew I wasn't going anywhere. I guess she thought the same. Eventually, the friend said she was going to bed, and we were left on our own. So we continued having a chat. She started asking questions about Bianca, who she was to me. Obviously, I told her the truth, which was that she was a friend who was visiting me from England!

The thing is, I actually liked this Filipino lady. There weren't many women in my life I actually took a shining to personality-wise, but she was one of them. She seemed to be very educated, and she was very pretty. At about two a.m. I convinced her to come upstairs with me, which meant I had to go through the whole process of booking a room again. The front-desk man didn't bat an eyelid this time; he was the picture of discretion.

When we got in the room we talked and talked for ages; she was very easy to talk to. Did I go for the kill? Of course

I did, but she wasn't having any of it. All she kept going on about was, "I want to know who you really are before I even think about sleeping with you."

****

DAMN! Smart girl! She wasn't allowing her emotions to get in the way of finding out what my true character was!

****

In the end, we just fell asleep on the bed.

When I woke up it was breakfast time. I quickly told her I would catch up with her later and found my way back to my room.

Bianca was getting ready to go down for breakfast. She didn't say anything and neither did I. I just went straight to bed. I don't know how long I was lying there, but a door slam woke me. It was Bianca.

"You fucking bastard."

"What's the matter with you?"

She must've somehow found out that I wasn't on the beach at all.

"One of the staff just told me you booked a room with that fucking chink last night… On the fucking beach, is that what you call it?"

"Stop chatting rubbish! I wasn't in any room last night." I was fuming at the fact that one of the staff had actually said that. "Who said that to you?"

She described the man, and I knew exactly which one she was talking about: the greasy-haired barman. I could tell he was the jealous type.

I jumped out of bed and got dressed. I marched downstairs to that fucker. He noticed me coming and I could see the fear in his face. Idiot, had he expected her not to say anything?

When I approached him I said, "Listen, I'm going to ask you this once. Did you tell Bianca that I booked into another room in the hotel with a woman?"

"No, sir, I did not… I don't know what you're talking about. Why would I say something like that?"

I had a good mind to punch him in the mouth, but I changed my mind. I went back to the room and found Bianca sitting on the bed.

"He told me he doesn't even know what you're talking about."

Without a word, she flew out of the door.

I got back into bed. I couldn't have been in the bed more than ten minutes when the phone rang. It was the hotel manager. He told me my girlfriend had just punched one of his staff in the face and that the police had been called.

When I got down to reception, the hotel manager was waiting for me; he explained what had happened. I pulled him aside and told him the real story, what was really going on, and how his member of staff was bang out of order for interfering in my personal business. To my surprise, he totally saw things from my point of view and was furious that his staff member had been so indiscreet. I persuaded him it was his duty to sort this issue out with Bianca, so he did; he told her that this was not the first time that this particular member of staff had done something like this and that he was already on his final warning.

"If I were you," said the manager, "I wouldn't listen to a word he says; it's clear to see he has some serious issues."

On top of squaring things with Bianca, he upgraded us to a five-star hotel up the road and gave us a full apology. *Now that's what I call first-class service!!!*

What happened after that? Well, everything went back to normal and I behaved myself. When the vacation came to an end, Bianca begged me to come back to London. *No way!*

When I got back to New York, my wife had what she thought was a surprise for me – she had a new tattoo. She had put a gate on her breast and written over it were the words 'Jay's property'. Now, don't get me wrong, I found it quite flattering; but in my opinion she had far too many tattoos already. I had one tattoo on my arm – it was a bottle of Dom Pérignon and a stack of money with a girl in a champagne glass holding a gun. What had made me get it? I'm not sure, but I think it described my life quite well. But some of hers I just found to be too distasteful... like the handprint tattoos going up her leg towards you-know-where. Who the hell would marry a woman with that on her body? Not bloody me, that's for sure! Well, not for love…

For the next year or so I cheated on my wife left, right, and centre. Every night I was out with the crew in the clubs. Occasionally, I would witness a shooting; one night a man died right in front of me, and he hadn't even been the shooter's target. But hey, that was the Bronx.

In the daytime I would sometimes collect the kids from school and spend some time with them. And sometimes I would go with Zane to drop off some drugs. After a while I saw how much money he was making so I invested some money in his drug business, but I refused to work it with him. I loved money, but not enough to risk prison again. At the end of the week he would bring me back what he had spun for me, which turned out to be a great set-up for me.

During this period everything was going great. England was out of my mind, but I kept in regular contact with my mother and my daughter, and occasionally I spoke to Stretch and Bianca.

Eventually, I decided to go and pay a visit to my uncle Kojac in Orlando, but before I went I arranged for my mother to bring my daughter out so I could take her to Disneyworld. I caught a plane down there a week before they were due to arrive so I could mess about with a woman who I had previously been boning.

When I arrived at my uncle's he was glad to see me. One of the first things he asked me was whether my 101 had come back. I guess he was puzzled by the whole thing and wondered if I had struck it rich in his absence. I reassured him that I hadn't seen it again since the last time I missed the lotto. In the back of my mind I wished it would come back.

For that week I hit the club and messed around with this woman, Belinda. She wasn't the best-looking of women, but she was probably the best lay I ever had, really. She had moves that brought me to heights of ecstasy that no woman ever had.

My mum and daughter arrived – with the Monster, which I wasn't expecting. Seeing my daughter made me extremely happy. I couldn't let her go. I noticed she was starting to look like my mother. That same evening my uncle's phone rang – it was Azaria. She was talking sh*t, saying that she was coming out to Orlando the next day because she wanted another baby from me. Well… you know what I told her to do – get lost!

The next evening, when Fate had gone to sleep, I went to a club and got smashed. When I got back and went in my bedroom I got the shock of my life – Azaria was lying in my bed with a great big smile on her face. My initial reaction was shock – I couldn't believe it – but it quickly turned to anger.

"What the fuck are you doing here?"

I could see the disbelief on her face – for some reason she had not expected that reaction from me. "Jay, I want us to have another baby," she replied very weakly.

Another baby? Are you sick? I wouldn't have another baby with you if you paid me, I thought. My eyes squinted as I looked at her in disbelief and disgust. I could not believe Azaria had the cheek to ask me for another baby after going with somebody I knew.

"Get the fuck out of my bed, now."

Just as she began to move, my mother walked in. "Jay, leave her alone," she said. "I told her to come out here."

"What the hell did you do that for? I can't stand her!"

My mother looked shocked.

"Listen, Mum, I don't care how this was arranged or why, but just get her out my bed now."

"And where do you expect her to sleep exactly?"

"I don't care. All I know is, she's not sleeping in here."

"Jay, please stop shouting at me and listen. You're waking everybody up. There is nowhere for her to sleep apart from in here."

I was furious; but she was right. I sat on the end of the bed with my hands on my forehead. My mother left the room and went back to bed. For some time I sat there in silence. I was angry with them both. I couldn't believe my mother had let Azaria come out to Orlando, as if we were some happy couple. It was obvious my mother wanted us to get back together and had no idea how much I couldn't stand her.

As soon as I had thrashed out all my thoughts I climbed into the bed with my back to Azaria.

She said, "Jay, why are you treating me like that?"

I just wanted her out of my sight. I was so angry, I just ignored her.

"Jay, please give me another baby. Isn't it better I came to you for it? You know I still love you."

I didn't answer; I put the pillow over my head to block out the sound of her talking.

She climbed on top of me. "What the hell is wrong with you? Everyone sleeps with the mother of their child – what is wrong with you?"

I looked her right in eye. I could no longer hold my silence. "I don't fucking care about anyone else, I'm never sleeping with you again!"

To my amazement she did the unthinkable and grabbed my baton. Now as you can imagine my split second reaction was rage, but the next was *boing, boing, boingggg!*

The next morning, I felt dirty. I was disgusted with myself for being so weak. In the end I told myself it was because of the alcohol I had drunk at the club before I came in. From that day until the day she left I barely spoke to her. I also made a mental note never, ever to make such a mistake again.

But I had a fantastic time with my family. Funnily enough, for the first time in a long time the Monster and I spoke – not that much, mind you, he just asked me general stuff like how I was getting on in New York, how I found it compared to London, and stuff like that. I just kept it brief. Somehow we even managed to play chess; he had drilled it into me from the age of seven. However, I was aware he wasn't showing his true colours, probably because Kojac was there.

The day Fate and my parents left I felt like crying. Being so far away from Fate was taking its toll on me. I kissed her and whispered in her ear that I loved her more than the whole world and that I would send for her soon. It was the tenth of September, 2001.

The very next morning I was due to fly back to New York but I had a change of plans – all flights were suspended until further notice due to some crazy attack on the Twin Towers, including mine. So I ended up back at my uncle's with Belinda, watching the whole fiasco on the news.

Two days later I was able to get a flight out. Belinda dropped me at the airport and kissed me goodbye. I had no idea what was about to happen!

When I boarded the plane I noticed that the plane was empty; there were maybe five or six people on the flight. I suppose it was to be expected, considering what had just happened. I remember joking with the flight attendant, saying I wanted to sit at the front so I could handle any terrorists on board; he laughed with me. It was a strange situation.

When I went to my allocated seat, I phoned Rikki to tell him what time I was coming in so he could pick me up at JFK Airport. As I was on the phone, one of the stewardesses politely asked me to turn off my phone. I assured her I would be two seconds, and she said, "Okay." When I came off the phone I settled into my seat and sank into some deep thought, biting on my phone antenna.

Suddenly, another stewardess shouted at me to get off my phone. Now, you know I'm not the kind of person who likes to be told what to do, let alone be shouted at; I wasn't even on my phone. I snapped back at her, "I'm not on my bloody phone."

At this point the plane was moving along the runway. But then I felt the plane come to a halt. The next thing I knew the pilot was sitting on the arm of my chair telling me that if he turned back the plane I was going to get arrested.

"Arrested? For what?"

The pilot didn't say another word. He began to walk back towards the cockpit. I could tell by his body language that he was going to turn back the plane. So I jumped up out of my seat and went towards him, to reason with him. It was at that point he broke into a sprint.

Here we go again!

When the plane docked back at the gate, a few FBI officers came on and demanded I get off the plane. I was so pissed off that it had gone this far that I was being nothing but arrogant. I couldn't wait to get back to the Bronx, and I knew if I came off then the plane was leaving without me.

"I'm not coming off this plane," I replied.

"Sir, I won't ask you again," Robocop continued.

"You don't have to ask me again. I just told you, I'm not moving. I've done nothing wrong."

I knew full well they were about to go for me. They didn't wait another second; they rushed me. With every drop of strength I had, I put up a fight. For some time they were struggling to get me restrained. At one stage I remember my head had ended up under the seat. But I knew they would win in the end.

Once they had me in handcuffs they began to walk me down the aisle to the exit. The plane was virtually empty, but I remember seeing one woman's face; she looked so worried – she must've thought I was a terrorist. When they had me outside the plane I heard them discuss what they could charge me with. Finally, one of the officers said, "Just charge him with assault."

Before I knew what was going on, I was carted off down corridors and thrown into a cell somewhere deep inside the airport with the handcuffs still on. I remember thinking, *What is the point of leaving the cuffs on? I'm in a bloody cell!*

Only then did I wish I had complied. It was now going to take me a lot longer to get to New York.

CHAPTER 24
A DOWNWARD SPIRAL

Forty minutes later they came back with a folder. The file had everything about my whole life. I couldn't believe it. I found it quite astonishing.

The officer with the folder said, "Bit of a menace, aren't you? Six years, that must have been a tough time."

I didn't respond.

Then he looked at another officer and said, "He's a bit of playboy too."

And instantly I looked up.

"You're a playboy, right?" He started laughing, as if it were impossible.

I still didn't answer, but I wondered if it was a result of Bianca and the bank incident – I wasn't sure. I couldn't believe it; they even knew I was a womaniser! It was officially on my record!

Then they started some bullsh*t about how they knew I had terrorist friends. Was I scared at that point? I was; I was worried they were trying to stitch me up. But they were just fishing. Terrorist friends my arse!

After the brief interview I was taken to the county jail – you know, the whole chains and jump-suit crap. They put me in a cell with about fifteen other men. Now, if you thought English jails were bad, this was a whole new realm of horror – the toilet was in the corner with no cover. There was a cell opposite with the same see-through toughened plastic; everybody could see everybody's movements. Talk about taking a sh*t with an audience! I didn't sleep a wink.

The next morning they took us down to this big room. I couldn't believe my eyes – on the left side of the room there were women in blue jump-suits. I thought, *What the hell! Women in the same prison as men!* But what really grabbed my attention was the fact that the judge was on a TV screen and that's how we had to communicate with him.

Eventually, it was my turn to deal with the judge. When he started to speak to me he said, "Mr Johnson, are you stupid?"

I guess he was referring to the fact the Trade Centre had just been blown up and, in his opinion, I had made a nuisance of myself on the plane.

"Are you stupid?" I replied.

The other cons started laughing.

I don't recall much else of what he said; all I know is he didn't give me bail. So I was taken back up to the cells.

Eventually, I was given a phone call, and I phoned my uncle and told him that I needed bail money and to call my wife and let her know what had happened. He wasn't happy with me, and he showed it in his delay in bailing me out.

I was taken to 'main population' and allocated a cell with around twelve cons. *What the hell is this?* I thought. They looked big, and I mean really big. I found out later they had suspended everyone from using the gym because the inmates were getting so big they were intimidating the staff!

There was one particular convict on the top bunk next to my bed. He was a big guy, or was he a big woman? I didn't know what the hell he was. All I knew was, I didn't want him or her to say one word to me. I made it clear by the look on my face. The whole time I was there, I slept with one eye open!

When it was time for dinner the door was unlocked and we all had to walk down some steps to the mess hall. I couldn't eat the food; prison food really sucks when you first go in, until hunger sets in and then it gradually becomes normal. Well, I wasn't that hungry yet so I just left it for the other inmates to fight over.

I was about to get up when the screw said, "You're the one who got arrested on the plane, right?"

"How do you know?"

"Your mug shot was all over CNN News."

I was shocked! It was the second time I had made the national news! I had been on the news back in England when I was in Feltham. Now I was on it again. And it was the second time I'd been arrested on a plane. There seemed to be a *pattern* emerging!

I got bail a month later. Belinda was there to pick me up. She kept going on about how she had been in bed that morning with her back to the TV when she had heard the anchorman say, "Man gets arrested going to New York." Before she'd even turned around and looked at the screen, she knew it was me – Mr Attitude!

When I eventually got to court, I pleaded 'not guilty'. The judge begged to differ, and found me guilty in a minute flat. He gave me a fine and ordered me to attend anger management classes – and I had to stay in Orlando until I'd completed them.

I was fuming at first, until I saw the probation officer – lady! – who kindly attempted to arrange for me to complete the classes back in New York. Unfortunately, New York State wouldn't accept it, so I eventually had to go back to Orlando to complete them. The classes were boring and unconstructive; I didn't think I actually had an anger problem anyway!

Eventually, after a long detour, I was back on home ground in the Bronx. But back in New York it was as if a dark cloud had come and hung itself over my head. A number of things happened back-to-back that sent me on a downward spiral.

When I arrived back at the apartment, the landlord was there to greet me; he whispered in my ear that while I'd been away a man had been visiting Cali on many occasions, late at night. I was shocked, but I didn't lose my temper. Did I say anything to her? Of course I didn't! But I still wanted conformation, so this is what I did...!

I waited until a couple of days had passed, then I applied the 'similar scenario' technique. I fabricated a similar scenario about my cousin and her boyfriend. First of all, I made sure she was very relaxed, so the body language would be easier to read. I was also looking for something specific that I knew would be a dead giveaway! The conversation went like this:

"Cali, do you know what I found out today? I can't believe it: my cousin is cheating on her man."

"Is she?"

"Yes."

I stopped the conversation right there on purpose. Now I was waiting for how she would continue the conversation, if at all. It was as I thought: she changed the subject!!! She didn't ask me how I'd found out. She didn't ask if my cousin's boyfriend knew, and so on. Obviously, she was doing the same thing and she felt uncomfortable. Innocent people show interest and want more detail; guilty people avoid the subject and quickly want to talk about something else. I had my conformation without her realising she had given it to me.

I was getting wiser; it couldn't benefit me to show her I knew what had been going on. After all, she was paying the rent for the roof over my head. It just hurt my pride a little bit. But I had no intention of staying with her; I just wanted my stay in America.

So what did I do? I went in and jumped into bed with her, and told her how much I'd missed her and how much I loved her. For a few months I played happy families, but secretly I couldn't stand her arse... Cheat on me? How dare she! I was Jay Johnson! I did the cheating, not the other way round! One night, around this time, I was out with Rikki when we bumped into Lucas, a friend of the crew. Lucas was angry. Rocco (remember, that delusional rap fanatic) had brought some out-of-towners to buy weed from him; when the transaction was complete and Lucas had gone home to put the money away, he'd realised he'd been given sixteen thousand dollars' worth of dud money. We stood there discussing whether Rocco had actually known it was dud money: personally, I believed he knew – everything in my body knew Rocco was a snake. Before Lucas left, he decided he was going to shoot Rocco in his ass to teach him a lesson.

Lucas was older than us. Although he sold drugs, he wasn't naturally the trouble-making type; he just felt he had to teach Rocco a little lesson. In many ways I wanted Rocco to be taught a lesson too; I guessed it was only a matter of time before he did some crazy snake move on me.

Lucas was true to his word. He shot him in the ass. When I saw Rocco next he was still walking funny, even though he had already come out of the hospital. I asked him what had happened, as if I didn't know!

His reply told me Lucas needed to be careful. "Lucas shot me… Does he think I'm a punk?" I could see it in his eyes: he wanted revenge.

One month later Lucas was found murdered in his car. The murderer was never caught. There was some talk that it might have been these guys from Brooklyn; I couldn't understand why no one suspected Rocco. Now, I can't say this for sure, but I would have put everything I owned on the killer being Rocco. But I kept my suspicions to myself.

Then Zane, who had been spinning around my money for me, got arrested. He had been turning over money for me for some time now, and always came through with the readies. I guess I got greedy and gave him a lump sum to work with. After he got arrested the police raided him and his girlfriend's house and the safe house, and they found everything. Zane ended up in Rikers Island Prison, and I ended up a hundred and twenty grand down. I was devastated. I didn't know where to turn. The authorities deported him back to Jamaica. Until this day I have never heard from him again. I did, however, see his girlfriend not long after he was arrested. She had already found a new man who happened to be one of the biggest money spenders in the Bronx!

They say, when it rains, it pours. Shortly after Zane got deported, Cali said she couldn't afford the fourteen hundred dollars per month rent any more, and that she was going to move back in with her grandmother. Now, I had some money left, about seven grand or thereabouts, but it wouldn't last long if I had to pay the rent.

I was in trouble, and I knew it.

This wasn't going to look good on my application to stay in the country. As much as I tried to convince Cali to stay, the reality was, it was impossible. So she went back to live at her grandmother's with the kids, and I went back to Cathy's basement. It was a huge U-turn. I was really under pressure. I didn't know what to do. I knew the rest of my money wouldn't last long. I had a few women who gave me some small change, but to be fair, a lot of the women in the Bronx were living on the breadline. It didn't help that I had grown accustomed to partying every night and doing the whole champagne thing. Many nights I was spending around a thousand dollars.

One night I called my mother. I was feeling down and I could feel the walls were closing in on me. She told me that Kain had been spread across the centre pages of the national newspapers; the police had finally caught up with him and he had been given a lengthy stretch. I had forgotten about him, but there was still some sense of relief.

I guess I was starting to realise that I may have to return to England. I loved New York and the lifestyle I was living there, but in one swoop it had been taken from me.

I had no idea what awaited me if I went back!

CHAPTER 25
ENGLAND – THE RETURN

Eventually, it happened – my money ran out. The lifestyle I'd been living vanished, and I couldn't cope with it. I was like a tormented child. I tried my best to hang on in there, but it didn't take long to make a snap decision: it was time to go home.

When I had made up my mind, funnily enough, I felt excited about it. It was like starting over again! And I was really looking forward to seeing my daughter.

The first thing I had to do was find somewhere to stay. I had lost contact with all my London women, apart from Bianca. And living with her was out of the question. In fact, we barely spoke any more. I think time, the healer, had guided her off the Misery Ride, and she had moved on. As for the rest, they had just faded away eventually. So I ended up calling Azaria, and asking her if I could stay for a bit until I got back on my feet. She said yes, and within a week I was on a plane back to England.

When I arrived, I couldn't believe my eyes – Azaria had had another baby! When I asked her who the father was, she said it was me, and that she had fallen pregnant that time she came to Orlando. In an instant my instincts prodded me that something wasn't right. I had heard no talk that I had another daughter from her or my mum. I looked at the baby; when I did, Lakisha, the girl from college, flashed straight into my mind like a snapshot. That reinforced my instincts.

I was wondering whether Azaria was mad. Didn't she remember that I made her have a blood test for Fate? What on earth would make her think I wouldn't do it again? Or was she relying on the fact that I had done it the first time to mean I wouldn't do it again? She was always telling me how intuitive I was… She was downright stupid, if you ask me! Before I was going to take that baby on, she would definitely have to take a blood test.

I didn't say anything then, but I made a mental note to make sure I had a blood test. At the time I had more pressing issues, like getting myself back on my feet.

All that first day I played with my daughter, and we slowly got used to each other again. I went to bed early that night because of the jet lag.

When I woke up in the middle of the night the time read 1:01 – it was back again. I was happy it was back, and simultaneously confused by it – what the hell was it all about? I went downstairs and turned on Azaria's computer. I started typing 'What is the meaning of 101' into the search engines.

A few things came up, but the one that grabbed my attention was this: "By using the correspondence table A=1, B=2… Z=26, we find that 'Sun of God' gives 101." I also found a website where two people were saying they had had the same experience, and were asking if anyone could explain it. Another person had answered their question with the response, "It means spiritual growth."

I must admit, it rattled me. Sun of God? Spiritual growth? What the hell was that all about? It spooked me for the rest of the night.

The next morning Azaria tried to jump me again, but I had already decided I was never sleeping with her again, and this time I meant it. She wasn't happy and she made it clear if I wasn't giving her any I would have to leave. I promised her I would be out as soon as possible. I knew I had to find somewhere fast, and with Azaria's temperamental nature (especially since her thyroid had been playing up), she was a bit of a loose cannon.

So the first thing I did was to go and see my godmother to get some money to tide me over. Bless her, she didn't even question what had happened to my money – and I loved her for it. I remember wishing at that point that I had used the money to do something special for her instead.

My next stop was to see Ms Carlton. When I got there she was overwhelmed with joy to see me and began quizzing me about my travels. As I was going through my Orlando and New York adventures, she put an envelope on the table. Straight away I knew what was in it.

She said, "Jay, I have no need for this. You will need it more than me."

I was tempted to take it back, but my pride wouldn't allow me to. I passed it back to her and said, "It's for you."

With all my efforts, Ms Carlton would not accept the money at all. When I left I went straight to the furniture shop and bought Ms Carlton some new sofas and a plant stand. I then went to the flower shop and paid for some flowers to be delivered on the same date as the sofas. When I finished

I smiled to myself, thinking about the smile that it would put on her face.

The next thing I did was to go back to my bus garage and get my old job back. That was the good thing with a PCV licence – bus garages were constantly recruiting. I had no intention of staying there; it was temporary – you must know that!!!

As soon as I was back on the buses, one of the drivers told me that his mother had a spare room to rent. I was round there like a flash.

Driving the buses was great for womanising, so I went straight into action to build up my database again. After a while I had loads of beautiful-looking women, but not many money-women.

When I had settled down a bit I bought an MG convertible car and went back round to Azaria's and demanded a blood test. I saw the shock on her face. *Damn fool!*

Eventually, I started hanging around with Lewis and some of the guys I had left behind. Not long after that, the *bang*, it happened. The meaning of 101 revealed itself! But it was a far cry from what I was expecting. I'll never forget this period for as long as I live. I wouldn't wish it on my worst enemy.

I had just popped into a local bar after work to have a drink when I bumped into an old friend called Corrie. I hadn't seen him in years; he was one of those people who I didn't hang around with but who I would always talk to when we bumped into each other. He was a family man and didn't do the whole party scene. He made his living from fraud, things like getting money out of people's bank accounts and stuff like that.

As soon as he saw me, he said, "Where you been, *galist*?"

I ran down the whole story: bank – Kain – New York – and that I had not long been back in the country.

When I'd finished, he said, "Listen, there's this girl in the bank. I want you to chat her up. I've got some serious links to get some serious money out of there. I've sent in loads of guys but they can't get her number. If anyone can do it, I know you can!"

"Okay, I'll do it!" I replied, but in the back of mind I wasn't really interested. He told me where she worked, in which bank, and then we moved on and talked about other stuff for a while.

When he was leaving he reminded me, "Don't forget that girl in the bank, okay?"

"I won't."

I forgot about her the moment he left.

Two weeks later, I had a call from Lewis. "Jay, there's a nice party down at Daniel's Lounge."

"I can't tonight. I've got work at seven," I replied.

"Okay then, chat tomorrow."

He hung up. Five minutes later the phone rang again. It was Lewis. "Jay, you've got to come down to this club. It's gonna be banging with chicks."

"Lewis, I can't, seriously! I'm tired and I've got work."

"Oh, okay." He hung up.

Now here's the thing. On many occasions he had called me to come out. At times I had told him I couldn't because I had to work, and he had never pressured me. But on this particular night, damn, he was like a pest. Before I could get back to sleep, the phone rang again.

"No, come on, Jay! I'm telling you, this party is going to be off the chain!"

"Lewis, what *is* the matter with you?"

"Nothing, why? Just get up and come on!"

I gave in. "Oh, all right!"

"I'll come and pick you up soon. That's what I'm talking about!" he laughed.

I had never been to this club before. It had a large lounge area with a bar and downstairs was just one big dance floor. As soon as I arrived I began to see all the familiar faces from my past. I got some drinks for Lewis and me, and then we sat down opposite the bar on the couch.

I couldn't have been sitting there for more than ten minutes when I saw this woman coming through the entrance; she slipped as she came through the door. I slapped Lewis's leg. "I have to have that girl."

She looked a lot like Azaria when I had first met her, although younger and fresher. Everything about her was put together perfectly. I remember thinking to myself, *I should wait a bit before I approach her*, and then, *I'm not waiting at all – somebody else might get her before I do!*

So I approached her at the bar and introduced myself to her and her friend. I can honestly say at that moment when I was at the bar I don't remember fancying anybody like that ever in my whole life, and it probably showed. I had never believed in love at first sight, but now I wasn't so sure.

She told me her name was Summer. I invited them over to have a drink with me and Lewis. They accepted, and the character he was, he had them fully engaged and laughing their heads off. I couldn't take my eyes off her – honestly, she had me hypnotised.

At one point some guy I knew came over and sat down with us, and for some reason her attention turned to him, or so it appeared. I could see he was getting hypnotised too. When she left to powder her nose, I made no bones about telling him to f**k off. I think at first he thought I was joking, but when I repeated it he finally got the message.

Eventually, I made my move for the number. I don't recall what she said, but I remember she wasn't having any of it. At some point she told me her stepmother was having a party up the road and asked me and Lewis if we wanted to come. I jumped at the invitation. It wasn't until after that party, when we were saying our goodbyes for the night, that she slipped me her number.

When I got in I had roughly two hours before I was meant to be starting work. I didn't go. I was tired and over the moon I had met this girl. Don't ask me why; I just was.

The next time I saw her was when we arranged to go to the movies. I remember she insisted on paying; I made a mental note of it. Was that the sign of a good woman? After the movies, I wanted to take her to bed but I didn't try it.

Over the next few weeks we got together maybe six or eight times, and every time it was outside her house. I would call her when I was outside, and she would come out and sit in my car and we would have a chat. We were properly dating.

It was probably during the fourth week of our dating that I was in a nightclub with Lewis and I was tipsy. I decided I was going to see her – it was pretty late and I had one thing on my mind! It had never taking me this long to get in any woman's knickers.

When I arrived, I knocked on the door. She let me in. I remember she poured me a brandy and coke in a plastic cup. We had a chat and it became clear I would not be getting any because her parents were in. I decided I was leaving, so she walked me to the door. I said goodbye and walked up the garden path.

As I got to the gate she said, "Aren't you going to give me a kiss?"

I smiled. I hadn't even got a peck on the cheek until now.

I turned around to go and give her the kiss of her life, and there it was. I couldn't believe it. The plastic cup dropped out my hand. She saw my reaction and asked me what was wrong. I was dumbstruck for a few seconds.

"Your door number is 101."

"Yes?" she replied as if I was stating the obvious.

"Oh," I said, collecting myself. "It doesn't matter."

I gave her a kiss and said goodbye. I drove home in a daze. What was that all about? Are you thinking what I was thinking? Maybe… not? Well, this is what I was thinking at the time. *No way on earth is that a coincidence. She must be the one for me. The number 101 is all about finding me my soul mate. I fancied her like crazy anyway and now her door number is 101. She must have been sent for me.*

Okay, you may be thinking, yeah, yeah, yeah? That was just coincidence. Well, wrap your head around this then! Not long after that, she told me to meet her at work, so just before she finished I went down to her workplace and discovered that she worked in a bank. Which bank? Yes, that bank!!! My friend Corrie had asked me to chat up some girl in the same bank because he wanted to do some kind of fraud from there. *No fucking way. It couldn't be, I* thought. It was! I called him and asked him to describe the girl. Yep, it was her all right!

Now, you could well be thinking that Lewis and Corrie, the fraud guy, conspired to get me to meet her. Wrong – they didn't even know each other.

The way I looked at it, 101, whatever the hell it was, had tried to get me to meet Summer through Corrie. By rights, following my previous pattern, I should have gone for the girl in the bank straight away. Remember, I had previously got twenty grand that way. But I wasn't listening, so it used another angle – Lewis! Wow! I know it sounds crazy, but how else could I look at it?

I fancied the hell of her, but now that 101 was involved I was convinced she was my soul mate. So what did I do? *I let down my guard, and nothing was left but emotions, of course!*

CHAPTER **26**
THE UNIVERSE DOESN'T SLEEP

I was head over heels in love like I had never felt before. I mean, I had been there before, but nothing felt the way I felt with Summer.

At first, when I realised I was falling in love, my initial thought was, *No, no, no, not again!* But it was always followed by, *She's got to be my soul-mate! This is something special, orchestrated from above!*

It was orchestrated all right!

In next to no time, we were living together. I had done the old doctor trick and got another flat. I got in with her family, and I was the happiest man in the world. I cut off all my women and even my friends – they barely saw me. When they did, they would take the piss.

"The *galist* is in love!"

"Wonders will never cease!"

"Remember you used to say MOB? Money Over Bitches? What *happened*?"

And so it went on. They had never seen me like this before, and it was a big shock. I guess that's why they couldn't help passing comments. Did I care? I couldn't have cared less; as long as I was with her I was happy.

I couldn't wait to introduce her to my mother, and when I did she didn't seem as happy as I thought she would be, especially as I was doing what she had been wanting me to do for years – settling down. I wasn't sure what it was – maybe it was motherly instinct; maybe she thought this was the one who was going to pay me back or hurt me in some way; maybe she thought it was just another one of my fly-by-night relationships; maybe she just didn't get a good vibe from her. Whatever it was, I could tell she wasn't over the moon. But no matter what anybody else thought or said, I was in love.

I wanted to spend every waking moment with Summer. When I went to work I couldn't wait for my shift to be over. No matter what I had to do, I would check what Summer wanted to do first. I can honestly say nothing much mattered to me apart from her, and all of a sudden I wanted to give her a better life. In next to no time I had this deep-bedded desire to become successful. I guess that's where that saying comes from: Behind every successful man is good woman. I'm not sure it means exactly that; I would say more that behind every successful man is a man who fell in love. I realised love can elevate you to another place in yourself that you never knew existed.

I believe the desire started when I came back from Brazil. Before I met Summer, I had saved up and booked the holiday; so I went along anyway. But I missed her so much that as soon as I went I wanted to come straight back. Shortly after I returned, I made a firm decision that I was going to be rich, and not only that but great too. Whether I was to be or not is irrelevant – the fact is that I believed it as much as I believed my name is Jay Johnson.

At that point, a book came across my path, *The Success Principles* by Jack Canfield. I don't think I would ever have read it before I fell in love and had this deep desire to be successful. I remember, halfway through the book, I started thinking about what it was that humans were fascinated with, what I could capitalise on? After maybe a day's thought, right or wrong I came to the conclusion that most people were interested in mobile phones and celebrities. With that in my mind, I started to try to combine the two.

For the next two weeks I went into what they call the zone. I had the ability to concentrate on solely that. I mean, I could hear when people were talking to me, and I could respond. But I was focusing so intensely on coming with up with something to do with mobile phones and celebrities that I barely noticed them. Let me put it another way – try staring at a one pence piece and holding your attention on it for as long as you can. You would probably hold it there for a minute or two before your mind drifted. Well, the kind of zone I was in, I could have held it there all day.

Two weeks later I was sitting in my living room thinking about something completely different when – wow! – it just popped into my head from nowhere. My brain had connected the two things. I later found out that apparently it's impossible to concentrate on two separate items or ideas without the brain connecting the two – that's how inventors come up with their ideas! Takes tremendous discipline to cut out all the other daily distractions, though.

My idea was a database on the phone with celebrity pictures. Let me explain... On your mobile phone you have T-zones, if you're on T-Mobile, or Orange World, if you're connected to Orange, as ways of getting on the internet. This is how it came to me – I happened to be on the T-Mobile network at the time. So imagine a database full of celebrity pictures when you clicked on to T-Zones. Then imagine you picked one of those pictures – in my case, I would probably pick Alicia Keys. You would then take a picture of yourself and upload it to that database. The database would then, for a modest fee of three pounds fifty, merge the two pictures and download it back to your phone, as if, in my case, someone had taken a picture of me and the beautiful Alicia Keys together. The celebrity would get a cut, along with the mobile service provider. I already knew that teenagers were crazy about celebrities and phones and that they were downloading fanatics, so I was fairly sure I was onto a winner. To make it worse, I kept getting flashes, like mental snapshots – I didn't know what it meant at the time but now I know it means inspiration – keep going! Take note!

The next thing that came to me was the name: ME AND MY ICON.

I ran it past Summer. She thought it was a good idea too.

That same night I stayed up on the computer researching who I should take this fabulous idea to. Every night, after work, I would do research.

Then things started to go wrong with me and Summer. I think the first sign I noticed was when I was coming from work and parking up my car, and I noticed she would always be at the front window on her phone. By the time I came into the flat, she would always be off the phone. It became a regular pattern. Sometimes I would ask who she was talking to, and she would always tell me it was her friend Barry, who I had never met or spoken to before. I remember my instinct prodded me on one of the first occasions.

Then one evening, when I was in bed and she was in the bathroom, a text message came through to her phone. I had never looked in her phone before, but at this point something was telling me to look at the text message. Every time I looked at the phone I said no to myself, but that feeling wouldn't let me go.

****

Now my past experiences have taught me that whenever I get a feeling that refuses let go of me, something is most definitely wrong! It is not to be ignored, whether in a relationship situation or anything else. It is something deep inside me that knows better than I do!

****

I looked and I couldn't believe my eyes. It was from this so-called friend Barry who, she had told me, was a long time friend. *Friend my arse!* The way the text was worded, it was obvious that Barry was more than just a friend. I knew something was going on.

I charged into the bathroom. "What the fuck is this?"

She totally ignored the question and replied, "Who are you talking to like that?"

"I'm fucking talking to you – what the fuck is this?"

She looked at the text, and was silent.

"Well?"

"Why the hell are you looking at my phone?"

Why the hell am I looking at your phone! I couldn't believe what I was hearing; here she was disregarding the content of the text! I went berserk. I held her so tight she couldn't move. She was staring at me with a look I hadn't seen before; it was a look of hate. Eventually, I let her go. She had a bruise on her cheek. She started going on about how I had hit her. I knew that tactic – it was more about diverting my attention from the text. I wasn't having any of it.

She said, "I'm leaving." She started to pack her stuff.

As mad as I was, I remember thinking, *How can this be? She is supposed to be my perfect partner* - 101 *showed me the way.* I started begging her to stay. *Dumb arse!*

She wasn't having any of it. She left, and took her stuff with her.

That night, when I finally went to bed, I couldn't stop thinking about Summer and 101. Before I fell asleep I told myself to forget the bitch and move on. When I woke up the next morning she was still on my mind, so much so that I couldn't even go to work. I couldn't get her out of my brain; I wanted to know what the hell had happened with her and that guy.

I was in deeper than I'd thought. If that had happened before, the woman wouldn't have had to tell me they were leaving – I would have put their arse out of the door myself! Yet here I was, convincing myself that maybe I was wrong!

The next day at work, everybody kept asking me what was wrong. They could see something was up from my body language. When I came home from the day shift, I called her and begged her to come home. It was crazy. I hadn't done anything wrong, yet I was doing the begging. In everything I did, I always put her first! At the end of the week she agreed to come and have a talk.

After lots of pressure about the text, she confessed she had slept with this Barry guy when I was in Brazil. Right there it clicked: that's why my instinct had prodded me when I saw her at the window on the phone. She had been talking to him but made sure I couldn't come in and hear her conversation. I was devastated. I can't put into words how hurt I was, so hurt I couldn't even get angry.

When she told me, she said, "I'm sorry. I didn't plan it," as casually as if she were saying, "I'm sorry I forgot to put the kettle on." Then she went to leave and said, "Sorry it never worked out."

My mind raced back to 101. I started convincing myself that this couldn't be the end. Against everything I believed in, the patterns were there! I begged her to come back home, and eventually she agreed. But a few weeks later, one night when she came in from the club, I could see or thought I could see that she looked flustered, as if she had just come out of a bed. My intuition said she had. I asked where she had come from and she said the club, but I wasn't having it. What confirmed it for me was the fact that as soon as I mentioned my suspicions to her she just said, "Oh… I'm going back to my mum's." I quickly dismissed everything, and begged her to stay.

From that point on I knew I was in trouble, but I couldn't do anything – I was in love.

****

Although I wasn't blinded by her shenanigans, I was still blinded – 101 had me as blind as a bat, because I had convinced myself that 101 was something special for me. WOW!

****

A few weeks later I woke up feeling sick, as if I wanted to vomit. It happened for the rest of that week. When I went to collect my daughter Fate for the weekend, I told Azaria that I had been feeling sick all week.

"Are you sure that bitch isn't pregnant by you?"

"Why do you say that?"

"Don't you remember? You had my morning sickness when I was pregnant."

It all came back to me in a flash and she was right – I felt exactly how I had the last time. Azaria had started to give me a headache when Summer came into my life. I guess she knew I had fallen for her, and she wasn't happy. She had tried everything to throw a spanner into the works; she had even wanted to fight her. But I always kept them apart.

That evening when I got home I asked Summer if she was pregnant and explained to her that I had got morning sickness when Azaria was pregnant with Fate. She dismissed it as ludicrous.

But that Sunday we went to her parents' house, and as soon as she got through the door her mother said, "Summer, are you pregnant?"

"No way! That's what Jay asked me the other day!"

"Then why has your nose swollen up?"

"I don't know. I hadn't realised."

That night, when we left her parents', we picked up a pregnancy test at the late-night chemist's. When we got home she went in the bathroom to do the test. My impatience got the better of me; as I walked into the bathroom she had her hands on her head, as if she was thinking, Sh*t... what the hell am I going to do now?

She was pregnant all right! I was over the moon! She didn't appear too happy, although she said she was.

So for three months I went through morning sickness again. On many occasions I missed work, and when I explained why to the general manager I don't think he believed me! I wasn't surprised – it was a bit of a hard one to believe – but the truth is it's not as uncommon as you would think. The phenomenon is called Couvade Syndrome. In severe cases the fathers-to-be even develop swollen stomachs that look like a 'baby bump' – incredible but true!

Although everything seemed fine, I was in torment. I couldn't let go of the fact she had slept with this Barry when I was in Brazil. It was making me lose sleep. How could this girl I loved so much do that to me?

I always put her before myself – I was truly in love – selfless.

****

Deep down, I was hanging on to this 101 thing. I kept telling myself it was going to turn out great in the end. But things just seemed to be getting worse and worse. She started talking to me like sh*t, and doing things that I used to do to other females. Everything I did, I always did with her in mind. But it was as if she didn't care.

I was trapped between a rock and a hard place; I just didn't know what to do. This love thing was stronger than anything I had ever seen or felt. On the one hand I could see she didn't love me, but on the other hand I was powerless to move on, even though she would swear blind she did love me.

****

I convinced myself it would work out in the end. I spent a lot of energy trying to make her happy.

The rest of my energy I used trying to get my business idea, ME AND MY ICON, developed. I sent it to all the major networks, and a week later I received an email from the marketing director of Orange. The email said that they were looking into the viability of the concept, and would be in touch with me shortly. I was falling over with joy! I knew it had passed the gatekeeper, which was a good sign.

When he did get back in touch, he basically told me that it was a great idea, but I would need to have rights to do something on such a scale, rights from the celebrities as well. As much as it put me on a downer, I was convinced the idea could work, so I set about finding a way to get the rights. I didn't have to wait too long – maybe three weeks – and then it got delivered to me on a plate.

As I was going through the gym door and some film crew was going in at the same time. Without telling them the whole of my idea I was able to get a contact out of them – they told me to go to Getty Images. As soon as I got home I went and looked them up. I was shocked when I saw the address for their head office – the door number was 101! Obviously, I thought, Wow! Is 101 helping me here?

That night I got Summer to do me a proposal package. The next day I sent it out to Getty, explaining that I had the mobile provider in place and that the only problem I had was getting the rights for the pictures. I was driving the bus when the vice president of Getty Images called me from the American branch. I was a bit confused as I had sent it to London. I stopped at the next bus stop and got out onto the pavement. I couldn't believe it; I was ecstatic – this was a whole new world to me, a direction I wanted to go in. He told me that he had received my proposal and that he was discussing it with some other people and would get back to me as soon as he could.

That evening, when I got home I told Summer about it all. She didn't seem that interested.

Summer had me by the balls, but even though I could see she wasn't in love with me, my guard was down and I couldn't do anything about it. How the hell had I got there? In an instant my mind flashed back to all the women I had hurt, deceived, used – all for my own selfish needs. It felt like I was feeling all their pain at all at once.

Then it clicked for me – 101 was my payback! "The universe doesn't sleep... Somebody will come and do the same to you... You reap what you sow in this life!" That's what my mother had told me. I became aware the universe had somehow got my guard down by using 101.

I would have found the whole thing funny if it weren't for the fact that I was well and truly on the Misery Ride!

CHAPTER 27
CATERPILLAR TO BUTTERFLY

For over a year, I became a recluse. I was going through a period of transformation, but I wasn't aware of it at the time.

It started when the baby arrived. A week before the baby was due, Summer and I agreed that she would stay at her mum's until the baby was two weeks old to get some support while I concentrated on putting my business idea together.

The new baby arrived; she was called Chelsie and she was beautiful. When the two weeks were up, I expected Summer and the new baby to come home. But she didn't arrive, so I asked her why she hadn't come home yet. It was then that she told me, as cool as anything, "I'm not."

At first I thought she was joking; but she was dead serious. I had no choice but to accept that it was over.

I booked a blood test for Chelsie. I didn't really doubt she was mine; I just wanted to make sure so I didn't lose even more sleep. It seemed like a good idea to also book a blood test for Azaria's second baby Chloe, who I knew in my heart wasn't my biological daughter. I wanted a clean slate, to know who was my responsibility and who wasn't.

On the day of the blood tests I picked up Summer and Chelsie, and then I went to Azaria's to collect Chloe. When

I got there, Azaria refused to let me take her. The fact that she didn't want me to take her only proved my doubt even more.

What I didn't know then was that Azaria had already taken a blood test for Chloe in my absence. She had returned to the same hospital that had performed the tests for Fate, and she had forged my signature. The test had come back saying I wasn't the father. Why on earth women say men are the fathers of kids when they aren't I will never know, but one thing was for sure – I wasn't about to father some kid that wasn't mine. *Or was I?*

In the end, it was just Chelsie who had the blood test that day. As I expected, the tests showed she was mine. But it changed nothing between Summer and me, and from then on we went our separate ways.

The thing is, my pain didn't stop there. This is the part where a man's ego tends to get in the way, and he'll never want to admit or say it – but I wanted to die! For weeks and weeks, I cried my eyes out. You may be thinking, what a wuss, but think again – if Mike Tyson can cry, anyone can…!

****

Now herein lies the reason why many men will not admit such incidents. Their ego makes them believe it is a weakness - wrong. Contrary to how it may appear, that kind of thought process comes from a position of weakness in the individual; it is really fear, fear of how other people will perceive them. The reason why I can admit I cried and everything else in this book is because I'm coming from a position of strength; I fear less! I can admit it and look anyone in the eye - overcoming any fear equals freedom and strength over weakness. Now I admit that for someone like me, who has always had a big ego, to gain that kind of inner strength and understanding took a miracle! I was unaware that miracle was just around the corner but was disguised as a disaster!!

****

I wanted her back, and I didn't care much about anything else. I even tried to go with some of my old women, thinking that would somehow fill the gap. Whenever I did, I couldn't even kiss them, let alone sleep with them. I was stuck somewhere between Summer and Summer! I tried everything in my power to get her back home, but she just wouldn't come.

Then I turned to praying every night and asking for forgiveness, not knowing my world was about to get turned upside down again. The only way I kept my sanity at the time was to throw myself into getting my business, ME AND MY ICON, developed, in the hope that it would elevate me to the top of the success chain. Then she would want my ass back, I convinced myself!

My thirst for success and knowledge jumped to a whole new level. I started reading a book a day and watching biographical programmes on successful people. I retreated to a place very deep inside myself. Every day I woke up, went to work, came home, read a book, worked on ME AND MY ICON, and went to bed. I kept going round and round like this for ages.

Throughout this period I was still yearning for Summer. What made it more difficult was the fact that we had this child together so I couldn't just cut her off; we had to keep seeing each other.

Eventually, the vice president of Getty Images got back to me – with some bad news. He told me there would be problems getting the rights because of some legal issue. What was I to say to him? I was naïve when it came to the business world. All the same, I wasn't ready to give up on the idea just yet – I had another flash of inspiration! I decided to get in contact with one of my brother's friends, Spencer, who had been the next door neighbour of a guy named Matthew. Now, Matthew had turned a millionaire overnight for something to do with telecoms. At the time I didn't know he was having some financial problems. (Yes and we all know who he is!)

I wish I hadn't contacted him; my world was about to tumble further into chaos. The day I met Matthew he started telling me that I had a good idea but that it depended on the quality of the software program and how well it would work in merging the pictures. He said he was making a phone call to someone who could create the program; he picked up the phone and dialled the number, but after a few seconds he said the phone went to answering machine. He was lying; he hadn't called anyone, my instinct told me. From that moment on, I knew I would have nothing to do with him.

It was around three weeks later, while driving the bus, that I got devastating news. My phone rang and I answered it; it was Spencer.

"You're not going to believe this. I've just seen your concept on my friend's website."

"What the fuck are you talking about? It's impossible!"

"Seriously, but my friend said he's willing to work with you and Getty Images!"

I put down the phone. I couldn't breathe. I kicked the passengers off the bus and drove to the terminal in a daze. When I got there, I called Spencer and I asked for the name and number of his friend's company. When I called I asked for Matthew; he must've been the one behind it.

The receptionist said, "Hold one minute. I'll just get him."

I couldn't believe my ears when I heard his voice on the phone – he was stealing my idea, or trying to involve himself. I went straight into the bus garage, signed off, and went straight home without saying a word to management. When I got home I put everything into my own warped perspective:

1. Matthew was at the company that was supposedly doing my idea already. If that was the case, why hadn't he said that before when I brought the idea to his attention? Lies.

2. Spencer was in on it. He was the one who had called to tell me.

3. I was going to murder them.

That night I cried again. My whole world was falling apart. The one thing I had pinned all my hopes and attention on after Summer had left me was this idea, and now it was being taken away from me too.

I called Spencer again for the name of the website. When I finally looked at it I couldn't believe it: it was exactly the same thing; they had only changed the name. It was a cheap way in. I was so upset. I later found out they were doing a cut and paste job.

The next day I struggled to even get out of bed. I just felt so sorry for myself. Eventually, I got up and called some solicitors and told them everything, to see if I had a case.

It turned out I didn't have much protection. Even though I had sent the idea to myself recorded delivery, a litigation case was going to be prohibitively expensive. Speaking to them made my blood boil.

I called Lewis. When I told him, the outcome wasn't good. Lewis made a call and got all of their addresses and family's addresses. With that I found Spencer and said, "Listen, I know you stole my idea. If I don't have some money put in my account tomorrow, I'm coming to blow your head off." And then I started to reel off his address and those of his family members.

"Jay, I didn't steal your idea! I had nothing to do with it, I swear!"

"Did you hear what I said…? I don't have anything more to say."

"But I didn't! I haven't got no money…"

"You know what? I'm coming right now. I've had enough of this shit."

I hung up. The phone rang straight away.

"What?"

"Okay, Jay. I'll give you my car and put three thousand in your account on Tuesday…"

"You fucking better," I said, and hung up.

Three thousand my arse! That was just the beginning.

That night Lewis dragged me out to a party and tried to set me up with some chick, but I was still reeling from my break-up with Summer; nothing worked – I still wanted her.

On Monday morning as I got out of bed my mobile phone rang. It was Scotland Yard telling me I had better get down to the police station immediately or they were coming to get me – it was my choice. When I asked why, they said for threatening to kill.

I quickly made tracks back home and removed some stuff from my flat in case they came around anyway. I called my solicitor and told her to meet me at the police station. When I arrived I spoke to my solicitor and told her what had happened. She strongly advised me not to say anything.

Just as the police asked us to come through to the interview room, I asked her what the time was. She said, "One minute past one." Oh God. It grabbed my attention immediately. Why the hell hadn't she just said one o'clock? For some reason, I took it as a sign to stay calm, because my blood was still boiling.

The police asked me some questions; I replied, "No comment." Eventually, they let me out on bail with strict conditions not to contact Matthew and Spencer by phone, or by any other means.

I didn't know what to do. I really felt like murdering them, but in the end I had to let it go. I swallowed down the anger, and pushed it inside. I decided there was more to 101 than just my comeuppance; my redemption was wrapped up in it too, somehow. I just needed to find out how.

For about fifteen months I became a complete hermit. I didn't return to my job; I couldn't find the strength. I had no sex, no women, no late-night visitors. I just stayed at home alone. I stretched myself out on my cream sofa under the window and read books. At times I would just lie there, deep in thought, reflecting on my life and the people around me. On many occasions I would walk into the hallway and sit on the steps with my head in my hands for hours, just feeling sorry for myself. I was at my lowest point ever.

Even though people always think their own pain is worse than anyone else's, the truth is, we never really know what someone else is going through. During this period I felt as if I was in a worse hell than anyone else had ever experienced, and that I was in there all alone. I was very confused: I had been convinced 101 was supposed to bring me some kind of good fortune, but now it appeared it had brought me the opposite. I had lost everything: my job, my woman, my daughter, my business idea that I'd thought was possibly going to make me a millionaire, even my friends because I had ignored them when I had been with Summer and now I couldn't bring myself to be around them – who wants to be around misery? My life didn't make any sense any more.

Then something strange started happening. I couldn't turn on the TV or put a movie on without feeling the characters' pain intensely; it kept bringing me to tears. It was as if I was literally in their shoes; it was insane. I had become hyper-sensitively empathetic. It didn't stop there, though. Whenever I started to feel empathy for someone, one half of my body was shouting, *What the hell are you crying for? This isn't you! You're a bad boy! Fix yourself up!* But the other half wanted to cry, and it did. This duality went on for months. I couldn't understand it. It was crazy. It was as if on my inside there was some kind of chemical reaction going on; the bad side of me was fighting against this new, empathetic side of me. Every day seemed to be one big battle.

At this point I was so weak, and I mean weak. I couldn't even go outside without feeling fearful, fearful that people could sense or see that I was weak. That same weakness led me into another state of mind: I was looking at the world differently; it was as if my whole ego had gone for a walk. Questions I wouldn't previously have asked myself were now getting my full attention: *Why do I have to be so tough? Why am I ready to jump down people's throats at the first sign of disrespect? Why do I think life is all about me? Why do I treat women like sh*t?*

These questions led me on to something I'm so grateful for that it makes my eyes water just thinking about it. I began to get what I now know are *epiphanies*. My awareness started opening up like a flower; it was as if I was being taken to another dimension. Wisdom flooded into my mind on a daily basis. I began seeing my character flaws and mistakes.

It started like this: many things that I had previously thought I had known and understood started to arrive in me visually, giving me a fuller understanding. For example, the very first thing I had my eyes opened to was attitude. I had been told thousands of times that I had an attitude, and I'd always taken it as some kind of perverse compliment – behaving badly wasn't such a bad thing, was it? But I received a vision that showed me the truth.

I saw in my mind's eye a memory of a time when I'd been on the youth team for Tottenham Hotspur football club. I was the shining star of all the players, but after a while I told the manager, "I'm not going to training any more." He stuck with me for a while, and kept picking me up for the Sunday matches, but after a while, he dropped me. I asked him why. "Because of your attitude."

Now I was reliving the episode but it was me *now*, not me *then*. I now wanted to go to training! I understood the manager was trying to make me a better player, even though I was already the star, because it would open more doors for me.

Right there and then, I saw the negative impact my attitude had had on my life. It blew me apart. I saw that my attitude was my mental view, my outlook on life. I had a choice: I could either view things negatively or positively, but the two different outlooks produced totally different results. My bad mental view, my attitude, had had a huge impact on my life, and it had cost me. Not taking my football talents to their conclusion was one of the big regrets of my life.

These kinds of epiphanies kept coming. With each one, I got a new understanding. I could clearly see I was doing things *back* to *front*! Suddenly, I was seeing all my character flaws.

Another one was integrity. I saw that my car was an empty shell; all the parts were scattered over the floor, and each part was a character trait of mine. Then, slowly, all the parts started moving into their correct place, and when everything was where it should be, the car windscreen flashed the word *integrity*. Then the car spun off.

In an instant I understood it: my character traits needed work, and when I had got them all performing well and working together in harmony, then I would finally achieve integrity – then and only then would I be unstoppable. Just by thinking it through, I realised that it is essential to tell the truth to get real results in the real world. Lies belong to the land of fantasy and make-believe, and I was done with those. Integrity, I concluded, is the ability to meet the demands of reality. If you don't possess the stuff that each real situation is demanding of you, you won't be working at your best – in my case, I felt I wouldn't be successful. Reality does not bow to us; we must meet the demands of reality. So I decided from that moment on I would dedicate every bit of my energy to developing my integrity.

They just kept coming, these violent realisations that daily opened little doors that had been firmly shut inside me. It became crystal clear to me that success or a good life cannot come off the back of anybody else, such as a woman. For me to be successful would require my own hard work, which would make me appreciate success more; there is no self-satisfaction to be had through anybody else's achievements, only your own – period. Anybody who thinks they can achieve through others is sadly deluding him- or herself, as I was.

Another realisation was that I wasn't stupid as my father had made me believe. He always said I wouldn't amount to anything and that I had two peanuts for brains, yet there I was, someone who had got the attention of one of the biggest companies in the world, Getty Images.

Here is a brief list of some other realisations.

Everything is available to me out there!

My emotions and my rational side must be working together in sync if I am to make good decisions!

My unhealthy pride is a weakness, not a strength!

My good instincts get muffled when my ego comes into play!

Successful people have a library at home: it is not a coincidence!

My inner thoughts will drive where I end up in life!

My belief is what creates my reality; I must gain control of my thoughts and make sure I believe in whatever I want!

My behaviour is just habitual; I can replace old habits with new, positive habits through repetition!

****

Now here is the most valuable bit of wisdom I understand.

First of all, there are some things I think I'm sure about and other things I will go to my grave believing, because I believe they are absolute truths! This is one of them. In fact, somebody please engrave it on my gravestone when my time is up! This unfortunately goes over the majority of people's heads. The reason it does is because it is so obvious that it is easily overlooked.

So what is this valuable bit of information? Everything starts inside you and radiates outwards, into the 'physical world'. For the purpose of my gravestone, please put 'Everything started in me and radiated outwards – what a life I created'. You're probably thinking, Euh!... Obviously! Exactly my point!! It is overlooked!!!

Okay, let me give you a clear cut example – when I was younger I would get into arguments and fights more or less everywhere I went (I didn't put all this in because it wasn't relevant to the message I wanted to get across in this book). I would go home and curse them and call them all punks. However, one day I asked myself, Can all of these people be punks? It soon became obvious that I was the common denominator: I was the punk. Once I acknowledged that, I no longer had the problem. My point is, I never changed anything on the outside; I changed the way I looked at the issue and then it changed outside. (I don't bump into punks any more!!)

This principle applies to everything in life!!! If it's not working outside then look back into yourself for the answer. The answer is never outside. Change your thoughts and the way you look at things and the results outside will change. Most people look outside of themselves to make a change – that is back to front! I have met so many women who are constantly saying, "I always meet jerks" – sorry to inform you, ladies, but your problem is not them, it is _you_!!!

****

They just kept coming. Every day I was amazed at how clear things were becoming for me.

Sometimes I couldn't help feeling angry that no one had taught me these fundamental truths at school. If they had, would I have taken some of the roads that I had chosen? I didn't think so.

It was on one of those days that I realised I wanted to reach out to the bad boys who were still walking those roads. I wanted to pass on what I had discovered, I wanted to let them know what I knew, because perhaps if they really understood what they were doing, they would change before it was too late? No matter how much I tried to let that thought go, it kept coming back – it was burning me at heart level.

I started writing down affirmations and reading them three times a day for months until it became a new habit and worked on auto-pilot. Now, this was the most painful thing: I had to unlearn almost everything I had been taught or had learned or had perceived negatively.

Here is my very first list of affirmations.

****

NO EXCEPTIONS TO THE RULE, JAY.

Never forget this, Jay – life is about value, not the value you _get_ but the value you _give_.

Discipline is key to me changing. If I want to get what I want in life, I cannot afford to be distracted by everyday stuff.

The purpose of my life is to discover my purpose. Without it, I'll just be going round in circles.

Be quick to listen, and slow to get angry. Whenever I feel emotionally moved, I will say to myself, "Now remove the emotion so the rational side of my brain can peek at the facts."

Whenever I feel I am about to get angry, I need to take the emotions (temporarily) out so I can see the situation clearly.

I won't let anyone or anything have rent-free space in my mind. I need those attention units for where I'm heading.

The past is the past. Leave it there; that's where it belongs.

Pay attention to everything.

Remember, sleeping around is selling myself short. Know my value. People who sleep around are just searching for love; they are just not aware of it. I understand that now, so there is no need to.

Treat everybody how I would like to be treated – that includes women too.

Don't look outside of myself for answers. The answers always inside me.

My thoughts are literally creating my reality, so it's essential I gain control of them.

Remember to be successful! There is no escaping the process. The universe has laws that govern: learn these laws and things will be a piece a cake.

Instant gratification is a surefire way to long-term failure. Resist – resist – resist.

I will never, ever lie or try to convince myself of something I know is not true. That is not living in reality; that is fantasy land.

I must stop harbouring feelings towards my dad. It only hurts me. He's a sad man who takes out his inadequacies on the people around him. I have to release the feelings.

****

All these things – the empathy, the crying, the epiphanies, the affirmations – all these things were happening concurrently. Let me put it another way: imagine the process a caterpillar goes through when it's inside a cocoon. The caterpillar goes through some kind of chemical change – well, that's exactly how I perceive what happened to me. I went through some kind of metamorphosis. When the process had finished, the ugly old Jay had gone and out came Jay the butterfly!

When a butterfly first emerges, though, it takes some time for it to be strong. The same went for me: I had transformed myself, but I was still weak. Slowly but surely, my strength and confidence came back. I was a new person, and ready to re-enter the big wide world!

Before I made that move, my mind kept jumping back to Ms Carlton and her saying I needed to let go of the anger I had for my father. I decided to write my father a letter. It was something I felt I had to do. I could feel he was still affecting me on a deep level.

****

Here is the letter I wrote:

Dad,

I know this letter may come as a surprise, and I assume, through habit, that your first instinct will be to throw it in the bin without reading it, saying something to yourself like "Damn fool", or hissing through your teeth. But I also assume curiosity will get the better of you and you will read it anyway, even if you pretend you didn't.

You're probably wondering why I'm writing to you. To make myself clear, this letter is more for me than it is for you. I have come to understand that although I know on the surface I have disliked you for most of my life and told myself I have put you to one side and you just exist, I now know that you still have a deep effect on my life, and the only way to rid myself of this anger is to release it. This is exactly what I'm doing by writing you this letter. But I also hope you will see things that were previously invisible to you.

Dad, one thing no one can ever take from you is that you're an extremely intelligent man, and I admire this in you. But on the other hand, you are an extremely arrogant, ignorant, impulsive man. We haven't talked for many years so you will still be under the impression I'm still the same person. You would be very wrong to make that assumption. I have wised up in ways you would never have imagined possible of me. And one of the things I have come to realise is that being unable with that intelligence to acknowledge or be aware of the simple things in life halves its impact.

For many years you have had an impact on me in ways I could never have imagined. As a child I harboured a secret hatred for you, which stemmed from the time you punched my mother in the eye. I hated you for that and still do now. The image has never left me. I always wondered why Mum never left you; I told her to on many occasions. I know it must've burnt you when I said that, but ask yourself why. If I felt you treated Mum right, it would never have even entered my head to say such a thing! Why? Because I will always have my mum's best interests at heart, no matter what. Funnily enough, deep down I will always have your best interests at heart too, but not before my mother's.

Why? It's simple – Mum showed me more love than you ever did. In fact, you showed me none. If you had shown me more love, then I guess it would be the other way round. I now know Mum wasn't strong enough to leave you. Probably in the early days she loved you; I would guess now it's more about dependency and habit.

As a child I was a bully and terrorised other kids. I now know this stemmed from you bullying me and telling me I was stupid all the time. I'm a bit older and wiser now, and I can see things more for what they were. Do you know what your behaviour does to someone's self-esteem? You know Fate is not the brightest child, yet I would never dream of telling her she is stupid! If her own father, who is supposed to know best, tells her she's stupid, what is she to believe? That she's stupid, of course!

You see, it's no good being intelligent if you miss the simple things in life.

I loved football, and I was very talented – I was told so time and time again. But instead, you tried to make me play cricket, the game you loved and were good at, totally disregarding the fact that football was my passion. It was so simple, but you couldn't see it.

Many times I have heard you tell people that they are fools and that you don't talk to idiots. I have come to realise that the biggest fools on this planet are the ones who see only their own point of view, and don't try to see things from another point of view. For many situations in this life, neither party is right or wrong – it just depends on the angle from which you are looking!

It may seem that I'm blaming you for everything. I'm not. I know some of the things you told me were for my own good – get a good education, that was one. I know I was unruly as a child, and you probably felt I was always undermining your authority.

You see, Dad, when something is not in your awareness, it means it is totally invisible to you. I couldn't see these things at the time. When I see how Paul is behaving right now, while I totally disagree with his behaviour I do sympathise with him, because I know he is blind to the advice he is receiving. He really can't see it. When I was younger, I really couldn't see it either. My selfishness, my bad attitude – I was blind to it all – it wasn't in my awareness at the time.

So for this reason, and this reason alone, I release every bad feeling I have towards you, because I know you couldn't see it and you can't see it now. People do the best they can at any given moment in time. If they don't meet your standards, sympathise with them, rather than think they are fools! They know no better and can do no better, otherwise they would, just as I knew no better then. Everyone comes into the world with different capabilities. You were fortunate in the intellect domain. And I now realise you did your best with the knowledge and awareness you had.

Dad, life is short, and I'm sure you'll appreciate that fact more than me. I know no one is here to stay, and that is why I had to get this out of my system today. I got out of bed at five o'clock in the morning to write this all down.

Like I said at the very beginning, this letter is more for me than for you. There is so much more I could put in this letter – but I now feel there is no need.

I have to forgive you, or else the subconscious effects you have on my life will keep resurfacing every now and then in my actions... my impulsive behaviour, my temper, and so on.

You may never understand this, but I have to do it now, in case I don't get round to it and I get trapped with these negative traits I don't like for the rest of my life. This may all sound a bit out there to you, but it isn't meant to be.

I wish you all the best from my heart. I hope you have been able to look at this letter from my point of view, as well as your own.

Don't worry; I don't expect a reply. I know your arrogance and pride will probably make that impossible. Habit! But I hope you do, and I hope you can also forgive me for the things I have done that offended you.

We all make mistakes; that is how we learn and better ourselves.

Yours faithfully,

Jay

****

My father pretended he never read it; he said to one of my mum's friends, "That boy wrote me a letter; I didn't even read it, I just threw it in the bin!" But he was lying; the next day my mum said she found it tucked down his side of the bed, and it was open. Whatever his thoughts were, I decided it was his problem; I was no longer going to let him affect me. I wasn't going to hold any more animosity towards him – so I released all my anger. *Pride can be a real killer!*

When I came back into the world, I knew I was stronger than ever before. I had a confidence that was second to none, but this time my confidence was inner and not outer. I was fearless more than ever before – something deep inside me realised that nothing or no one could really harm me; only giving into the emotion of fear lets that happen. My ability to stay calm no matter what astounded even me. In other words, I was mastering my own emotions.

As I began to bump into old faces, one of the first things I noticed in myself was a lack of tolerance for old friends. I could see clearly where their lives were heading, and I knew that I was heading a different way. I could see that if I stayed around them then some of my old ways could rub off on me again, and I was not prepared to let that happen. In an instant I could see why parents are so concerned with the friends their kids hang out with; friends have a huge impact on the way we turn out.

The first time I bumped into Lewis, he was on at me to come to a club we had been to many times before. When I told him I wasn't going, and that I would never be going there again, he looked shocked and asked me why.

"I don't want to mix with the kind of people that go to that club. They don't have the right mentality. At any time gunshots can go off. I don't want to be involved."

He looked puzzled for a second. Then he said, "Listen, blood. You can't make a man *scare* you from going to the club. We should be able to go anywhere we want!"

"I agree with you, Lewis, and I can assure you that I'm not scared and we *should* be able to go anywhere we want! But the *reality* is that some places you go to increase your chances of getting into problems a whole lot more, and that place is one of them... I *know* where I'm going and I'm not letting anyone who doesn't have the awareness stop me from getting there. They are fighting a battle they cannot win. Somehow we got tricked into thinking ghetto life is good. Look at it from another angle and you'll see the reality – it's the bottom of the pile."

He paused as if to digest what I had said. Then he said, "You've changed."

"That's right. I've wised up, and I suggest you do the same."

So he tried to get to me by the only angle he knew. "There's going to be loads of chicks there."

"I don't care about women any more, Lewis. I want one woman, one who complements me, and I complement her. I'm finished with sleeping around; it only makes me feel empty inside anyway. You'll realise it one day."

Lewis couldn't believe his ears.

When we parted, I was happy that I had not succumbed to playing the role he expected me to play. I was finally free to make my own plans and to not care what other people thought about me. It felt great!

The more people I bumped into and chatted with, the more I kept hearing that I had changed. A few said the same thing: "I have never seen anyone go from one extreme to the other so fast." Even women I'd been with could see the change. I knew that I had changed, but it was music to my ears hearing *other people* tell me that.

My mother was proud of me, and told me, "You've always got everything you wanted but you didn't go for the right things. Now that you want to be at the top, I know you'll get there because you won't stop until you achieve it." Then she started crying.

I became closer with my daughters, and more understanding towards their mothers, especially with Azaria because I could see her issues. It was harder with Summer; although I had got over the pain, mentally I felt I was still married to her, deep down. I guessed the love I felt for her would probably not die until it was replaced.

One of my ex-girlfriends, who years before I had put on the Misery Ride, became one of my closest friends. She was working for one of the biggest companies in Europe at the top of the executive ladder. I asked her to write me an honest account of how she viewed my transition, as she knew the old me and was very much around the new me, looking in from the outside. I wanted an unbiased analysis.

This is what she wrote:

Jay,

I ask myself – can someone really change from being a womanising, manipulating fucker? Looking back, I didn't think it was possible and I still ask myself the same question today, more out of disbelief. I can only relay my doubt back to my mum's advice when it comes to men – people can change on the surface, but deep down, a leopard never changes his spots! Well, she was both right and wrong in the context she used this saying. Let me explain...

You re-entered my life in the same way you left it – unexpectedly. Nearly two years had passed when I received your phone call, greeting me as though it had only been a few days since we had last spoken.

I couldn't believe you had the audacity to call after disappearing without even a phone call on return from our holiday. I didn't want you back in my life again. I just kept wondering – what the hell was it you wanted? I was sure you weren't just calling to see how I was.

You were obviously after something; the last conversation we had ended with me feeling threatened. A series of calls followed and in your own cocksure way you offered a feeble apology for disappearing the way you had done.

I didn't want to waste any more energy hating you, so it was fairly easy for you to charm your way back into my life, in true Jay style.

Over the course of the next few months I saw your drive and determination grow. Your focus had shifted from women and good times to success. Success! You wanted to be rich, long-term and NOW.

I look back at how I cursed you and called you all the names under the sun and it's funny because I can clearly recall these names and yet, today, for those who know you now, they would think I was talking about a completely different person.

It's easier for me to use these names to show the differences in you between then and now:

· Self-centred

Then – You were Number One and everybody else came second.

Now – You encourage growth amongst your friends. You share your knowledge freely and offer people advice on how to improve, whether it is directly improving themselves or offering advice on a situation. You take the time to listen to others. Today you are more self-ful rather than selfish.

· Pig-headed

Then – You were obviously very bright and socially aware from a young age but this was channelled negatively.

Now – You use your experiences and intuition to guide others, specifically the youths. Gone is the dog-eat-dog mentality of every man for himself. You are continually expanding your mind through your growing library and wisdom. Library – can't believe I said that, but yes, your library. And not forgetting the time you spent on qualifying as a life coach. It was a challenge but your focus and determination got you through.

· Cold and calculated

Then – You didn't care who you trampled on to get what you wanted, even in life-and-death situations!

Now – I've seen you soften to people's feelings. This has been a major change, you being empathetic towards others. I didn't think you had a heart, but now you react to people's pain and, more importantly, you take note of how your actions affect others.

· Liar

Then – You said anything to get by.

Now – You avoid situations where you may be put in a position where you have to lie. In fact, you'd rather not be around people who are dishonest. Honesty means so much to you now that you are willing to cut those people out of your life who are dishonest.

· Does not suffer fools gladly

Then – Your tolerance level was unbelievably low. In fact I would say it was zero.

Now – Your tolerance levels have improved. You are not so quick to dismiss people or cut them out of your life. I've seen you cut people off only to realise that what is obvious or plain as day to you may not be the same to others.

· Manipulator

Then – Somehow you had this ability to influence people. You used anyone and everyone to your advantage so long as it got Jay what he wanted.

Now – You channel the gift you have of being able to persuade people in a way which helps others. You are a true philanthropist.

And finally... the Ladies' man!

Now you may think this has changed, but you are still very much a ladies' man! You have this strange magnetism which keeps drawing women to you, even the ones you have abused in the past.

You are a true social butterfly and I don't think this will ever change until you find the right woman for you.

So yes, there are some things that never change, but can a manipulative, cold, calculated, womanising thug turn into a caring and moral man...?

You are living proof that he can.

Regards,

As this new person, I was able to see through other people's eyes. I was able to see people's weakness and strengths. I began to pick up on a whole lot of stuff that is way too detailed to put into this book – it will make a whole book on its own.

I now had this burning desire to succeed, and it made me pay attention to the fat cats of the world. I could see that ninety-five per cent of people think and act in the opposite way to the five per cent who are successful. As the days went by I began to see more and more.

On one occasion I bumped into a youth who reminded me of the old me. His name was Tony, and he was the type who carried his gun everywhere and was full of confidence and wouldn't take bullsh*t from anyone. Because of the whole experience I had been through I could see it was all a front and knew he was destined for prison or the morgue. I felt compelled to talk to him.

"What you carrying a gun for?"

"Times is serious out here, cus. I'm not letting no pu*syhole disrespect me."

Now I already knew his thought processes, because he saw things how I used to see them. I knew his actions and thought processes were rooted in his belief. I knew if I was going to change his outlook I would have to change his belief. If I could change his belief, I knew he could be successful. I knew his ways would change.

It felt like planting a tiny seed. Like a seed it would need time to grow – no matter how much you bend down and beg for it to sprout, it just takes time. The seed, given a chance, would grow on its own and open his awareness; and once that happened and his awareness was open, I guessed that little things would trigger the next level in the process: little leaves would unfurl, little roots would burrow, until his belief had changed. That was how I understood what had happened – what was continually happening – to me. I wanted to trigger the same process in Tony, so there I was trying to plant the seed.

I needed an in – an angle that motivated him. I used the money angle.

"Let me explain some things to you. I just want you to listen, and after, you can tell me your thoughts."

I unleashed some insights I had had that I guessed would connect with the way his thought processes worked. I translated them into his language. I knew that was critical if he was to understand me.

"First of all, let me tell you something, blood – there is nothing fabulous about being ghetto fabulous. It's an illusion! It just seems right because of the way you viewed things growing up. But the truth is, it's the bottom of the pile. We've viewed it as some kind of glorious thing but it's not. It's far from it. The percentage of bad men anywhere is minute. Do you think this minute percentage have got it right or does it make more sense that they got it wrong?

"Here's what the man at the top views when he sees people like that. He's calling his friend over and saying, 'Oh, Larry, look at these fools acting as if they got shit. I would kill myself if I was in their shoes!" Your fighting and going to war with people over nothing, pretending it's something! It's shit. You want to make it big, right? Well, that road you're on is no road; it's a vicious circle. You'll never win because you're doing everything back to front.

"First of all, if you want to make it big you're going to need help. Those guys you hang around with can't help you. I can guarantee in five years' time they'll either be on that same corner chatting the same shit, or in prison, or dead. Let me put it another way – when you see the fat cats in their suits, you automatically think, Punk! Right? All of us do. But let me assure you they think the same about us. But they're not pretending – we are. When you walk around with your jeans hanging down, guess what? You only attract those same people who have their jeans hanging down. But those aren't the people who can elevate you to the level you really want to be at. In fact, you repel those people who can help you away.

"You have to start acting and thinking like where you want to be. You have to rise above it if you really want to make it big. Life will pay you – and anybody else – whatever we bargain with, no more and no less. If we bargain with peanuts, that's exactly what we receive. This is a simple law, with no exceptions.

"As for the gun, you need to get rid of it right now, because I can tell you what will happen. Someone will come along and you'll feel they've disrespected you and your emotions will take over and you'll probably shoot them. Your rational brain won't step in for one second until it's too late. It won't tell you that there are cameras right there; it won't tell you that this situation can be sorted out without the violence; it won't tell you that what this guy thinks about you is his problem, not yours. I've seen it too many times – your rational side kicks in afterwards, when it's too late, when you're sitting down in a cell for life.

"It might appear to you that it makes you a big man, but I assure you, you will be forgotten about because people just get on with their own lives. You can't afford to get caught up in what other people think of you. I've seen it so many times – a man jumps up into another man's face like an emotional woman!"

And so I went on...

At the time I wasn't aware I spoke with passion; but people started to tell me I did.

When I was finished talking to him, I could tell I had moved him; how much, I wasn't sure. It wasn't until the next time I bumped into him that he showed his eagerness by asking for more. The third time I saw him, I could see slight changes in him. He said, "You should be chatting to the kids in school; I think you would move them."

The next time I spoke to him I got a shock – he called me on the phone and thanked me for showing him what he couldn't see, and he told me he had got rid of his gun and that he couldn't stand being around his mates any more because it was so clear to him where they were going.

I knew the seed had been planted, and that it would grow. But I also knew in the back of his mind he was thinking, *But what am I going to do now?* I wanted to be sure he didn't slide backwards into it again. So I tapped into what he was passionate about. I discovered his strength was his creativity – he had loved drawing when he was younger, and was exceptionally good at it. So I suggested to him that he do an interior design course. I could tell it was like a lightbulb going on.

This started happening with loads of youths. I was having an impact on everyone I came into contact with, and I loved it. There was a particular youth I had thought I had no impact on – but I was wrong. Months later, out of the blue, he texted me: "I'm so glad you came into my life. I love you more than my own father and brothers – my life has changed so much. Thank you." Now this was a guy who had spoken nothing but slang talk when I met him – even in text messages! I was getting texts from youths and sometimes even mothers thanking me for changing their kids.

It wasn't long before I was aware I had been given a gift. I knew right there and then that this was my purpose. My first thought was, *This isn't going to make me rich.* My second thought was, *People have got rich from the most ridiculous of things.* My third thought was, *Whatever happens in my life, I will never stray from this path.* I would be insane to go against my strongest strength. It was clear to me that people got rich by going with their talent, gift, or strength, not from their weakness, and on top of that it came naturally to me and I loved it. I could see I was having an impact on everybody I came into contact with. But the most amazing thing was, I realised as they grew they were having an impact on other people, so it was like a chain reaction!

I knew I had to find a way to get to the really bad kids. But I knew that if I was going to do it as a profession, it had to be in a big way, at a top level. I knew it would be difficult for me as I had no proven track record, but I could see that my ability was profound. Nobody yet in high places was aware I had this unique gift, but I was ambitious.

As for women – well, what was extraordinary was that I had become even more of a magnet to women. The outside of me had not changed, apart from the way I dressed. I was still being perceived as a handsome rude-boy thug, but because of my experiences I had softened a lot, I was humbled, I was listening much more than talking, I was paying more attention to detail, I was packed full of wisdom and understanding, and I had discipline in spades. I was getting out of my seat to shake hands or kiss on the cheek, and making notes of people's passions, their birthdays.

Then when I actually opened my mouth, it threw women sideways because the outside did not fit with the inside; it basically had them intrigued. I also quickly learned that the only people who needed to know my business were the people who absolutely needed to know; I came across as enigmatic, but instead of removing me from being the centre of attention with women it seemed to have the opposite effect. So without realising it I had wrapped an aura of mystery around myself.

To add to all of that, I had become super-aware there were *patterns* to people's behaviour. It's important to note: people who have the highest pattern recognition are quickly able to ward off negative people and situations from their life. They are happier, have better relationships, make more money – they generally get further in life.

****

Here are a few examples of what I refer to as patterns. Any one of these patterns should serve as a yellow light or red light to you, and you should then be planning your exit strategy. A yellow light means caution, pay attention. A red light means stop right now! It's time to exit! Conflict, pain, or the Misery Ride is on the horizon.

1. <u>He Does Not Let You Know Where He Lives</u> (YELLOW LIGHT) - Now, it's possible there is a valid reason - perhaps he's ashamed of his accommodation. But he's probably hiding something from you, or just doesn't have long-term interest in you.

2. <u>He Only Calls You at Night</u> (RED LIGHT) - There is no reason on earth for that, unless he only has free calls at night and he's broke.

3. <u>He Says He's Always Busy</u> (RED LIGHT) - You are one hundred per cent not the one for this man. No one on this planet is that busy. When a man really likes a

woman he will fit her in, regardless of his schedule.

4. <u>He Always Seems to Have Excuses for His Cock-ups</u> (RED LIGHT) - He's really just a cock-up kind of guy. That's his character. It will take something dramatic for him to change - so don't waste your energy.

5. <u>He Pays You a Visit Every Month or Totally Irregular Visits</u> (RED LIGHT) - It's a no-brainer!

6. <u>You Suspect He's Lying and He Gets Defensive When You Confront Him</u> (YELLOW/RED LIGHT) - This can be a tricky one depending on a few factors. First of all, you have to be sure you're not the paranoid nagging type, because that can very well cause anyone to get on the defensive, big time! However, if you're not, there is no reason for him to lose it in such a way. If he does, the reason is that you're on to him and he's trying to argue and force his way out of a corner. If he actually responds calmly, pay attention to the body language and then drop it. Spring it on him again when he least expects it - if the body language repeats itself, there's good chance he's lying. But most of all, if you get a feeling that does not let go of you, it's your intuition - you're right!

7. <u>He Tells You He Is the Most Faithful of People</u> (YELLOW/RED LIGHT) - Once again, this one depends on the context. I have personally used it as a way of

throwing women off the scent when I was the total opposite.

8. <u>He Makes Every Excuse Under The Sun That You Can't Meet Any of His Friends or Family</u> (RED LIGHT) – You're not good enough in his eyes.

9. <u>He Makes Excuses As to Why He Can't Go Out With You</u> (RED LIGHT) – You're good enough to give him money or sex but that's it – no-brainer!

10. <u>He Always Wants to Check Your Phone</u> (YELLOW/RED LIGHT) – Maybe he doesn't trust you, so ask yourself why. Maybe he knows what he's like, which makes him paranoid that you might be messing around too!

11. <u>There Is a Code on His Phone</u> (YELLOW LIGHT) – Is he protecting his phone if it gets lost, or is he stopping you from getting into it? Point blank, there is no excuse as to why you shouldn't have the code to his phone.

12. <u>He Deletes All Phone Messages / He Puts His Phone on Silent / He Never Answers His Phone When You're Around</u> (RED LIGHT) – No-brainer!

13. <u>He Repeatedly Starts Fidgeting Straight After Sex and Makes a Swift Exit</u> (RED LIGHT) – You're just there to be used for his pleasures. If he loves you it is just as much about spending time with you as it is sex.

14. <u>He Makes Excuses, Moves the Bar for What's Right and Wrong, and Likes to Win Debates</u> (RED LIGHT) – Get out of

there. He's too difficult to deal with and you will constantly feel as if you have no say.

15. <u>He Makes an Unnecessary Fuss About Being Called on a Withheld Number</u> (YELLOW LIGHT) - He needs to know when you're calling him in case he's somewhere he's not supposed to be.

16. <u>He Gives You a Fake Name</u> (RED LIGHT) - A good sign he may have another woman.

17. <u>He Flirts a Lot and Has a Roving Eye</u> (YELLOW LIGHT) - He's still searching; you are not enough for him. If you were he wouldn't do it, period. There is a difference between someone being charming and smooth, and flirting.

18. <u>You Ask His Friend What His Name Is. The Friend Replies, "Ask Him!"</u> (YELLOW LIGHT) - Pretty much indicates he uses several names.

19. He Gives You a Number That Is Not His Primary Number (YELLOW/RED LIGHT) - Maybe it's a precautionary measure at first (YELLOW), but if, after a while, he does not give you the main one it's a red light.

Too many yellows serve as a red, in my opinion, depending on how they fall.

Now, you may be thinking that some of these things are obvious, and to some extent I would agree! But I assure you, they are not so obvious when the heart is taking over. That's why I say it is imperative to see these patterns before you get emotionally entangled.

A womaniser tends to think he hasn't any flaws; he believes he is the sexiest and smoothest operator around. Use that weakness to your advantage and give him the rope to hang himself, and I assure you he will if you're paying attention.

Of course, there are many other yellow and red lights – it's your duty to see them. Don't allow them to go unnoticed; no one else can do it for you.

Please do not go actively looking for patterns – life has an uncanny way of showing you what you're looking for! But don't turn a blind eye to them if they turn up. If you do, there is a very good chance you have crossed the line, the point of no return from where there is no way back – and he'll have you exactly where he wants you.

Remember to start any relationship in the way you mean to go on. There's a fine line between showing your love and spoiling him. If you spoil him, he will expect it constantly, and it will be your fault, not his.

****

By becoming aware of these patterns I was quickly able to see someone's true character, no matter what they were trying to portray. I was in no rush because I now knew it takes time to see people for who they really are. Some women would get frustrated because I wasn't trying to get them into bed. But I was looking for Ms Right, not Ms Right Away.

Around this time, I stepped out of a clothes shop and a man I had never seen before stopped me and said, "You have an amazing aura."

"I can't stop now, I'm afraid," I replied.

The next thing he said stopped me dead in my tracks. "The experience you are having is from God."

Now he had my attention. How the hell did he know I was even having an experience?

"God is helping you, helping you to fulfil your purpose – you have been given a gift. You know, you're going to be a legend."

I politely said I was in a rush and made my way to my car. I remember walking off and thinking, *Why the hell did he stop me?*

Deep down I believed I was going to do something special with my life. Maybe everybody feels that way, I don't know. I thought again about 101, and I found it hard to believe it was just about payback. Maybe part of it was, but surely that experience was about something bigger?

Not long after that I went into the gym sauna and there was a middle-aged lady sitting in there. As soon as I came in she said to me, "You have an amazing aura. Do you know what I mean by that?"

"Yes." I was wondering where she was going with it.

"You're special. Do you know that?"

"No," I replied, not really wanting to answer.

"You have always been a good person, underneath the surface."

With that she smiled and quickly exited. There was something about her smile I couldn't put my finger on. I sat there puzzled for some ten minutes pondering how this lady could possibly know whether I was a good person or not – she didn't even know me! For the rest of that day I felt confused about those words, "You have always been a good person, underneath the surface."

Three weeks later I received devastating news. Totally unexpectedly, Ms Carlton had died. The sorrow I felt shocked me.

CHAPTER 28
INCREDIBLE!

I received a phone call from a secretary of Thompson & Thompson solicitors regarding Ms Carlton. I was told to come to the office on Ms Carlton's request. On my way there I couldn't help think about Ms Carlton's death and all the advice she had given me.

At the reading I was given a hand-written letter from Ms Carlton:

Dear Jay,

I feel blessed to have known you. Although I lost my own son, God brought you into my life and I was given the opportunity, I feel, with you, to make amends. I have said often that you are just like my Jamie. Jamie had a kind heart and I know you have too.

I hope over the years you have listened to the advice I have given you. You need to put the past behind you and release the anger you have for your father and only then will you really become the better person I know you are.

You are special and an intelligent person and I believe in you and hope you start to believe in yourself. Put your intelligence to good use, Jay, because I know, I can feel it, that you are destined for great things.

Behind all the ups and downs you have had, the mayhem and the many hearts you have broken in your life, I can see you have always been a good person, underneath the surface.

Take good care of yourself and your children and most important of all, be happy.

Love Joan (Ms Carlton)

My eyes jumped back to the words 'You have always been a good person, underneath the surface'. I read them over and over again… These were the same words the middle-aged lady had said to me only weeks earlier whilst I was at the gym. My mind was a blur; I had to double-check with the solicitor when exactly Ms Carlton had died. It turned out it was the same day as my encounter with the middle-aged lady in the gym. What to conclude from that is entirely up to you!

At that point I felt teary-eyed so I got up, thanked the solicitor, and went to leave. It was at that point he asked me to sit back down. What came next was totally unexpected. He opened his drawer and pulled an envelope. Then he turned to the side and picked up his glasses, bent his head to look over them, and said, "Mr Johnson, you have been named as the sole beneficiary to a Ms Joan Margret Carlton's estate."

At that point I thought, What estate? She lived in a council estate! "What do you mean by estate?" I asked.

He then explained to me that her estate was all of her personal possessions and everything she owned.

I thought, Great! She left me the sofas!!

He then proceeded to tell me what Ms Carlton's estate consisted of... at this point!

How much? You got to be kidding! How much?

I could not believe my bloody ears. I sat there in total disbelief.

It didn't make any sense to me. As far as I could tell, she had never had any money. Curiosity got the better of me and I had to ask her solicitor how this money had come about. He explained to me her money had been left to her by her husband some years back, but oddly enough she had never touched one penny.

I left that office thinking, *God is great!* I came to the conclusion that in her mind Ms Carlton had redeemed herself through me. And what a coincidence that I happened to change just before she had passed away!

The first thing I did was go to Ms Carlton's grave and say thank you and tell her how much I missed her already.

My life turned around, and in the blink of an eye I was able to do the many things I had always wanted to do. I phoned my nephew and asked him if he fancied a holiday to Mexico on me. Of course he said yes. So I booked it. It was on that very same flight that 101 popped up again.

I remember the flight had just got airborne when my nephew pulled out a book. As soon as I saw the title it grabbed my attention: *Cracking the Millionaire Code: What Rich People Know That You Don't* by Robert Allen, co-author of *Chicken Soup for the Soul* with Jack Canfield. I had already read one of Jack Canfield's books, *Success Principles*, and I had loved it. *Chicken Soup for the Soul* is in one of the bestselling book series in history; but it was rejected by over one hundred publishers before a small publishing firm took it on. I never forgot that story; it always made me think about how bad those publishers who had turned it down must have felt!

I took the book off him and started reading it. Can you imagine the shock I got when I tuned to page xiv and read:

By the way, you may soon be wondering why we use the number 101 so often? We believe that 101 is an enlightened number and has served both of us very well - one of the most successful series books in history, Chicken Soup For The Soul, contains 101 heartwarming stories. Therefore, we will be using the number 101 in several different contexts throughout this book.

Don't take my word for it – go and read the book yourself!

I started thinking about the whole 101 thing from the beginning. Maybe Summer wasn't a bad thing after all. In fact, maybe she was the best thing that had ever happened to me? I had had a painful time, but I came out a better person for it. Not only that, but a seed had been planted – I wanted to make something of my life from my own doing and believed a hundred per cent that I was going to do exactly that. So was that what 101 was really all about? Helping me to get there? Helping me know who I really was? Remember that guy who had stopped me in the street and said God was helping me? Looking back at everything, it didn't seem so far-fetched.

And guess what? My nephew never asked me for the book back! It was if he was just meant to give it to me. We had a fantastic time in Mexico. We became really close after that holiday; I helped him with his blind spots and got him off the streets. Back then he was playing wannabe gangster; now he owns his own business.

When I arrived back in England I relaxed for a bit before I headed off to you know where – yes, the one and only Monte Carlo. I fell in love with the place as I knew I would – the glamour and the beauty won me over. Then I went to all the other great places I wanted to visit, but I always returned to Monte Carlo. I wanted to live there.

Now the windfall I had received wasn't enough to set me up for life; it was just enough to make me enjoy life for a while. What I had been through had been tiring and I decided I needed a break.

It was on one of these very same holidays to Monte Carlo that I was given a solution to a problem. I remember the day very clearly. Dressed in a perfectly tailored Gucci suit, I got off the plane at Nice Airport. Confidently, I made my way over to the heliport terminal, and clambered into a helicopter. The engine and the propellers engaged in a fast spin as the helicopter lifted off into the air.

When I arrived at my destination, I jumped down onto the Monaco heliport tarmac. I slid into the back of a limousine and made my way to Monte Carlo Casino Square. There, I exited the car and walked towards the entrance of a luxurious hotel, passing Bentleys, Ferraris, and many of the finest cars ever made in history. I am so used to seeing them; I have been there many times before.

As I checked in at the front desk, I charmed the lady. I could see she was blushing, but she couldn't take her eyes off me. She gave me my room key, and as I walked away I turned and gave her a slow wink. Her face lit up, and I could feel her eyes on me all the way to the lifts.

I arrived at my room, the concierge trailing behind me. I opened the door to my suite and tipped him a hundred euros. Then I carefully put my luggage in the corner of the room. I took off my jacket and lay down on the bed. I didn't bother to check whether everything was okay in the room. I had been here so many times before, and they had never had anything out of place.

I was more concerned with making a phone call.

"Hi, hun. What time will you be arriving?"

The lady friend at the other end of the phone replies, "Hello, my darling. I'll be arriving at around eight. Do you fancy going to Jimmy's tonight?"

"Actually, Jimmy's sounds good."

"Okay, I'll catch up with you later, my darling. Oh, I forgot to ask you – have you made a decision about sending your book off to a publisher? I really think you should."

"I can't. My conscience won't allow me to do it. I'm not that person I was back then."

"Well, I've been thinking. You're very good at spotting people's blind spots. Why don't you write it to show the blind spots of a womaniser? That way you're giving something back."

"Yes…" I muse on it for a minute. "Yes! Sounds like a good idea to me. I'll think about it."

"Okay, we'll speak about it later. Ciao."

I hung up and in an instant I knew I was going to do exactly that.

The next week, I took out the old manuscript I'd written all those years ago in jail, *Galist Exposed*. It would need a new title, for starters.

I set to work.

EPILOGUE

For a long time I wondered whether to write this book. I can now only hope it has been worthwhile – which to me means that it has brought some kind of value to you, the reader.

I genuinely hope it has given you some deeper insights into how a womaniser thinks and operates. Not all womanisers are after the loot; however, they still think broadly the same, about themselves and their needs. I guess the main reason for writing this book was to highlight blind spots; now you know about them, you are going to see them everywhere! And most importantly, I hope you are going to see your own. And finding them will help you grow.

I'm sure some people who read this book will be thinking, *No, not me, I don't have any blind spots!* I have met these types before and way more often than not they have more than most! The minute you start thinking you don't have any, you have definitely got them!!!

There are a lot of things in this book I look back at with disgust. Do I regret them? My philosophy in life now is that no one should have regrets; some will agree and some won't. I'm not proud of my past and it is unfortunate I had to hurt so many people to become the person I have become today. If I had a chance to live my life over again I would like to think I would not be a jerk and make those same mistakes again.

As I sit here I can't help thinking I'm so grateful 101/ God came along, because I'm so glad I am no longer the womaniser thug I was.

I feel more comfortable with who I am today. I believe under the surface this was the person I was all along, but I let other people and the world around me influence me. I wasn't strong enough to just be who I am!

I'm still a little bit confused about what 101 really meant in my life. But what appears to be glaringly obvious to me about that experience is this: I had to be brought to my knees, a low point. In other words, my cup was too full – there was no room for me to learn or take in anything new. I thought I knew it all, even when I was clearly being given signs from people. Change would not have been possible for me unless I was taken out of my comfort zone; I had to hit a real low. I was a Know-it-all Charlie, blind-spotted by life. Now I'm a Know-nothing Neil! With that mental outlook, I see more and learn more!

All I know is that a seed was planted, and I experienced spiritual growth, and it hasn't stopped. I get insights regularly and I'm still growing. I really do believe that when I reach a certain level I'm going to be one hell of a force, that somewhere along my life line it will be clear for me and everybody to see what the end purpose is. But that is still to come.

A big part of me thinks it will be to do with helping the youths who are walking that no-good path. I'm so passionate about it, and looking at how bad it's getting there definitely needs to be someone like me who has a fundamental understanding of how to bring about that change.

I have also come to the realisation that money does not make me happy. What makes me happy is to be doing what I know I should be doing. Right now, that is bringing the wannabe gangsters back to reality! Time will tell whether that will be the case. I am now working on a few projects towards this dream of mine.

All of my kids are around me – the ones that were mine – Fate and Chelsie – and the one I have taken to my heart as if she is – Chloe – and I love them all more than they will ever know. I have also made some new friends whom I value incredibly and I know have integrity.

I'm currently single through choice – although I must admit there are women trying to win me over. Fortunately or unfortunately, I see right through people; I know The One has not yet crossed my path. My guess is, she'll think she's a lucky lady when I find her.

But I'll be the lucky one.

THE BEGINNING!

THE GUIDING PRINCIPLES...

HUMAN NATURE

Remember, every single person on this planet is motivated by self-interest. It's human nature and not a bad thing; it's only bad when used selfishly! And that is currently commonplace amongst womanisers.

I.   No matter who a person is, whether he be a womaniser or anybody else, the pull of someone's true self is stronger than acting out a fake character. Womanisers wear different masks, but if you pay attention, glimpses of the real him must and will always come to the surface. Appearances can be deceiving. Never take someone on face value, whether they are pretty, or sweet, or innocent-looking: it's a character flaw to do that. It is quite difficult not to, as apparently we perceive people fifty-five per cent visually, but judging someone from the outside can be very deceiving. I have also judged people negatively by their appearance and later found out they were absolute angels. It works both ways to trip you up.

II.   Your emotions are there to be mastered; do not succumb to them.

III.   Resist telling him he is your world and giving the impression it would be difficult to be without him. If you don't make him work for you, he won't value you: it's that simple. You must at all times think highly of yourself. Do not put anyone on a pedestal (in the beginning) – you will lose their interest. People value what they have to work for! Let him feel he had to work to get you!!

IV.   Look out for repetitive thoughts. They are a red light that means, Stop! Evaluate the situation more *carefully*! The subconscious part of your brain knows something isn't right. This is your intuition raising the alarm.

V. Your intuition is your inner guidance system. Listen to it; it deserves your attention! Your intuition, gut feeling – whatever you want to call it – tells you something is not right with the situation. The problem is, so many women don't want to listen even when friends are pointing out he's no good. You don't want this to be true, so you allow the emotional side to come up with all the reasons to justify why your friends are wrong.

RELATIONSHIPS

To stay in a relationship when you are no longer happy or when you have continuous doubts is one of the greatest wastes of time in life – period!

I. If you're in a relationship right now and you are not happy, there is a huge probability your intentions are not in line with his. When your heart is telling you to stay and your head is telling you to go, you are only playing games with yourself. This conflict can only bring dissatisfaction: the head and the heart must be in harmony if you are to feel happy.

II. Ask yourself the question, *With what I feel and know now, if I had the chance to choose over again would I make the same decision?* If the answer is no, don't waste any more time. Get out of there. Life is too short.

III.   Do not, I repeat do not, let fear stop you from leaving a relationship that is not right for you, or your children. On the other side of every fear is freedom!

IV.   If he is in love with you, he will be selfless towards you. Never let him, or anyone for that matter, become a priority in your life when in your heart you know you are only an option in his.

V.   Start the relationship as you mean to go on.

VI.   Jumping in at the deep end is nothing more than letting your emotions run away with you.

VII.   Life only gives you what you are prepared to accept. When they are being abused mentally or physically so many women accept the apology, which usually ends in, "I love you." Remember, the words "I love you" are just words. It's the action behind these words that demonstrates real love.

VIII.   Stay away from men who have double standards: men who say it's okay for them to do something, but not okay for you to do it.

IX.   Refuse to pretend or wish something is not true when in your heart you know that it is.

THE BRAIN

The brain has two sides: the emotional and the rational. You will be working much better if you use both of them in decision making.

I.   The brain works in patterns. Be alert to patterns; they don't lie!

II.   People who have the highest pattern recognition are quickly able to ward off negative people and situations from their life. They learn from mistakes quicker, are happier, have better relationships, make more money – they generally get further in life.

EMOTIONS

Emotions distort your view on situations. Emotions are in the now. They won't tell you that there is always someone around the corner who will treat you better; only your rational brain will alert you to things like that!

That does not mean you must be emotionless. Feel the emotion and then temporarily remove it by saying to yourself, "Now remove the emotions." This is so the rational part of the brain can have a peek at the facts!

Emotions are neither good nor bad: they're neutral. It's the way you apply your emotion that is good or bad. You must learn to master your own emotions; no one else can do it for you.

I.   Never convince yourself there is nothing you can do to change things. This thought process is not rational, it is emotional. Life does not decide whether you have a good relationship; you decide – you are in control. But don't make the mistake of thinking you're the woman who can change the man. What makes you think you can really change this man? This way of thinking is emotional. The rational side of the brain will alert you that only the man can decide he's ready to change – not you!!

II.   Womanisers generally don't like to be around your parents. The reason is that your parents are not emotionally involved so they can see what you can't and can usually spot a womaniser a mile off. If your parents don't like him, well...!

MANIPULATION

If anyone is manipulating you, they are using one of these emotional pulling angles: stroking your ego or playing on your desires, your fears, your guilt, or your curiosity. Any one of these emotions can blind you and sway you from seeing the reality!

I.   Having looks and charm on their own is a huge price to pay for misery, but it's the charm (stroking your ego) that gets your emotions fired up! Remember, the more you like someone, the easier it is for you to be manipulated.

II.   When you feel you are falling for a man, this is the time you should be most alert, because from the womaniser's point of view this is when you are most vulnerable. This is the time he will start to abrasively manipulate. And it is at this point, if you are not very careful, that you will be as blind as a bat!

III. Be aware of men who are always coming up with sudden scenarios that end with money!! They are playing on your emotions. Always ask yourself what the other person's motive is – there always is one, good or bad. Remember, there are two forces at play when anyone speaks to you, the inner and the outer. When anyone says anything to you it is motivated by the inner force. You should be listening to both as very often the two don't line up. Master this one skill and you will start to see right through people!!!

IV. Manipulators get away with a lot of manipulation because the recipient underestimates how far they will go to win! They are also good at calculating what your next move is.

V. Too much vanity and an unhealthily large ego are both major character flaws. They are traits womanisers often show.

VI. Make sure you are interpreting what he is saying correctly (don't start reading in something else); don't live in fantasy land! For example, he says to you, "Let's have a break. If we're meant to get back together, we will." You now interpret this as, "We're going to get back together." Fantasy land! He did not say that! In fact, he knows that you are thinking this but he's not correcting you. He's doing what I call 'dangling the carrot'. He's giving you just enough to keep you hanging. He doesn't want you, but the minute you stop paying him attention it's as if he wants you again, and so it carries on. This will feel confusing to you, as if you're getting mixed signals. The truth is, you are not getting mixed signals –you're just interpreting the signals as mixed because of the emotions and the rational side of you being at battle. Understand, this person doesn't want you: he is just stroking his own ego with the fact that he can have you whenever he wants.

VII. When you ask him a question pay attention to his body language. Then change the subject and when he's comfortable ask him again. If he repeats the same body movements, there's a good chance he's lying.

VIII. The phrases "Trust me" or "Would I lie to you" are common for womanisers, so my tip to you is to be cautious whenever you hear these words. Whenever I hear them I think, *Who are you trying to convince? Me? You?* Of course, there is always the odd exception that proves the rule, but nine times out of ten I would have to say beware!

IX. If you suspect, don't forget to use the similar scenario technique. Fabricate a similar cheating scenario and see how he responds to it. Remember, guilty people will avoid the subject and will want to talk about something else. Innocent people will want to know the details.

DENIAL

Don't blame anyone for anything that happens to you in your life. You are responsible on some level for everything that happens to you, good or bad. If you find yourself blaming anyone for anything, you're not learning the lesson. Everything starts in you and radiates outwards!

X.   Guess what? If you keep meeting the same kinds of jerks, sorry to say this, ladies, but you are the common denominator: it is not them, it is you. Change your mental outlook and the jerks will disappear!!

XI.   Whether you have encountered any womanisers before or not, don't be ignorant of the fact and think there aren't that many around and I was a one-off. I assure you there are far more than you can imagine. They're just not admitting it!!! They come from all backgrounds and cultures. Don't believe it? Watch *Judge Judy* for a couple of weeks!

XII. Avoiding reality is nothing more than living in denial. Ladies, please understand that if you want to get the results you want in relationships then you have to deal with what is in front of you. Understand, whatever you want in your life – money, car, ideal partner, house, and so on – ultimately boils down to one thing: *you just want to be happy*. Making excuses to yourself only delays the inevitable, the reality, in your terms – your happiness!!!

To conclude... Don't regret the past; just make sure you take these lessons forward in your future. Don't let tradition or other peoples' beliefs stop you from living your life and getting what you want. There is a lot of social pressure on people to conform to the accepted standards! Understand this: if you were meant to follow other people and conform you wouldn't have a brain that is independent and thinks separately from everyone else's!

One serious word of warning, though: do good, because the universe definitely doesn't sleep!!!

Remember: Everything Starts in You and Radiates Outwards

Share this book with your sisters, daughters, nieces, and every teenager and woman you know who can truly benefit from understanding the need of truly knowing and loving yourself first and your potential male counterpart, boyfriend, or husband second, before allowing yourself to fall in love with him.

Before I sign off, I am very aware you have more than likely had every emotion rung out of you whilst reading this book. Contrary to what you may believe, I wrote this book out of guilt. Strangely it was never motivated by money, but to get my karma back on track... as you all know that saying "what goes around, comes around" and I believe that more than anyone!

I have had many requests for Woman VS Womaniser II, which I really hope you will enjoy as much as this book but in a completely different way. My spiritual growth has by far surpassed what you have read so far in this book, but I'm savouring it for WvW II. I have always sensed there was more to discover about life and I've always tried to seek it. So let me give you some clues to what you can expect... – More bizarre encounters - Third eye activation – Deeper understandings – Tricks women have tried since reading about me – and a whole lot more!

If you would like to be notified when this book is available please sign up at www.thisisjcjohnson.com.

In order to conquer my quest to help as many women as possible, I humbly ask you to write a review. This will fundamentally help another woman considering whether this book is for her.

To be continued...